MIND OVER MIDI

MIND OVER MIDI

Edited by Dominic Milano

A Volume In The *Keyboard Magazine* Basic Library

**By the editors of *Keyboard Magazine*
GPI Publications
Cupertino, California**

HAL LEONARD BOOKS
8112 W. Bluemound Road, Milwaukee, WI 53213

GPI Publications

President/Publisher
Jim Crockett

Editor, Keyboard Magazine
Dominic Milano

Production
Cheryl Matthews (Director), Joyce Phillips,
Joe Verri

Typesetting
Leslie K. Bartz (Director), Pat Gates,
June Ramirez

Corporate Art Director
Wales Christian Ledgerwood

GPI Books

Art Director
Paul Haggard

Senior Editor
Brent Hurtig

General Manager
Judie Eremo

Graphics Associate/Designer
Rick Eberly

Index
Steve Sorensen

Assistant
Marjean Wall

Director
Alan Rinzler

ISBN: 0-88188-551-7

Photo Credits

Cover design and photo by Paul Haggard.
Computer graphics by Rick Eberly.

Page 6: Ebet Roberts; 60, 66: Jon Sievert; all
others courtesy of manufacturers.

CONTENTS

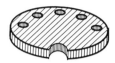

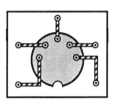

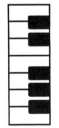

INTRODUCTION

An understanding and hands-on knowledge of MIDI has become essential for the modern musician. Musical Instrument Digital Interface has become the glue that binds together a new kind of modular music system, creating artistic potential and practical application of tremendous creative magnitude. In performance, composition, and recording—it's now possible to create guitar, keyboard, drum, or computer controlled setups consisting of any number of synthesizers, drum machines, sequencers, samplers, signal processors, and sound reinforcement equipment.

MIND OVER MIDI presents a comprehensive and practical introduction to this crucial new technology. A collection of seminal articles reprinted from the pages of *Keyboard Magazine*, MIND OVER MIDI is a valuable reference for beginning and advanced users of MIDI which also offers specific lessons and technical tips from leading writers, designers, and performing artists.

MIDI is here to stay, an indispensable new creative tool. MIND OVER MIDI will help you use its enormous potential to expand your own artistic options and to express more completely all the music in your mind.

1 **BEGINNINGS**

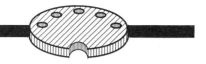

A LITTLE HISTORY

It seems like only yesterday that I first heard rumors of a proposed electronic music interface standard, later to be called the Musical Instrument Digital Interface. This was in mid-1982, not too long after the winter NAMM (National Association of Music Merchants) show. I remember clearly that my first reaction was one of apprehension: My main business was doing custom interfacing of synthesizers, sequencers, and drum machines for musicians around Los Angeles, and I feared that a standard interface would put me out of business. So much for foresight.

It was at that NAMM show that "techies" from the major manufacturers of electronic music gear—Sequential, Oberheim, Roland, Yamaha, E-mu, and a dozen others—got together to discuss a proposed interface called the Universal Synthesizer Interface, an idea that Dave Smith of Sequential was putting forward. That particular proposal was later integrated with some work along the same lines that the Japanese manufacturers were working on. As far as I know, the first actual public announcement of what was to become of the MIDI standard was Bob Moog's October 1982 column in *Keyboard*. The first commercially available synthesizer to be equipped with MIDI was the Prophet-600, which was first shipped in December 1982.

January 1986

All the material in this book has been reprinted and edited from the pages of *Keyboard Magazine*. Month and year of original publication is indicated throughout.

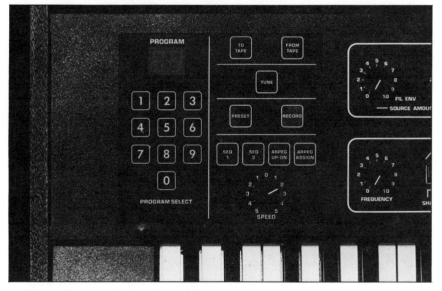

Sequential's Prophet 600 was the first commercially available synthesizer equipped for MIDI. Shown here is a closeup of the programmer control panel.

The effect on the buying public was a bit slow to develop, but was irreversible. For years, synthesizer players had put up with a host of incompatible interfaces (or no interfaces at all) on their electronic equipment. The one-volt-per-octave analog control voltage standard had helped a bit with monophonic synthesizers, but never caught on with polyphonic instruments. As a result, sequencers from Oberheim couldn't be attached to drum machines from Roland or synthesizers from Yamaha, and there was a *lot* of frustration about the whole situation. By late 1983, the word "MIDI" had come to be a mantra that was going to make everything all right.

Naturally, nothing is ever that simple. Due to a disagreement on certain aspects of the then-fledgling MIDI proposal, the first attempt to attach the new Yamaha DX7 to the Prophet-600 at the June '83 NAMM show didn't work well at all. There were snickers about the MUDI (Musically Unusable Digital Interface). It should be kept in mind that at that point, MIDI was just a "proposal." There were parts of its implementation that hadn't been nailed down yet. The transmission rate of 31.25 kilobaud (thousands of bits per second), the current loop opto-isolator, and the type of connector were really the only givens. It wasn't until August 1983 that the actual MIDI 1.0 specification was defined at a meeting in Japan with Sequential, Roland, Yamaha, Korg, and Kawai in attendance. With the publication of the MIDI 1.0 spec, things could really start to move forward. More and more manufacturers saw the opportunity (or felt the pressure) to jump on the wagon, and by the June '84 NAMM show, MIDI was everywhere.

Still, we haven't had totally smooth sailing since then. Since MIDI is not part of some police-state decree, there are differences in implementation. These are mostly too esoteric to explain here, but they can definitely cause communications problems when two devices are MIDIed together. Like most other people, I refer to MIDI as a "standard," but for it to really *be* a standard would bring up severe legal problems of an anti-trust nature. (I'm not a lawyer, but that's what I've been told.) So MIDI is a specification for a method of interfacing, not a law. Exactly which parts of the specification actually find their way into a given instrument or device depends on complex tradeoffs that the engineering and marketing departments of each manufacturing company must decide on.

Consumers must keep in mind that the mere presence of a MIDI connector on the rear panel of a synthesizer doesn't guarantee that it is

The Yamaha DX7 was the first commercially successful digital synthesizer.

going to fit smoothly into their dream system, any more than buying a VHS videotape machine guarantees that you'll have freeze-frame capability. VHS is also a specification, which covers tape format (physical size, speed, and so on), not the features of the machine itself. We can't afford to let MIDI make us lazy; these are complex times in electronic music, and we have to do our homework. The worst problems seem to be smoothing themselves out by now, and the "standard" is definitely in a more mature state. Certainly it is more grown-up than the RS-232 "standard" used in the computer industry. Nothing will bring tears to the eyes of a computer store clerk faster than a request to try out one brand of printer with another brand of computer if he or she hasn't actually tried the hookup yet. There must be at least a dozen variations in the electrical scheme, to say nothing of the various baud rates that abound. I know that I hate to have to integrate a new RS-232 device into my mess of computers—and I'm an engineer. So I don't feel bad at all about how far MIDI has evolved in only a couple of years.

MIDI was originally intended to be strictly a keyboard-oriented interface. In fact, Dave Smith's USI proposal was designed only for note-on and note-off commands. Fortunately, before it got off the ground, the proposal was enhanced a great deal to add many other functions, such as pitch-bend, after-touch, and other performance features. There came to be quite a few left-over commands, mainly in the controller family. In fact, in the original MIDI 1.0 spec, only two (modulation high bits and low bits) of the possible 122 commands were actually defined. A total of 32 pairs of high/low commands were set aside as continuous controllers, 32 were assigned as switches (such as sustain on/off), and 26 were left totally undefined. In addition, three of the "system common" messages (such as song select) and two of the "system real-time" messages (such as start or clock) were left for future definition.

The fact that all of these commands were left undefined is a double-edged sword. On the positive side, it allows for the growth of MIDI into an unknown future. There are already some very interesting proposals cropping up with regard to controllers, particularly from the non-keyboard instruments that are starting to move in the MIDI direction. Fortunately, the room for growth is there. The negative side, however, is the possibility that one manufacturer may pick a code to be, for example, a breath controller command, while another picks the same code to be a stereo pan control. As it happened, the Yamaha DX7 used seven of the then-undefined codes for some of its controllers (breath, volume, sustain pedal, and so on). With the sort of clout that Yamaha in general and the DX7 in particular brings to bear, these seven quickly became de facto specifications and are now, in fact, part of the "MIDI 1.0 Detailed Specification" that was published in October 1985. Not all manufacturers, however, are likely to find their decisions so universally accepted. While I don't know of any actual usage conflicts, the possibility is there.

Two factors should help keep things sane. First, there is a trend among manufacturers to make controller functions somewhat flexible. You can, for instance, define exactly which MIDI command is issued upon moving the pitch-bend wheel on most of the new remote keyboard units. In fact, that definition is often part of a stored patch, so that you can, for example, bend pitch during one part of a song and control volume with the same wheel later in the song. Of course, this puts some demands on the musician to know what it all means, but owners' manuals are starting to include MIDI command data, so the information is available. A second important development which should help keep sanity in view is the formation of the MIDI Manufacturers Association (MMA) and its counterpart, the Japan MIDI Standard Committee (JMSC).

Another wide-open area for MIDI exploration that was built into the original specification is the system-exclusive message mode. With commendable foresight, the designers of MIDI saw the desirability of giving each manufacturer an area of total freedom within the MIDI format. The only rules in the MIDI spec about system-exclusive data is that it must start and stop with specified codes. The start code includes an identification code indicating the manufacturer, so that, one hopes, no confusion can arise. In most cases, the manufacturer will include a model ID as part of his "header," followed by some sort of command structure, then the actual data. Any data, in whatever amount may be needed, can come in the middle. It is strictly up to the manufacturer to decide what to do with this capability.

The other requirement of the MIDI Detailed Spec (and philosophy) is that the manufacturer publish (perhaps in the owner's manual) an explanation of what the system-exclusive codes do. This is in keeping with the "open architecture" aims of MIDI. Initially, system-exclusive was used only as a parameter data dump, a sort of high-speed cassette dump facility. All that is needed is a computer with MIDI connectors and the proper software, and hundreds of patches can be stored on a single disk. As a logical extension of this, software packages started to appear that took the data from these dumps, figured out just what all the parameter settings were, displayed these graphically on the computer screen, and provided a method of editing them. Knowledgeable musicians could now change the parameters on the computer and send them back into the synthesizer, all in a fraction of a second. Envelopes could be drawn graphically rather than entered as numbers, volume levels could be displayed as vertical "sliders" like those on a mixing console, and so on. This marriage of music and graphics was only a dream a couple of years ago, and now anyone with the bucks can go to the store and buy it. Because of its strong graphics, the Apple Macintosh is an ideal computer for this type of application. I personally am very pro-Macintosh, and look with excitement to future developments happening around the Mac/MIDI link.

Other computers now have large amounts of software available that speaks MIDI through interface devices of one sort or another. MIDI has even developed the sort of acceptance that led Atari to put MIDI connectors directly on their 520ST and 1040ST. MIDI is also available for the Commodore Amiga and the Apple IIGS. That makes four different graphics-intensive computers with powerful microprocessors and MIDI available now for under two thousand dollars.

Aside from the parameter data dump aspect, there are almost unlimited possibilities on the horizon for the creative use of system-exclusive commands. Of course, the ID code is unique to a given manufacturer, but part of the open-architecture philosophy of MIDI says that use of another manufacturer's system-exclusive code is entirely permissible. If I could design a $200 synthesizer that had exactly the same functions and parameters as the DX7, I might want to be able to take advantage of all the existing software for parameter storage, display, and manipulation that was designed to work with the DX7. So I would naturally have its data dump use the Yamaha system-exclusive format and ID. What I could not do is add or change a couple of commands within the Yamaha format. Nor could I use the Yamaha ID for an entirely new purpose, such as add a new model ID to it to identify my unit. All extensions of a system-exclusive format must be made by the ID "owner," for obvious reasons.

Proposals are now pending for the assignment of three system-exclusive ID codes to applications rather than manufacturers. There have been requests for a code that could be reserved for use within schools, research facilities, and so forth. In these cases, the reasoning goes, it is unlikely that equipment designed and built in-house will be used with equipment from another similar organization, so no unique ID is needed. Since the number of unique ID codes is very finite (only 128, without some extension of the existing method), it is unreasonable to assign a unique ID to every possible school or organization. So this proposal at least keeps these in-house applications from interfering with commercial equipment. I can already imagine the MIDI-to-satellite links that will come out of places like Stanford and MIT.

There are two proposals that have been accepted as additions to the spec, but they still require the formality of ratification at the the time of this writing. The first of these proposals is for extensions to the present real-time codes, since none of the current real-time codes can have data associated with them. Originally called M-SMPTE, but now known as MTC (MIDI Time Code) for legal reasons, this would be a sort of SMPTE-like arrangement that would allow an actual "time of day" to be transmitted for synchronization purposes. By setting this ID aside now, we can let sequencer software designers know that they might like to have the option in their programs to store this particular data along with other MIDI data, and not filter such system-exclusive data out, as most sequencer programs currently do. (They do this so that the limited note storage doesn't get filled with useless data. For instance, if the transmission modes are not set correctly on a DX7, it will dump all of its parameter data for a patch out through MIDI whenever a program change is made. Each set of parameter data is equivalent in number of MIDI bytes to about 22 note-on commands, so it's useful for these to be ignored at the sequencer input. If, however, special system-exclusive real-time commands come into use, they would need to be stored as part of the sequence.)

The second proposal, for a system-exclusive ID reserved for non-real-time applications, is pending. The immediate proposal for usage of this code is for the dumping of sampled waveform data according to a specification developed by Chris Meyer at Sequential, Dave Rossum at E-mu, and others. The purpose of this spec is to allow a sound sampled on one machine to be dumped onto another. The new Prophet-2000 includes this feature, the E-mu SP-12 sampling drum machine should have it by the time you read this. The proposed specification includes the ability to handle anywhere from eight-bit to 28-bit (!) samples, and includes data indicating the sample period (time between samples, in nanoseconds) and loop points (where in the sound you loop to get a sustain). This whole subject is more exciting to

Dave Smith of Sequential first proposed the Universal Synthesizer Interface which evolved into MIDI.

me than almost anything else within MIDI. The ability to take sampled data out of an Emulator and stuff it into a Kurzweil may not seem to be a world-stopper, but wait till the computer programmers get involved! The Digidesign people have created quite a stir with their Sound Designer package for the Emulator II and the Macintosh, and once a standardized MIDI sample dump protocol is worked out, more such programs, allowing not only waveform editing but digital synthesis, are sure to follow.

The only danger in such uses of the system-exclusive code is the possibility of uncontrolled expansion. One of the duties of the MMA and the JMSC will be to coordinate any proposed expansions.

I'm afraid I don't have a crystal ball, but I will try to give a few guesses about what you might see happening with MIDI during the next couple of years. For one thing, the present trend of putting MIDI functions on delay lines, reverbs, and such devices will continue. In these boxes, some or all of the normal front panel knob and switch functions are programmable. When the unit receives a MIDI program change command, the new patch is brought up. In more extensive implementations, system-exclusive commands can reach in and tweak a given knob, so that continuous control of the sound parameters can be accomplished from a computer, or even (if everything is set up correctly) from the modulation wheel of a synthesizer.

Expect to find MIDI-controlled equalizers before long. MIDI-interfaced audio mixing boards have just become a reality, making automated mix-down accessible for even a home eight-track studio. Some mixers will

5

probably have only gain as a controllable feature, but more expensive ones will have panning, routing, EQ, and so on either accessible in real time or stored as patch data. I can see a day when essentially every piece of audio equipment you need could have MIDI on it, if you are willing to pay. Why the extra expense? Not because of MIDI itself, but because of the implications of putting a function under computer control. Let's look at a simple flanger. When you adjust the amount of feedback, you turn a knob on a pot that lets some amount of the output signal go back into the input stage. Of course, MIDI can't turn a knob, so the pot (50¢) has to be replaced with a voltage-controlled amplifier or digitally-controlled amplifier ($2 to $10). And you need interfacing electronics, and a microprocessor, and memory to hold the data, and a lithium battery to power the memory, and so on. But it can be done.

Jan Hammer in the studio with (clockwise from left) a Fairlight CMI Series II (CPU, keyboard, computer controller), LinnDrum, Fairlight monitor (with light pen for drawing waveforms), Roland Jupiter 8, Memorymoog, Yamaha DX7, and Sundown guitar amplifier. In the background is a Sound Workshop Series 30 mixing console.

The SMPTE-to-MIDI link should actually get somewhere soon. While it is reasonably simple to convert SMPTE to MIDI clock signals, there is little being done on the sequencers available right now that would allow the sequencer to lock onto an arbitrary point on the SMPTE time signal. Usually, you have to wind the sequencer back to the beginning every time. The sequencer in the Emulator II lets you start in the middle of a tune if you're syncing to SMPTE, but you have to buy the whole instrument to get the sequencer. I expect to see a good stand-alone sequencer with full SMPTE capabilities any time now. Keep in mind that a good sequencer program is one to two man-years in the making. A company is not going to sense the need for one this month and show it next month.

Almost everything mentioned above applies to stage performance as well as studio work. The concept of MIDI-linked effects and mixing is already in use with groups like Toto, and it will find its way into local club bands too. Now that more and more bands are accepting the idea of being rhythmically tied into sequencers and drum machines, total real-time control of the whole sound path is going to become the norm. For bands who like the idea of letting adrenalin (or artificial substitute) dictate the tempo, I expect that we will be seeing an extension of the tap pad input of tempo. Perhaps a piezo pickup for the bass drum, and bullet-proof software that won't get confused no matter what the drummer does. (Don't call me up asking where you can get this one. I'm just predicting the future.)

Stage sound systems haven't gotten on the MIDI bandwagon yet, for the most part, but we should be seeing them any time now. Once again, this is predicated on the idea of a timing lock with a sequencer or drum machine. Once a mix is settled on, it can be reproduced exactly every night. When the band goes to the next club, it can start with the previous mix and edit it to get it just right for the new room, then save to cassette or disk.

I hope that MIDI will find its way into other aspects of the stage act. MIDI control of stage lighting is something I have been promoting for some time now, and expect to see accepted more and more. The idea of locking intricate lighting cues to the music is irresistible.

I haven't really said anything in this article about the music education applications of MIDI, partly because I am not involved in it. I gather that the whole field is still in its infancy, and it should be an area of great growth. With MIDI, the teacher has a simple way of attaching some reasonable number of keyboards to one central computer. Ear-training, sight-reading, and theory exercises could be given by the teacher and the whole class's work stored for later review while the teacher spends time with an individual student. Intelligent programs could even do the grading of the pupil's response, and be able to give back the appropriate exercises for improvement in weak areas. While the idea of teaching machines is almost ancient, this setup needs only off-the-shelf synthesizers and computers, plus the right software. And since many schools already have Apple computers, they are halfway there.

MIDI guitar controllers have been around (from Roland) for some time now, but the next year will surely bring half a dozen other manufacturers into the fray, some using the pitch-to-voltage method, others using wired frets. Reed players will find some sort of MIDIized Lyricon substitute from Japan very soon. The Bill Perkins trumpet-to-MIDI interface is still lurking out there looking for a manufacturer. Nile Steiner's EWI (Electronic Wind Instrument) with MIDI is being produced by Akai. And of course Fairlight and Roland are pushing their pitch-to-MIDI converters, which will bring vocalists, flautists, and nearly everybody else into the action.

Composers will find uses for transcription/notation software along the lines of Personal Composer (for the IBM PC) and Southworth's Total Music package (for the Macintosh). A good transcription program has to verge on artificial intelligence, so it's not an easy project. But MIDI makes it attractive to pursue.

Most of all, what I hope to see in the next couple of years is a greater understanding of what MIDI is and what it can and can't do. MIDI is not magic. It will not write great music, any more than it will take out the trash, but a lot of musicians expect miracles. MIDI is still quite new. And there are hundreds of small music stores that are just now getting acquainted with MIDI as something more than a name of a jack on the rear of a Casio. I expect that the larger manufacturers will put a lot of money into the education of retail store personnel.

—Jim Cooper

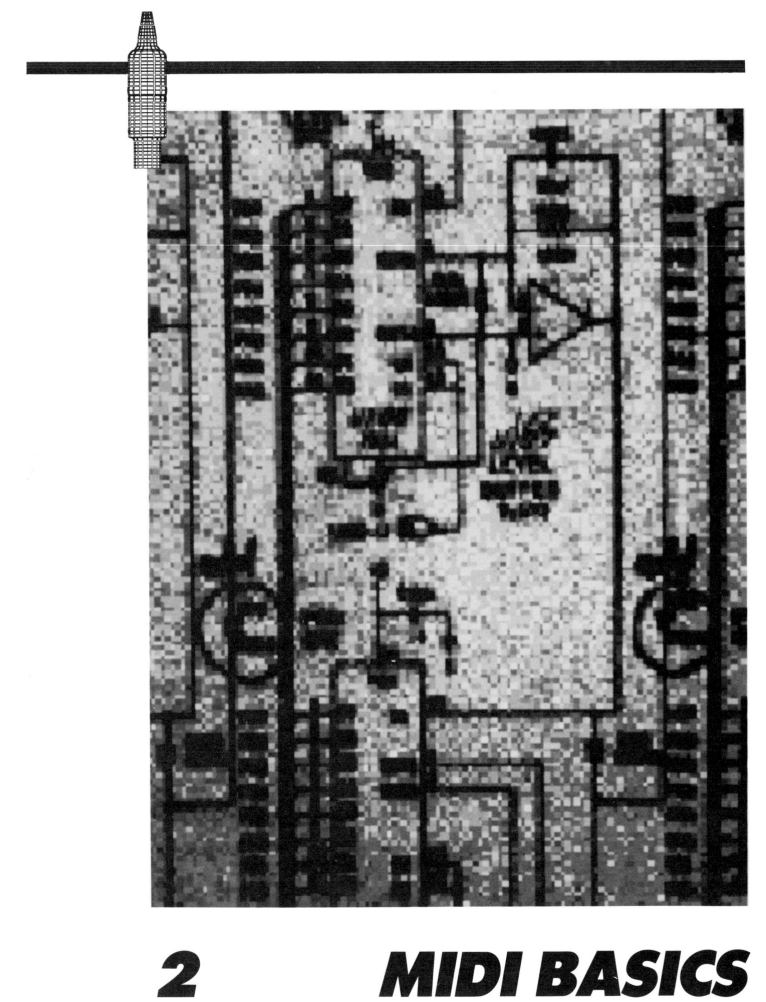

2 MIDI BASICS

WHAT MIDI DOES

July 1983

MIDI-equipped instruments may be interconnected so that information on sound changes and operating modes is shared by the networked instruments. Electronic keyboard instruments, sequencers, rhythm machines, auxiliary manual controllers, and personal computers are all examples of devices for which MIDI was designed. In its simplest application, MIDI permits a musician to play two or more instruments from a single keyboard, in order to layer tone colors. In its most comprehensive application, MIDI provides the means for realizing a multi-track recorder or a computer-based composing system by connecting several instruments to a master computer or controller.

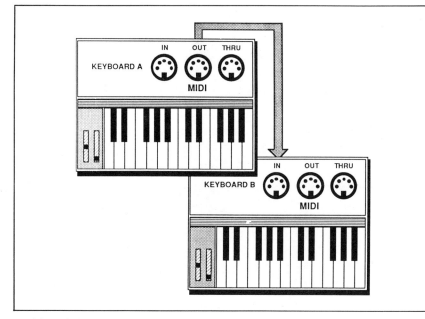

Figure 1. Master synth transmitting information through its MIDI outport to a slave synth's MIDI inport. Events played on the master keyboard can be doubled on the slave.

Most information is transmitted over a MIDI network on one of 16 'channels.' These are not physical channels such as separate cables, but rather are electrical labels that are attached to packets of information. According to the MIDI specification, each equipment manufacturer has the option of determining whether or not a given instrument has the ability to select which channel(s) it will respond to. Three modes of operation of MIDI instruments are provided: *omni, poly,* and *mono.* The modes are defined in terms of how an instrument responds to channel select information. If an instrument is in omni mode, it responds to information that is sent over any channel. If it is in poly mode, it will respond to information on the channel to which it is assigned. If it is in the mono mode, each voice within the instrument may be programmed to respond to a different channel.

Let's illustrate this with some specific examples. First, suppose we have three MIDI-equipped keyboard instruments. Instruments B and C are receiving keyboard information from A. If B and C are in omni modes, they respond to all keyboard information. The player has thus 'ganged' all three instruments so that they all play from the A keyboard. Keyboard information may include which key has been depressed, the velocity at which it was depressed, which key was just released, the velocity of release, and the value of the key pressure (after-touch). If A does not have a touch-sensitive keyboard, then no velocity or pressure information is transmitted. Similarly, if the voice circuitry of B or C is not equipped to respond to key velocity information (for instance to make the note loud or soft), then it simply ignores that information.

Now suppose A is a two-keyboard instrument, and that the top keyboard transmits on channel 1 and the bottom instrument transmits on channel 2. If the instruments are in poly mode, B is assigned to channel 1 and C is to play B from the top keyboard of A, and C from the bottom keyboard of A. Each instrument may or may not have the ability to select which channel it responds to in the poly mode. If an instrument is not equipped with channel-select capability, then the specification says that it must be permanently assigned to channel 1.

Finally, let's suppose that instrument A is replaced with a personal computer that is programmed to implement the functions of a multi-track recorder. Let's further suppose that B is a polyphonic synthesizer in which the parameters of each voice are individually addressable by its microprocesser, but that the voices in C are internally ganged so they all produce the same tone color. What this means is that B is capable, by virture of the

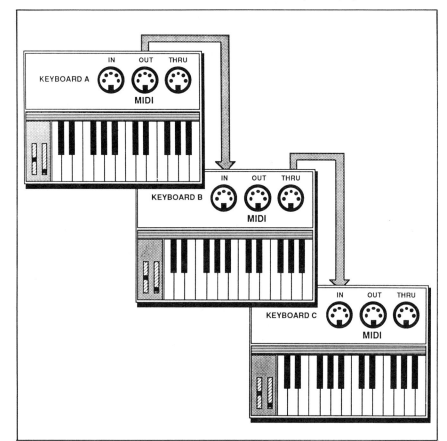

Figure 2. Three-keyboard, daisy-chain setup. A master synth is transmitting to a slave synth, which passes the signal through its MIDI thru port to a second slave. Events played on the master are layered on both keyboards B and C.

flexibility of its hardware, of producing many different tone colors simultaneously, whereas C is not. Now, if the computer sends a signal to B that tells it to switch to mono mode, the computer can send data for different tone colors over different channels (as many as one per B voice) to instrument B. C, however, must continue to receive in poly mode. That is, all keyboard information comes to it on one channel.

Of course, equipping an instrument with a MIDI interface does not expand its sound-producing capability. A MIDI-equipped monophonic synthesizer, for instance, will play no more than one note at a time, even though the MIDI information says that several keys are down. Similarly, a MIDI-connected drum machine will respond to timing and program select information, but has no use for keyboard information. In general then, MIDI-equipped instruments will respond to information that is applicable to them and ignore the rest.

In addition to key information, MIDI allows voice parameter, mode select, program change, and auxiliary controller information (like pitch-bend, modulation amount, and volume) to be transmitted over a specific channel. The specification tells what codes stand for which keyboard keys, so playing Middle *C* on instrument A will produce the same note from instrument B as if Middle *C* on the B keyboard were played. However, the specification says nothing about codes for voice parameters. The reason is simple: While synthesizers all use the same type of keyboard, their panel controls are unique, and not standardized at all. One manufacturer may have a four-part envelope generator where another has a two-part envelope generator. Or the filter controls on two instruments may be radically different, even if they are different models of the same brand. Thus, manufacturers are free to assign their own codes to their instruments' voice parameters, but are required to list these codes in their instruction books.

In addition to the types of information that I've listed above, all of which can be sent through specific channels, the MIDI specification provides for several types of information which are transmitted without channel labels. The first of these is timing information by which drum machines, sequencers, and other real-time controllers can by synchronized. Then there are some labels that can be used to call up portions of a piece of music ('measure,' 'tune,' and 'song') that have been preprogrammed. Finally, a block of codes is reserved for use by individual manufacturers to implement functions not explicitly defined in the specification.

Inside MIDI

First of all, MIDI is a bi-directional interface. According to the specification, a MIDI-equipped instrument must have an input port and an output port. MIDI input and output ports both use five-pin DIN sockets, the kind that are frequently found on stereo equipment, cassette recorders, and electronic musical instruments. MIDI cables (which, according to the spec, may be up to 50 feet long) are terminated in mating DIN connectors. To play the tone generators of one keyboard instrument (the 'slave') from the keyboard of another instrument (the 'master'), one simply runs a MIDI cable from the MIDI output of the master to the MIDI input of the slave. To play either instrument from the other's keyboard, one uses two MIDI cables to connect master output to slave input, and master input to slave output. Figure 1

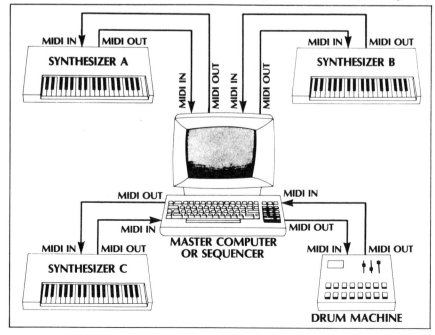

Figure 3. MIDI star network.

shows four MIDI-equipped tone-producing instruments connected to a master sequencer in a 'star' network. Here, the master sequencer can receive performance information from any of the keyboards, and can program any synthesizer selectively without first transmitting a channel select code.

The MIDI spec suggests, but does not require, that a third 'thru' port be provided in MIDI instruments. The thru port provides a signal that is a replica of that fed to the instrument's input port. Thus it is practical to control several slaves from one master by means of a chain network like that shown in Figure 2. In this system, a master sequencer or controlling computer can

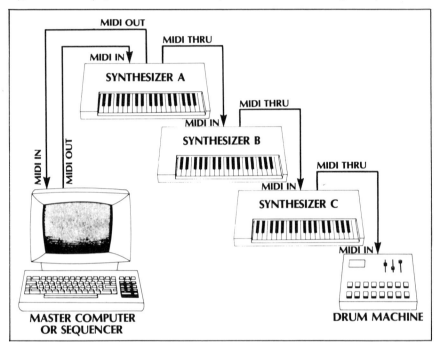

Figure 4. MIDI chain network.

provide keyboard or voice parameter information to any of the synthesizers, as well as timing information to the drum machine. In addition, the keyboard of the first synthesizer can provide information to the sequencer.

Either a star or a chain network allows a musician to configure a multi-track recording and playback system in which only MIDI signals are recorded by the sequencer. The chain network requires fewer MIDI cables, but channel selection codes must be transmitted by the sequencer if individual synthesizers are to be selectively addressed.

Second, MIDI (as the name makes clear) is a *digital* interface. That is, information is passed from one instrument to another as a series of digital codes. In many modern electronic keyboard instruments, especially the larger polyphonic instruments, virtually all control within the instrument is in digital form, and under the direction of one or more microprocessors. A MIDI interface merely taps this information (also under microprocessor direction) and dispatches it according to the rules laid down by the specification.

Third, MIDI is a *serial* interface. Digital bits follow one another in single file through a cable containing a single pair of wires. In contrast, a parallel interface (which, by the way, several equipment manufacturers currently use) uses a whole bunch of wires, through which the digital information marches eight or 16 bits abreast. In a MIDI interconnection, the bits are spaced precisely 32 microseconds (millionths of a second) apart in time. The basic packet of MIDI information consists of ten bits: and initial 'start bit,' a 'flag' bit that identifies whether the packet is data (a number) or status (what a data number is supposed to mean), a seven-bit code for the status or data itself, and finally a 'stop bit' bringing up the rear. It takes 320 microseconds for a byte (packet of information) to transmit through a MIDI interconnection. In contrast, several dozen bytes can be transmitted through a parallel interface in a same amount of time.

Pushing our 'marching' analogy a little harder, let's compare MIDI information to a Boy Scout troop marching single file through the woods. This particular scout troop was sent out by the microprocessor when the musician played Middle C loudly on his MIDI-equipped axe. The troop is divided into 'partols' (packets) of ten. The first patrol is headed by the patrol leader (start bit). Next in line is the carrier of the 'status' flag. After him comes seven marchers bearing the message "key data, channel #1" (it takes seven 'scouts' just to carry that message!). The assistant patrol leader (stop bit) brings up the rear, just so everyone knows where one patrol stops and the next one starts. Next come two more patrols of the same size, both with flags saying 'data.' The second patrol carries the message, "Middle C," while the third patrol carries the message "loud." Soon the troop emerges from the woods (the MIDI interconnection cable) and arrives at the microprocessor of the slave synthesizer. The slave microprocessor (perhaps like politicians on a reviewing stand) identifies the troop by examining the first patrol, then sends the second and third patrols through the slave synthesizer circuitry to tell a voice generator to make a loud Middle C. The whole 'march' takes about a thousandth of a second.

When you play a MIDI-interconnected system, you never have to deal with the individual bits. Unless you get into computer programming, you don't have to know codes, or worry about status and data. All that is taken care of by the microprocessors of the instruments you are playing. The MIDI scouts that I described above are closely related to those that march off your bank card when you use a 24-hour teller. However, unlike the bank machine that coughs up money when you need it, a MIDI network should be able to carry a great deal of information, some with very high accuracy, but all of it so fast that the delay is imperceptible. Under some conditions the delay in transferring information may become audible.

—Bob Moog

DATA TRANSMISSION TUTORIAL

The concept behind MIDI is really very simple: If musical instrument manufacturers can agree on a straightforward method to hook up their various boxes, then everybody will be better off. MIDI (for Musical Instrument Digital Interface) is actually an outline, on paper, stating how this interface should be accomplished. Somewhat simplified, the main points of this outline are as follows:

Connector Type. The preferred type is the common five-pin DIN connector that has been in use on European hi-fi equipment for years. If a given manufacturer wants to substitute a different connector, such as the XLR, he should make adapter cables available. The MIDI specification says that pins 4 and 5 are used for the digital signal. Pin 2 is hooked up to ground on the sending side only, so that no ground loops are formed.

Electrical Specification. The basic method the electrical signal uses to get from one place to another is called a "current loop" (see Figures. 1 and 2). As the name implies, the electrical current actually travels in a large loop. The current originates at the sending side from the resistor in Figure 1 (which is connected to the power supply), just as it does from the battery in Figure 2. It travels down one wire until it gets to the receiving unit. There, the

December 1985

13

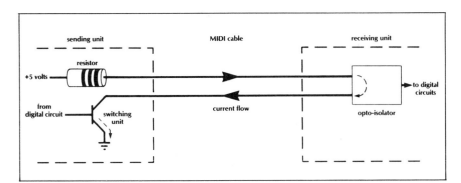

Figure 1. The MIDI signal travels between the power supply and the opto-isolator in a current loop.

current flows through the opto-isolator (more on that later) almost exactly the way it does through the light bulb. After the current flows from the receiving unit, it travels back to the sending unit via the other wire, until it gets to the switching unit, which corresponds to the knife switch in Figure 2.

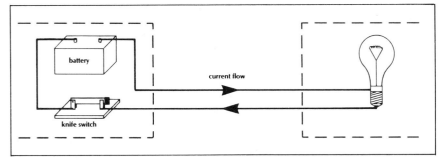

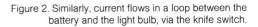

Figure 2. Similarly, current flows in a loop between the battery and the light bulb, via the knife switch.

Assuming this switch is on, the current then flows to the other side of the power supply voltage, just as with the battery. If the switch is off, naturally no current will flow in the first place, current being clever that way. So just as we could send Morse Code to someone watching the light bulb by alternately opening and closing the knife switch, we can send messages to the receiving unit by turning the switching unit on and off. Of course, this switching unit is hooked up to the microprocessor inside the sender, and is being switched thousands of times per second, but the principle is just the same.

The opto-isolator corresponds to both the light bulb and the watcher in the analogy above. This little integrated circuit has a light-emitting diode (LED) inside, along with a light-sensitive transistor. When the LED turns on in response to the current flowing through it, the transistor can notify the rest of the digital circuitry of the fact. Why go to all this trouble? The answer is that the opto-isolator provides isolation. With this scheme, there doesn't have to be any actual electrical contact between the sender and the receiver. This does wonders for the elimination of the infamous Group Loop. I hate to imagine what would have happened if MIDI hadn't had this isolation concept built-in from the beginning. It would have been buzz city.

Method Of Data Transfer. MIDI uses a type of data transfer called "serial." Just as with the dictionary definition, serial transfer means that individual parts, called "bits," are sent in a continuous manner at a regular interval to form a data "word." A serialized novel in a magazine reveals one portion of the story each month, and you won't know the whole story until you get to the end. In MIDI, each bit is sent in 1/31,250 of a second, and it takes a total of ten of these bits to form a whole data word. The word itself is only eight of these bits in length, the other two bits, called "start" and "stop" bits, being used for synchronization purposes. To use our serialization analogy again, you could conceive of a trilogy of novels being published in a magazine. Each novel is an entity in itself, but it takes three of them to tell the complete story. In just this way, MIDI often needs more than one data word to complete the command.

We said earlier that bits are sent at a rate of 31,250 per second. The accuracy of this rate is important. To whip the serial novel analogy to death, let's imagine that the magazine has no date printed on it, and that the publisher puts it on the newsstand whenever he jolly well pleases. We, the readers, go to the stand faithfully on the first of each month and buy the magazine, trusting that it is the new issue we are buying. You can see that sometimes we may end up rereading a previous bit of the novel, and sometimes may miss a bit altogether. The bit rate of 31,250 per second had to be at least this fast or the dreaded MIDI delay would be far worse. And if it were much faster, the digital circuitry inside the units would have been much more expensive. Unfortunately, this bit rate is not one of the common computer RS-232 communications rates (they're much too slow), so it usually requires that a custom interface be designed for any given computer.

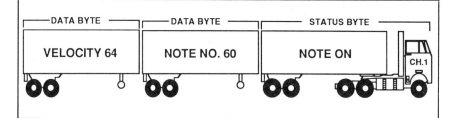

Figure 3. The first part of an event message's status byte contains its channel designation. Receiving instruments scan incoming messages and respond to those tagged with the channel number they're programmed to receive on.

Message Protocol. Well, now we have established the type of connector, the type of electrical signal, and the method of actually forming the data. What next? We need to define carefully just what form this data will take to, say, define the playing of Middle *C*.

MIDI uses "messages" to tell the receiving unit what to do. A given message may be a single data word long (to start a drum machine), or many thousands of words (to do a sequencer data dump). In each case it starts with a "command" word that tells the receiver generally what to do; for instance, to play a note. In most cases, the command is followed with "data" words that tell the receiver the specifics, like which note to play and how loud to play it. Along with the command will often be the channel data used to "steer" the command to one specific instrument. For an explanation of channels, see below. Let's try an analogy to describe the message concept, specifically regarding note commands.

A composer hands three slips of paper to a messenger who rushes to the concert hall. Opening the door, he reads aloud from the piece of paper. "Piano, play," he reads from the first "*Eb* above Middle *C*," he reads from the second. "And play it *forte*," he reads from the third. The messenger then rushes back to the composer, who gives him three more slips of paper. The messenger rushes back to the hall, opens the door, and reads: "Flute, play the," "*B* above Middle *C*," and "Play it *mezzo forte*." On subsequent trips back and forth the messenger reads: "Piano, release the," "*Eb* above Middle *C*," "slowly," and then, "Flute, release the," "*B* above Middle *C*," "quickly."

I think you get the picture. In each note-on message there are three separate data words: First is the actual command that says to play or release a note, along with the channel information steering the command to the correct instrument. Then the actual note is defined. And finally, there is a loud/soft definition which, in keyboard terms, is the velocity with which the note is struck or released.

If the messenger loses one of the slips of paper all bets are off, because the expectation of three slips (data words) per message gets thrown completely off; a velocity value would be confused for a note value. And what would happen if the messenger lost the "Flute, release," message altogether? Our poor flute player would expire before the *coda*. More importantly, a non-humanitarian would argue, the music would suffer because this *B* would sound continuously until the flute player passed out.

15

And since synthesizers rarely pass out, their notes will sound forever, or until the instrument is turned off, whichever comes first. Of course, the solution to all this is not to lose messages, but in high-speed digital complexities, the worst does happen occasionally. We'll go into that in more depth shortly.

Modes Of Operation. There are four main modes of operation defined in the MIDI specification, having to do with whether or not the receiver pays any attention to the channel part of the message, and whether ther receiver is going to respond in a monophonic or polyphonic manner.

—Jim Cooper

CHANNELS

September 1985

Now lets take a look at the basics of MIDI channels. First, it's important to understand that MIDI is a digital communications system that's used to transfer information from one instrument or device to other instruments or devices. The data being sent between instruments is *not* audio information, but digital information that allows the microprocessors inside instruments to talk to one another. MIDI channels, of which there are 16, are used in conjunction with the MIDI modes to allow you to send information on one channel to a specific instrument or instruments while sending other information on another channel to a different instrument or group of instruments *over what amounts to (electronically) the same cable.* The idea is analogous to what happens with a television set. Many different TV stations are broadcasting simultaneously. Your antenna, or cable system as the case may be, picks up all these channels at once, and your set allow you to selectively tune in to the station you want to watch at any given time. If you connect other TVs to the same antenna, you can tune them in to different stations as required. However, with MIDI, rather than receiving a continuous flow of information that's located on different frequency bands, the way a TV set does, the MIDI information flow is digital. That means that all the

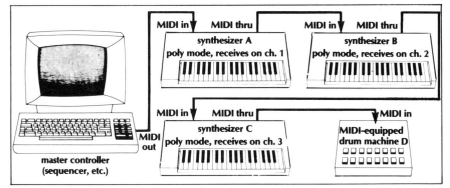

Figure 1. A MIDI chain network, with different instruments set to receive on different MIDI channels.

information is packed together as computer code flowing down a single transmission line. Different parts of that code identify each piece of information as belonging to specific channels. This means that there are a couple of ways that time delays might develop. The first involves a buildup of lag between instruments that are chained together one after the other.

In a typical MIDI keyboard setup, information has to be passed along from the first instrument in the chain to the second, from the second to the third, and so on. It might only take a fraction of a second for this transfer of MIDI data to occur, but when you have a lot of instruments in the chain, it all adds up to perceptible time delays. The way to get around that problem is to use a MIDI thru box, a device that converts one MIDI in to several identical

MIDI outs.

In this way, each instrument can receive data at the same time, removing the build up of delays caused by having multiple instruments chained together one after the other. The other potential cause of time delays is when you try to transmit too much data over MIDI. This isn't so much of a problem, simply because you'd have to turn dozens of notes on and off at extreme speeds (64 triplets at 200+BPM) to begin to perceive any delays.

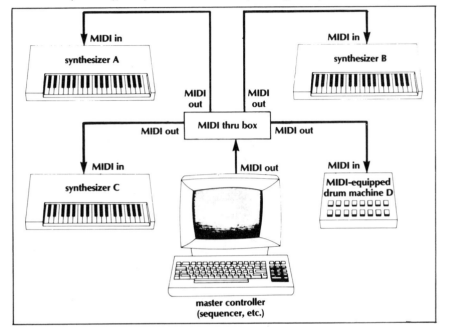

Figure 2. A MIDI star network, using a thru box.

Here's an example of how you might use MIDI channels in practice. Say you have a multi-track, multi-channel MIDI sequencer of some sort. It's the master controller. Then you have a couple of MIDI-equipped synthesizers as the slaves. You can have the MIDI sequencer putting out a bass line on MIDI channel 1, being assigned to instrument A which is in poly mode (mode 3, omni-off/poly), channel 1 and set to sound like a bass. Then you can have instrument B sound accompaniment lines on channel 2, and instrument C can do lead lines or effects on channel 3. Of course, if you want to have two instruments sounding the bass line, you can set them to poly mode and assign them both to MIDI channel 1, so what gets sent to instrument A, also goes out to instrument B. Using the MIDI thru jacks, you will still be able to send timing information along to a MIDI-equipped drum machine, so it can keep time with the master sequencer. Note that the drum machine doesn't need to be assigned to a specific channel in this case, because all it is doing is responding to timing information. However, if you were to want to control it from a keyboard, you might want to set it up to receive on a particular channel corresponding to that of the keyboard you were going to use to play it.

—*Dominic Milano*

MIDI MODES

There are actually only four modes; however, you'll run into quite a few variations on what they are called. MIDI modes determine the relationship

July 1985

between the 16 available MIDI channels and the synthesizer's voice assignment. These modes are determined by combinations of two of the three possible mode messages—*omni, poly,* and *mono.* Note that the term *message* refers to software codes, which might be generated within the instrument or come in from some external source over a MIDI line. The omni-on message tells the instrument to accept information from all 16 MIDI

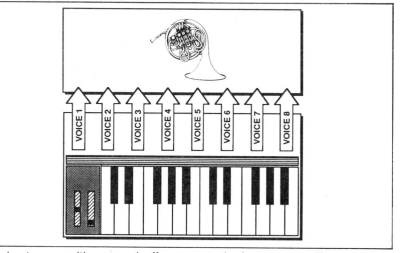

Figure 1. Mode 1: Voice assignments in a synth receiving in omni mode. The synth responds to all data received, regardless of channel designation, and all its voices are assigned to the same pitch.

channels at once; with an omni-off message, the instrument will respond to information on one selected MIDI channel. The poly and mono messages are mutually exclusive and determine how many voices are assigned to each channel depending on the omni setting. Here's a rundown of how mode messages combine to make the four MIDI modes:

Mode 1. Omni-on/poly, *a.k.a.* omni mode. The omni-on message tells the instrument to respond to information coming in on all 16 MIDI channels, while the poly message tells the instrument to respond polyphonically. Of course if it's a monophonic synthesizer like the OSCar; it will only respond monophonically.

Mode 2. Omni-on/mono. One of two modes known as mono mode. It assigns all incoming information, recognized from any and all channels, to one voice. This mode is used for playing an instrument monophonically. This is the mono mode available on Roland's MKB-300 and 1000 MIDI keyboard controllers (not pictured).

Mode 3. Omni-off/poly, *a.k.a.* poly mode. An instrument in this mode will respond only to information on a designated channel; voice messages are assigned polyphonically. This mode is used to control different instruments, playing different lines at one time from a master control source like a sequencer.

Mode 4. Omni-off/mono, *a.k.a.* mono mode. Each voice (or a number of voices specified by the transmitter) within an instrument may be programmed to respond to a different channel. This mode is used when controlling multi-timbral instruments like Oberheim's Xpander and Matrix-12, Casio's CZ-101 and 1000, and Sequential's Multi-Trak.

Most instruments power up in omni mode (mode 1). Front panel controls are often provided for switching into the other modes. Some Roland instruments send out omni-off, poly (poly mode) messages when they are turned on. If these instruments are the last to be turned on, all the instruments able to respond to mode-change commands connected to a Roland master controller will switch from omni mode to poly mode.

Two other "modes" have shown up on a variety of instruments, and have been given different names by different manufacturers. Known as *cycle* or *overflow mode* and *multi mode,* the first instrument to use them was the

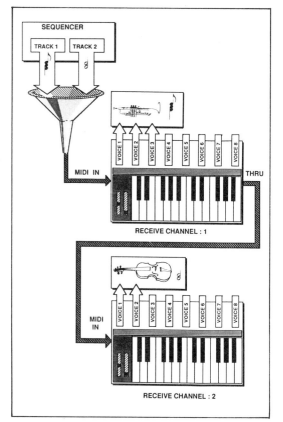

Figure 2. Mode 3: Two keyboards receiving in poly mode. The keyboard receiving over channel 1 plays track 1 data only; the keyboard receiving over channel 2 plays track 2 data only.

Kurzweil 250. Cycle mode allows notes being sent out over MIDI to be alternated between multiple synthesizers by sending them out on alternating MIDI channels. In the Kurzweil, this is used to make it possible to link two or more Kurzweils together and play them as if you had one big 24-or-more-channel instrument. The multi mode allows you to assign different MIDI channels to different keyboard setups within the Kurzweil, causing incoming control signals to address different sounds within the Kurzweil multi-timbrally. This is similar but not identical to mono mode (omni-off/mono, mode 4), which requires you to assign specific voices to specific channels.

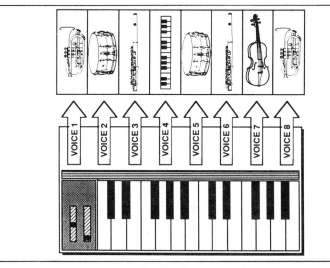

The K250's multi mode dynamically allocates voices to separate keyboard setups, so that if, for example, 12 voices of piano (one of the Kurzweil's keyboard setups) are required at one instant and six voices of slow strings are needed the next, they will be sounded as required. Note that since these "modes" aren't officially sanctioned in the MIDI spec, they aren't MIDI modes *per se*.

—Dominic Milano

Figure 3. Mode 4: Voice assignments in a multi-timbral synth receiving in mono mode. Each voice plays data from a different channel and can usually be assigned to a different pitch.

MIXING AND MERGING

In addition to the standard MIDI in, out, and thru, there are a couple of devices that offer a MIDI merge connection. MIDI merge or mix connections, as some manufacturers refer to them, combine the signal that's present at the MIDI in with the data being transmitted on the MIDI out. Most devices that offer this function are controllers of one sort or another. A few that come immediately to mind are the Roland MKB-1000 and MKB-300 MIDI keyboard controllers, the Yamaha KX88 MIDI keyboard controller and Roland's MSQ-100 MIDI sequencer. There are a number of manufacturers making MIDI mergers, including JL Cooper, Yamaha, 360 Systems, and MIDIMix. Most devices, including those mentioned, don't actually offer separate connectors for their merge/mix outputs. For example, the Roland products allow you to toggle the function of one of the MIDI outs to act as a simultaneous thru and out, sending incoming information along with new information being transmitted by the instrument itself to the MIDI output. The KX88, on the other hand, passes incoming information out the output all the time. How is this feature useful? Imagine using a MIDI sequencer to control a couple of MIDI synthesizers. The setup can be seen in Figure 1.

Now imagine wanting to use a MIDI keyboard controller to play live with the sequencer. Without the merge/mix function, you'd have to have another

October 1985

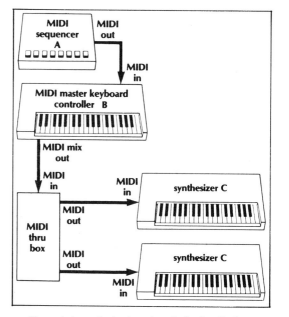

Figure 1. A master keyboard controller functioning as a MIDI merger.

Figure 2. A sequencer simultaneously receiving MIDI clock information and MIDI note information.

synthesizer that was completely independent of those being controlled by the sequencer. With the MIDI merge/mix feature, you can use the keyboard controller to address a specific synthesizer or MIDI sound module over a separate MIDI channel using the omni-off/poly mode (mode 3), while the sequencer information is being passed along to the other instruments in the system on separate MIDI channels. In the diagram, the information from the sequencer (A) is going into the MIDI keyboard controller (B). The signal from the keyboard controller (B) is mixed with the incoming signal from the sequencer (B) and passed on to the appropriate synthesizers in the chain (C). Which musical lines are sent to which synthesizer is determined by the MIDI channel settings. For example, the sequencer might be sending out the bass line on channel 1 and some accompaniment on channels 2, 3, and 4. You might be playing a lead line on channel 8. All this is being mixed together at the MIDI output of the master keyboard controller. From there it is sent on to a MIDI thru box (in order to avoid the inevitable delays caused when chaining a lot of instruments together in a line), and each synthesizer or sound module responds to the information on the channel to which it has been assigned; *i.e.* the bass synthesizer is set to channel 1, the accompaniment instruments are set to channels 2, 3, and 4 as required, and the instrument producing the lead sound is assigned to channel 8. If all this sounds like it takes a humongous array of instruments to achieve, you're wrong. It can be done with some kind of multi-track sequencer or sequencing software and two Casio CZ-101s in addition to the master keyboard controller in our example.

Another application can be seen in Figure 2:

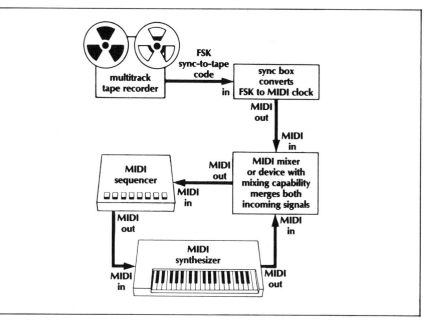

The sync tone coming from the multi-track tape recorder goes through a sync box (a Doctor Click 2, Korg KMS-30, or whatever) in order to convert the FSK tone to MIDI clock information, which is used to drive the MIDI sequencer in sync with the tracks on tape. However, the sequencer's one MIDI in will be tied up with the incoming MIDI clock signal from the sync box, making it impossible to add any overdubs while simultaneously listening to what's on tape. A MIDI mixing box, or MIDI device with that function, solves the problem, by letting you mix the MIDI clock signal from the sync box with the note data from your MIDI keyboard.

—Dominic Milano

TIPS

MIDI Cables. The MIDI 1.0 spec recognizes 128 notes, numbered 0 to 127. Middle *C* on a piano, for example, is MIDI note number 60. The lowest *C* on a piano is MIDI note number 24, the *A* below it is MIDI note 21, and the highest *C* is MIDI note 108 (see Figure 1). A knowledge of this will come in handy in cases where you want to know if a synthesizer will respond to a range wider than the range of a typical five-octave keyboard at concert pitch (this is something different from trying to figure out if a keyboard can be transposed, so don't be confused). Say, for example, you've got an 88-note MIDI keyboard controller or you just put MIDI on your piano, and you want to control synthesizer X with it. How do you know if synthesizer X will respond to the entire 88-note range of your controller and not wrap around at the outer

November 1985, updated September 1987

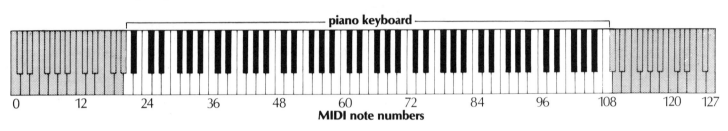

Figure 1.

octaves? A quick look at the MIDI implementation chart for synthesizer X will tell you what the note range is in MIDI note numbers. Another use of note numbers is encountered on most drum machines, like the Alesis HR16, which allow you to trigger their drum sounds from notes on a MIDI keyboard. The HR16 allows you to reassign drum sounds to different notes using MIDI note numbers, so you've got to know what numbers correspond to what notes in order to use this feature.

The Alesis HR16 drum machine allows you to trigger its drum sounds from notes on a MIDI keyboard.

MIDI Delay. The term means three different things. First off, MIDI delay is used to refer to what happens when microprocessors receive some kind of MIDI information, like a command or instruction to turn a note on, take a

21

moment to think about it, and then do it. That moment of thought is most often imperceptible, but when you're dealing with a set of instruments MIDIed together, it's going to take each of their respective microprocessors a moment to think about turning that note on. Since no two instruments are alike, the chances are excellent that no two of their microprocessors are going to take the exact same amount of time before they execute the command. This leads to slight lags between the various instruments. The typical time lag is on the order of a couple of milliseconds. You can see that when enough instruments are chained together one after the other, the delays can get pretty extreme. However, this is not all MIDI's fault, as many of the unenlightened are wont to say. Part of the blame must be placed on the microprocessors in the various instruments. For example, an Oberheim OB-8 takes something like 15 milliseconds to scan its own keyboard once, and this is by no means an atypical example. That means that you are going to have some minute time delays between when you hit one key and another *on the same instrument!* So if it bothers you to have delays that are a couple of milliseconds long—and yes, some people claim to be able to perceive delays that are under ten milliseconds—either you're going to have to convince manufacturers that they need faster microprocessors, or you're going to have to learn to get along in an imperfect world like all the rest of us. Other MIDI time lags can occur when you severely overload the information flow by playing lots of notes really fast, piling up gobs of continuous controller information, and things like that.

So those represent the typical meaning of the term MIDI delay. Another meaning for the term is when it is used to refer to devices that take incoming MIDI signals, intentionally delay them by some variable amount of time, and send them out to external gear, creating what is essentially a MIDI real-time digital delay system, not to be confused with "MIDI echo," which is another term for "MIDI thru." Currently, Dr. T offers a software package that performs these functions, and Akai is offering a hardware device, the ME-10D, that acts as a MIDI DDL. Another variation on this idea is a device by Akai, the ME-20A, a MIDI arpeggiator that takes incoming MIDI note information and arpeggiates it.

The third meaning of MIDI delay refers to traditional digital delays that are equipped with MIDI, like Roland's SDE-2500 and Yamaha's D1500. In

The MIDI programmable Roland SDE-2500 digital delay.

this case, MIDI is used to change program numbers on the DDL, enabling you to tie different delay settings to different synthesizer patches.

Local On/Off. Local on/off is a MIDI function that allows you to electronically disconnect an instrument's keyboard from its own internal sound-generating circuitry so that notes played on its own keyboard only cause slave instruments to sound. No sound will come from its own sound circuitry. This is a very useful feature, in that it allows you to cue layers of sound and in and out simply by turning local control on and off. Many of the first instruments to be MIDI-equipped did not feature this function simply because they were the first generation of MIDI instruments, most of which were designs to which MIDI was added almost as an afterthought. More recent instruments are much more likely to feature local on/off, simply because manufacturers are starting to include more complete MIDI implementations on most of their instruments.

The fully-programmable Yamaha DMP7 mixer includes built-in digital reverb, equalization, and other signal processing.

Dos And Don'ts For Connecting MIDI Cables. We routinely connect and disconnect cables from machines that are on and have yet to run into a problem, knock on wood. It's hard to imagine you will either. However, it's possible—remotely—that you could get hold of a bad cable, *i.e.* one that's been mangled enough to cause the ground to accidentally get tied to one of the information lines. If this were to happen you could possibly blow a resistor (or worse), because MIDI is a current loop, and one side of the two information lines (pins 4 and 5 of the five-pin DIN connector) only has 220 ohms resistance to the five-volt line inside the instrument. If that voltage gets into something it shouldn't, you could have problems. For quick connection and disconnection during live performance, you might want to have a service specialist install a switch on the instruments to turn MIDI on and off. Another solution is to pick up one of the many switching boxes available. Companies making such devices include J.L. Cooper Electronics (1931 Pontius Ave., West Los Angeles, CA 90025), Roland (7200 Dominion Circle, Los Angeles, CA 90040), Zaphod Electronics (220 Diablo Ave., Mountain View, CA 94043), Future Now (Box 3904, Kansas City, KS 66103), and Syco Systems (2 Conduit Place, London W2, England).

—Dominic Milano

3 BEYOND BASICS

BITS AND BYTES

All MIDI information is based on sending and receiving eight bits of data at a time, grouped together to form a byte. Each bit can communicate either of two possible states, on or off (also referred to as 1 or 0). You may already know that these eight bits can be arranged in 256 possible combinations (two raised to the eighth power), in much the same way that three normal numerical digits can form 1000 combinations—the numbers 000 to 999 (ten raised to the third power). This idea is illustrated in Figure 1.

February 1986

Figure 1.

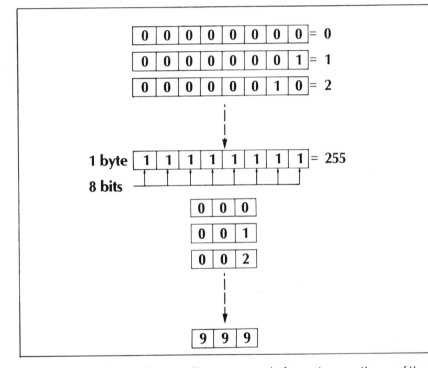

A MIDI command is usually composed of one, two, or three of these bytes sent one after another. Generally system-common commands are one or two bytes in length, and channel commands are three. The system-common commands are instructions used by the entire synth/sequencer/drum machine system, such as synchronization commands. In each case, the first byte sent is a status byte (referred to as a "status command" in the Spec, but called a status byte here to avoid confusion). The following one or two, if used, represent the "which" and "how much" portions of the command. For instance, a note-on command consists of three bytes (Figure 2). The first is the status byte directing the synthesizer to play a note (and supplying the channel number as well). The second byte in the overall command tells the receiver which note to play. The third byte carries the velocity value.

To make life easier on the software that responds to MIDI commands, a protocol was established to the effect that the status command byte's "most significant" (leftmost) bit is always a 1. In all following data bytes, the most significant bit is 0 (Figure 3). With this scheme, the software always knows, if it sees that the most significant bit is a 1, that it should start acting on a new command. It can also tell by decoding this status byte how many data bytes should follow.

This clear distinction between status bytes and data bytes makes possible a programming trick called "running status." The idea behind running status is that once a status byte has been received, the receiving instrument can continue running under that command until a different status

note-on status	byte 1
note number	byte 2
velocity	byte 3

Figure 2.

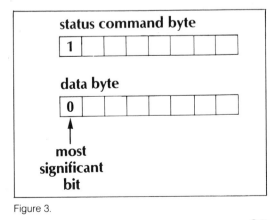

Figure 3.

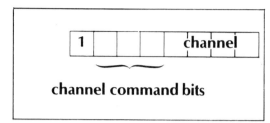

Figure 4. Three bits are used to define which channel command is being transmitted.

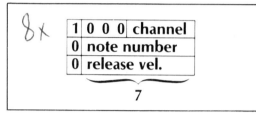

Figure 5. Note-off command.

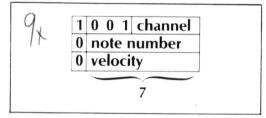

Figure 6. Note-on command.

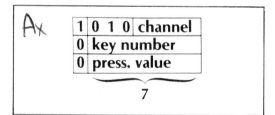

Figure 7. Polyphonic key after-touch.

byte is received. For instance, we can play a burst of notes by sending the note-on status byte just once, followed by a pair of data bytes (note number and velocity) for each actual note. A new status byte would be sent only if a new command, say, a pitch-bend command, were required. This speeds things up by about a third of a millisecond for each note, which can make a difference if a lot of notes are being sent.

What happens if you need a note-*off* command in the middle of all these notes? Note-off has its own status byte. But running status would have to be interrupted to send this. A faster way of doing the same thing is to send a special version of the note-off command—a note-on command with a velocity of zero. This can be used for this purpose assuming that the sending synth doesn't also send a release velocity, which would require a separate note-off status byte with its own associated velocity data. Most synths don't send a release velocity, however.

By setting aside the most significant bit of the MIDI byte as a status-or-data flag, we are left with seven bits, or 128 different combinations. This means that, if we are sending note-on commands, we can still specify any of 128 notes with 127 different velocity values (remember, we use the value of 0 to simulate a note-off). Since only seven bits would be too few to do a good job of handling pitch-bend (bending up and down one octave, 128 divisions makes for increments of about 1/5 semitone), two data words are used for bending, one for coarse and one for fine control.

As with data words, each status byte is left with seven "variable" bits, or 128 combinations. You might think that this is more commands than we could ever need, but the situation is not so generous. Most of the MIDI commands belong to a group called channel messages (Figure 4). These commands have the ability to steer themselves to any of 16 possible destination devices by using four bits to define a channel number. If we use four bits to define the channel, and one bit to define the status of a command, that leaves only three bits to spare or eight combinations.

In numerical order, the possible types are: (1) note-off, (2) note-on, (3) polyphonic key after-touch, (4) controller, (5) program change, (6) channel after-touch, (7) pitch-bend, and (8) system.

The last category, system commands, has no channel number attached to it, so there are actually 16 different non-channel-oriented command combinations to work with. But let's look at the other seven commands in some detail.

Note-Off Command. The command (Figure 5) requires two data bytes. The first defines a MIDI note number, from 0 to 127. Note number 36 corresponds to the lowest note on most five-octave keyboards. Note that this number doesn't define a frequency, only the number of a key on a keyboard. The actual pitch depends on several other things as well, primarily the patch currently in use.

The second data byte communicates the release velocity of the note, or how quickly the musician removes his or her finger from the key. This might be used, for instance, to define the decay rate of each note played. The implementation of this feature is still pretty rare. I expect we will see more of it in the future. The Oberheim Xpander, for one, is a slave device capable of incorporating this value into a patch.

Note-On Command. We have covered this one (Figure 6) pretty well already. As with the note-off command, one data byte defines the note number. The second data byte, when implemented, carries the velocity with which each note is struck. A velocity value of 0 is interpreted as a note-off command.

Polyphonic Key After-Touch. This command (Figure 7) is expensive to implement on a keyboard. Each key must have a pressure transducer attached to it, so that the musician can hold down a chord, adjust with his or her fingers the pressure applied to each note, and get a different response for each. Sixty or 80 of these pressure transducers, along with the conversion circuitry necessary to bring the data to the microprocessor, add significantly to an instrument's price; don't expect to find this feature in a $1,000 synth any time soon. On the other hand, adding this feature to a slave device is a less expensive matter of software. Several of the newer tone generator units can make use of polyphonic key after-touch.

Two data bytes are necessary for this command. The first defines which key is being pressed. The second defines the current pressure value.

Controller. This command (Figure 8) is sort of a catch-all for everything not defined elsewhere. There are two data bytes attached to any controller command. The first defines which controller is being used, and the second usually gives a value for the position of that controller. And what is a controller? Sixty-four of the 128 possible controller numbers handle the standard control devices: mod wheel, breath controller, volume pedal, and the like (excluding pitch-bend and polyphonic after-touch, which have their own controller codes). Actually, only 32 *different* controllers are allowed, but each can make use of two commands: a "most significant" data byte (MSB), and a "least significant" data byte (LSB). This doubles the number of controller numbers allotted for the 32 controllers. In many cases, the increased resolution afforded by using two bytes is unnecessary; for the time being, at least, the LSB is usually ignored. In the case of the common "continuous controllers," the value generated by the controller is passed in the MSB.

Another 32 of the controller numbers are set aside for on/off functions, such as footswitches or data entry switches. A low number (0) indicates an open switch, and a high value (usually 127) indicates a closed switch. Another 26 numbers are left undefined—for now.

The remaining six numbers are used to send channel mode messages. These commands are used to change the reception mode of the receiving device: for example, telling it to go from mono to omni mode. In Figure 9 the defined controller numbers are listed.

Program Change. This command (Figure 10) uses a single data byte to define the program number to which the slave device is supposed to change. This command is pretty straightforward, except for some confusion regarding what the numbers actually do. For instance, there are many MIDI devices out there that program from the front panel in octal—that is, the digits displayed range from 1 to 8, with no 9 or 0 used. To the best of my knowledge, in all such devices program 11 corresponds to program change number 1. Now, octal 11 is usually associated with an actual numeric value (at the data byte level) of 0. And an octal 88 shows up as a program change 64, while sending an actual value of 63. Straightforward?

Just to add to the confusion, there is nothing in the Specification covering what to do if the slave device only has, say, 32 patches (the DX7, for example) and receives a program change 50 command. Should it switch to its external cartridge, or ignore the command, or wrap around and start over from 1? Some machines, such as the JX-3P, stick their factory presets in the lower locations, and the user-programmable areas in the higher program numbers, making the latter inaccessible to master devices with a limited range of numbers. In addition, there are programmable outboard signal processing devices that have only a few MIDI program positions. Coming up with a method for coordinating all of this is a real problem. By the time you read this, there will be at least three devices on the market that will allow the musician some significant flexibility in setting up MIDI program change commands.

Channel After-Touch. This (Figure 11) is the common type of after-touch command. At any given moment it establishes one overall value, sent in a single data byte, for the pressure applied to the keyboard. It is sent out on the channel currently assigned to the keyboard. Exactly what happens in response to this command at the receiving end depends on the capabilities of that synth and on its current patch. After-touch may control overall

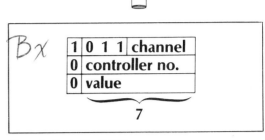

Figure 8. Controller change.

(1)	mod wheel.
(2)	breath controller.
(4)	foot controller.
(5)	portamento time.
(6)	data entry.
(7)	main volume.
(64)	damper pedal (sustain).
(65)	portamento on/off.
(66)	sostenuto.
(67)	soft pedal.
(96)	data increment.
(97)	data decrement.

Figure 9. Controller number definitions. All other numbers are undefined.

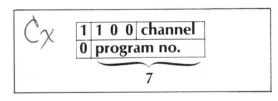

Figure 10. Program change.

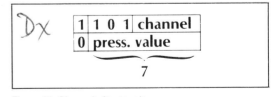

Figure 11. Channel after-touch.

27

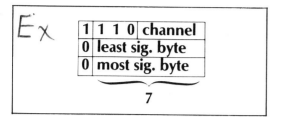

1	1	1	0	channel
0	least sig. byte			
0	most sig. byte			

7

Figure 12. Pitch-bend.

volume level, modulation level, brigthness, LFO speed, or other parameters.

Pitch-Bend. Because of the popularity of pitch-bending, this controller was given its own command (Figure 12), distinct from the controller group. This command sends two data bytes. The first is the least significant byte, and the second is the most significant byte. This allows 14 bits of resolution for pitch changes. For a normal controller command to send this level of resolution, it would have to send six bytes: an MSB controller command and an LSB controller command, each three bytes long. With a lot of pitch wheel activity, this would use up a fair amount of the MIDI cable's "bandwidth," the amount of data that it can send each second. Most synths don't actually take advantage of all this resolution, and just send the number 0 for the LSB. This yields 128 steps of bend. As mentioned above, these increments cover about 1/5 semitone, if you bend up or down a full octave. This is probably okay for most bending, but it is intolerable for very slow pitch transitions. If the bend range is only up or down a third, however, the increments will be much smaller and it will be difficult to hear the discrete steps.

—Jim Cooper

A DATA ANALYZER PROGRAM

August 1986, updated September 1987

Working with MIDI is sometimes like groping in the dark. The data passed over the MIDI cable, each byte of which is crucial to your music, is maddeningly intangible. Nothing is more frustrating, when things aren't going right, than not being able to see what's going on in that inscrutable cable.

I wrote the program *Peek* to solve that problem. *Peek* monitors a MIDI output, and when it detects any activity there, it translates the MIDI data to a legible form and displays it on the screen.

Peek is simple, but it has proved invaluable. I've used it to deduce the voice-dump formats of the DX7 (both of them), all of the controller codes, and a wealth of other useful and undocumented details. Whenever I have a new question about what's going on in the guts of the beast, I just boot up the program and push a few buttons.

There are programs on the market that do the same thing with more flash and filigree. So why bother to write your own? Well, the commercial programs can cost as much as $100.00, and for a program this simple, economy is a strong motivation to do it yourself. Of course, it takes a bit more ambition to write code than to write a check, but it pays off readily. Writing one simple home-brew program can teach you more about your gear, and about MIDI, than using a whole raft of sophisticated commercial programs.

Also, *Peek* is adaptable. Written in Turbo Pascal for the Roland MPU-401 MIDI interface, it will run on any computer that supports the Turbo Pascal compiler and the MPU-401. It will read data from any MIDI device. Unlike a store-bought program, you can customize it to suit yourself. Once you understand its workings, there's nothing to keep you from modifying it for a different interface, or even writing it in a different language.

But most important, *Peek* gives you the first monkey wrench in what I call a MIDI toolbox: a collection of utilities that can be used for routine maintenance, trouble-shooting, and problem-solving. Some of the MIDI tools you might want to keep in your kit are a channel mixer/splitter, a data filter—any program that helps you make the most effective use of your time and equipment. You'll find, once you've written one or two such tools, that it's easy to write more, because you can use tools to build more tools.

In their classic book *Software Tools,* Brian Kernighan and P.J. Plauger define a tool as "a program that helps develop other programs." They say, "Whenever possible we will build more complicted programs up from the simpler; whenever possible we will *avoid* building at all, by finding new uses for existing tools, singly or in combinations." I hope to introduce you to this powerful concept by way of *Peek.*

My choice of Pascal as a language may seem quixotic, since BASIC is the standard "free" language that comes with just about every microcomputer. I have nothing against BASIC, but I do have excellent reasons for not using it here.

First, BASIC is notoriously slow. A BASIC-language version of this program, reading MIDI data in real time, would hardly keep up with the data flow. Furthermore, every computer has its own particular dialect of BASIC. Apple BASIC is not the same as Commodore BASIC, which is not the same as IBM BASIC, which is not even the same as IBM-compatible BASIC! Turbo Pascal, by contrast, is extremely fast and consistent on all machines that run it. It is also inexpensive and popular, with a user base of close to a million, meaning that support and advice is likely to be available for some time to come.

Finally, Pascal is the language best suited to the concept I want to illustrate, that of software tools, because Pascal is a *modular* language. A Pascal program is made up of numerous small, independent modules—little tools, in fact, working together to perform a desired task.

The art of modular programming consists in breaking a complex task down into many simple sub-tasks, and solving each sub-task individually. It's a divide-and-conquer strategy. First you decide *what* needs to be done. Then you break the big what down into a lot of little whats. Then you figure out *how* to do each part. This is the messy part of programming, where you can spend a lot of time debugging, but once it's done, you can forget all about the how and just use your debugged tool for *what* it does.

Here's how the design process went for *Peek.* The first outline of what I wanted to do was absurdly simple:

1. Get one byte of MIDI data.
2. Display it on the screen.
3. Repeat the process.

As I worked out the whats, the outline grew more detailed. For instance, I had to decide on the display format. I chose hexadecimal format because it's the usual way of representing MIDI data. It became clear that each byte would have to be separated from the next by spaces. So the outline became:

1. Get one byte of MIDI data.
2a. Translate it into hex format.
2b. Write hex characters to the screen.
2c. Write 2 spaces to the screen.
3. Repeat.

Roland supplied the tools to solve step one. The MPU-401 manual provides the machine code for getting a data byte. I translated it into Pascal. The four necessary routines are in the program as the procedures PutData, GetData, PutCmd, and ResetMPU.

Let's read through the finished program in Listing 1. If you don't think you're up to reading Pascal, just follow my comments to the right of the program lines.

As always in Pascal, the main program is at the very bottom, because all data and procedures must be defined before they can be used. At the top, certain variables and constants are declared, including *drs* (Data-Ready-to-Send), *drr* (Data-Ready-to-Receive), and some port addresses, all gathered from the MPU-401 manual.

Next come four procedures and a function. These are the tools at the heart of the program.

The main program of *Peek* is very concise. The first line, "PutCmd ($35)," sends Roland command $3F, which sets up the MPU-401 act as a simple UART, or data conduit, instead of as a "smart" controller.

After the MPU-401 is set up, the program loops endlessly through the same two statements in the "repeat-until" loop: "GetData(MidiData)" and "if . . then write (Hex(MidiData)." These read the MIDI data port and write every incoming byte to the screen.

Well—almost every byte. The "if" statement is the only devious part of the program; it assures that the MIDI date is written to the screen only if it's not equal to $FE. Why is that? Well, it's one of the unforeseen details that can emerge in the debugging process. When I first tested the program with my DX7, the screen immediately filled with $FEs. I hadn't touched the synth. It appeared that the DX7 was sending out a continuous stream of $FEs, even when idle. Very strange indeed!

After digging through the MIDI spec I found that $FE is the active sensing code. Some synthesizers, the DX7 obviously among them, send this code continuously to confirm that the MIDI link is operative. So I learned something about my DX7 even while testing *Peek*! However, a screenful of $FEs was not what I had in mind, so I added that "if" statement to make *Peek* simply ignore all $FEs. Note, however, that first I made sure that MIDI never uses $FE for anything but active sensing! When you're in the *how* stage of programming, attention to such details is vital.

The program ends after any computer key is pressed, breaking the "repeat-until" loop. Note that the variable *done* must be set within the innermost loop of procedures called by the main program in order to properly register a computer keypress. The last line resets the MPU to its "smart" state for any subsequent applications.

You can see how trivial the main program is. It was simple to conceptualize, and simple to write, because all the real work is done by the procedures and functions. The procedures GetData, PutData, and PutCmd are fundamental subroutines which I use in every program I write for the MPU-401. They are the core of my MIDI toolbox. Because I have thoroughly tested and debugged these procedures, it was literally no work to include them here. The function hex translates a data byte into hexadecimal notation. You don't have to worry about how it works; take my word for it that it does. Again, this is the nice part of using tools: Once you have a solid, working module (like the MPU procedures, or Hex), it will always perform the same task flawlessly., with no further attention from you.

To be perfectly honest, I didn't even write Hex—I lifted it from another program. This is excellent programming practice. Never write code if someone else has written it for you. The whole idea of using computers, after all, is to save work.

Four screen outputs from *Peek* are shown in Figure 2. The first is the result of playing a *C* major scale, starting on Middle *C*. Let's look at the first six bytes. $90 is a MIDI status byte for a note-on command; it is always followed by two data bytes, in this case $3C (the MIDI note number of Middle *C*) and $38 (the velocity value; keyboards that don't sense velocity always send $40 for this second data byte). This three-byte sequence is then repeated, excpet that the velocity is $00, which is interpreted as a note-off. The remaining notes in the scale are played the same way.

The second example resulted from a slight movement of the pitch bend wheel. $E0 is the MIDI status byte meaning "The pitch-wheel is moving." It is followed by two data bytes indicating the position of the wheel.

The third example is the result of selecting a patch. Clearly the DX7 sends all the parameters of the selected patch over MIDI, as if it were transmitting to a slave. It only does this when system-exclusive information is set to "available." When sys-ex info is unavailable, it sends only the code for the button you're pushing.

```
type
  str1 = string[1];
  str2 = string[2];

var
  j, MidiData: byte;
  done: Boolean;

const
  dataport=$330;                   { These are port addresses for the }
  statport=$331;                   { IBM version of the MPU-401.       }
  drs=$80;                         { They must be changed for other    }
  drr=$40;                         { machines.                         }
  ack=$fe;

procedure GetData (var MidiData:byte);  { Gets one byte from MPU. }
  begin
    repeat
      j := port [statport];
      if keypressed then done:=true;  { checks for computer keypress }
    until ((j and drs)=0) or done;    { to allow exit from loop!     }
    MidiData := port [dataport];
  end;

procedure PutData (MidiData:byte);      { Puts one byte to MPU. }
  begin

    repeat
      j := port [statport];
      if keypressed then done:=true;
    until ((j and drr)=0) or done;
    port [dataport] := MidiData;
  end;

procedure PutCmd (cmd:byte);            { Sends commands to MPU. }
  begin
    repeat
      j := port [statport];
      if keypressed then done:=true;
    until ((j and drr)=0) or done;
    port [statport] := cmd;
    repeat
      GetData(j);
    until (j=ack) or done;
  end;

procedure ResetMPU;                     { Resets MPU to power-up state. }
  begin
    repeat
      j := port [statport];
      if (j and drr) = 0 then port [statport] := $ff;
      j := port [dataport];
      if keypressed then done:=true;
    until (j=ack) or done;
  end;

function Hex(b:byte):str2;
  const
    hx : array [0..15] of char = '0123456789ABCDEF';
  begin
    Hex := hx [b shr 4] + hx [b and 15];
  end;

{ **** MAIN PROGRAM **** }

begin
  done:=false;
  resetMPU;
  PutCmd ($3F);                         { Put MPU into UART mode. }
  writeln ('Now peeking ...');
  repeat                                { Begin loop. }
    GetData (MidiData);                 { Get MIDI data from MPU.}
    if MidiData <> $FE then             { If it's not an active-sensing byte...}
      write ( Hex (MidiData),' ');      { ... then write it to the screen.     }
  until done;                           { Repeat till keypressed. }
  resetMPU;
  writeln;
  writeln ('MPU reset.  So long!');
end.
```

Figure 1. The Pascal listing for Peek: A MIDI data analyzing program.

```
a) C major scale.

90   3C   40   90   3C   00   90   3E   40   90   3E   00   90   40   40
90   40   00   90   41   40   90   41   00   90   43   40   90   43   00
90   45   40   90   45   00   90   47   40   90   47   00   90   48   40
90   48   00
--------------------------------------------------------------------

b) Pitch wheel movement.

E0   02   41   E0   06   43   E0   08   44   E0   0A   45   E0   0C   46
E0   0E   47   E0   10   48   E0   12   49   E0   14   4A   E0   16   4B
E0   14   4A   E0   10   48   E0   0E   47   E0   0A   45   E0   00   40
--------------------------------------------------------------------

c) DX7 voice select.

F0   43   00   00   01   1B   31   63   1C   44   62   62   5B   00   27
36   32   01   01   04   00   02   52   00   01   00   07   4D   24   29
47   63   62   62   00   27   00   00   03   03   00   00   02   62   00
01   00   08   4D   24   29   47   63   62   62   00   27   00   00   03
03   00   00   02   63   00   01   00   07   4D   4C   52   47   63   62
62   00   27   00   00   03   03   00   00   02   63   00   01   00   05
3E   33   1D   47   52   5F   60   00   1B   00   07   03   01   00   00
00   56   00   00   00   0E   48   4C   63   47   63   58   60   00   27
00   0E   03   03   00   00   00   62   00   00   00   0E   54   5F   5F
3C   32   32   32   32   15   07   01   25   00   05   00   00   04   03
18   42   52   41   53   53   20   20   20   31   20   2B   F7
--------------------------------------------------------------------

d) DX7 power-on.

00   80   F0   90   25   00   90   31   00   90   3D   00   90   49   00
90   55   00   90   26   00   90   32   00   90   3E   00   90   4A   00
90   56   00   90   27   00   90   33   00   90   3F   00   90   4B   00
90   57   00   90   28   00   90   34   00   90   40   00   90   4C   00
90   58   00   90   29   00   90   35   00   90   41   00   90   4D   00
90   59   00   90   2A   00   90   36   00   90   42   00   90   4E   00
90   5A   00   90   2B   00   90   37   00   90   43   00   90   4F   00
90   5B   00   90   2C   00   90   38   00   90   44   00   90   50   00
90   5C   00   90   2D   00   90   39   00   90   45   00   90   51   00
90   5D   00   90   2E   00   90   3A   00   90   46   00   90   52   00
90   5E   00   90   2F   00   90   3B   00   90   47   00   90   53   00
90   5F   00   90   30   00   90   3C   00   90   48   00   90   54   00
90   60   00   90   24   00   B0   06   38   E0   00   40   B0   01   7F
B0   04   01   D0   01   C0   13
```

Figure 2. Sample screen outputs from the Peek program.

The fourth example resulted from simply turning on the DX7's power while *Peek* was running. I haven't figured it all out, but there's a note-off command for every note of the keyboard, and some controller set-ups as well. There are also a couple of garbage bytes at the beginning, which suggests that it may not be a good idea to power up a DX7 while it's on-line with other MIDI equipment.

These examples should give you some idea of *Peek*'s usefulness. Besides satisfying your curiosity about how your instruments speak MIDI, it can track down bugs that would be difficult to find any other way. The owners' manuals won't tell you, but *Peeking* at the MIDI data stream might.

In the interest of brevity, the version of *Peek* presented here is rudimentary. I'm sure you can think of some enhancements, such as the ability to store a screen to disk for later viewing, or an improved display format that decodes the MIDI status bytes into English (so you don't have to remember that $90 means note-on), or even the ability to send MIDI data back to the synth. Adding such features shouldn't be hard. And once they're properly coded, they can be used as building blocks in other programs. For instance, once I had finished *Peek,* I saw that I had most of the tools for a simple patch dump/load program; I just needed to direct the output from figure 1c to a disk file, rather than to the screen, and to add a module that sends it back to the synthesizer. Add an editor module, and presto, you have a full-feature patch librarian.

I'm not quite suggesting that you write your own multi-track sequencer program—that's an enormous job. But for simple functions or special needs, writing your own programs makes a lot of sense. And if you do it with the concept of the software tool firmly in mind, you might jsut find, someday, that you've collected enough tools in your box to take a crack at that sequencer.

An enhanced version of *Peek* (for the IBM-PC or compatibles only) is available for $10.00 from Carter Scholz, 2665 Virginia St., Berkeley, CA 94709.

—Carter Scholz

THE SONG POSITION POINTER

June 1986

Song Position Pointer (SPP) is a special command in the "System Common Messages" group used to cause a slave device such as a sequencer or drum machine to jump to the middle of a song. It is a three-byte command, having one status byte (F2 in hex, 242 in decimal) followed by two data bytes. The first data byte contains the seven least significant bits and the second byte contains the seven most significant bits of a 14-bit number. This could therefore be in the range of 0 to about 16,000. This is the number of sixteenth-notes into the song that we want to jump.

Why would we want this? For the same reason that you would hate to rewind a tape recorder to the beginning of a song every time you wanted to punch in to edit a track. The idea of song position pointer is that if you have a sequencer and drum machine synced up with the sequencer as master, you could work at editing a middle section of the sequence, and have the drum machine start at the right point every time. Another usage which you will see more in the future is to slave sequencers and drum machines to a SMPTE time stripe on tape. Any sequencer or drum machine that can't directly read SMPTE will have to get its timing info from a unit that does, or a SMPTE-to-MIDI converter such as the Roland SPX-80. If the slave unit can accept SPPs and the master unit can generate them, then you will be able to rewind the tape part-way and sync right up.

There are a couple of problems with all this that you should be aware of. Primarily, not all sequencers and drum machines recognize the SPP. This is an advanced feature that didn't find its way into any of the older designs, and is not necessarily present in newer designs either. Without the SPP recognition, the unit will have to run from the beginning each time. (Unless it reads SMPTE directly, of course.) The other problems are more subtle, and will probably cause a lot of hair-pulling in the future.

When a slave unit receives the SPP, it must figure out how far into the song to "jump" based on the number of sixteenth-notes. How does it figure this out? Well, the storage of data in a sequencer can take place in a number of ways. In one, a so-called Real-Time Clock (RTC) can be started at zero at the beginning of the song and be incremented at a rate of, say, 96 times per quarter-note. Each time a MIDI command comes in, the sequencer grabs the present contents of the RTC and stores that, along with the command, into memory. Then on playback, the RTC is started at zero and allowed to count. When the count is the same as the contents of the next memory storage location, the attached command is sent, and the memory pointer is bumped to the next one. With this scheme it doesn't appear to be too complex to calculate what the RTC should be for the desired point and just whip through memory looking for the first occurrence of that RTC, and start there. Simple, isn't it.

The problem is that this procedure doesn't take into consideration a lot that may have gone on before that point in the song. For instance, a long note may have been held into that point, a program-change command may have been missed, or a pitch-bend may be in progress. In order to be sure of not missing the "history" of the first part of the song, the sequencer must actually play (without sending MIDI note commands) the song up to the desired point. In the parlance of tape recorders, this is called "chasing." Even though this doesn't have to take place at normal tempo, it can take

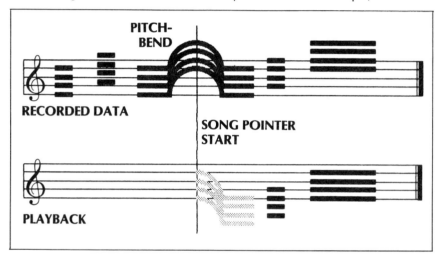

Figure 1. This shows what can happen when a Song Position Pointer tells a sequencer to start a sequence in the middle of a pitch-bend command. The remainder of the channel's data will be transposed possibly by a microtonal interval.

from a few seconds to a minute to reach the desired location, depending on how far into the piece it is.

Drum machines have a different problem. They don't generally use a RTC, but rather store a number in memory that indicates the number of internal clock times since the previous drum "event." This scheme is more efficient for drum machines, but makes it impossible to do anything other than actually play the song (albeit at a very fast rate) to find the desired point.

Now this delay is not a problem in itself, unless either the musician or the master device doesn't wait. According to the Detailed MIDI Spec 1.0, "There is no way in MIDI to know when the sequencer has selected or found the new song position. Therefore, it is up to the operator of the sequencer to see when the sequencer has found the new song position and then he can send a Continue message." This is usually done by pressing the Continue or Stop/Continue button on the master device. Each brand of slave machine will have its own way of notifying the operator that it has found the right point and is waiting, either via a beep, an LED, or a message on the readout.

I know that this manual operator intervention doesn't make everyone happy: Designers of units that send SPP would like to just send the pointer, a Continue command, and then Clock commands at the correct tempo rate, and not have to worry about whether you've pressed your button or not. In my capacity as president of the MIDI Manufacturers Association (MMA), I have received at least two "concerned" calls from software writers. Keeping in mind that this wait has to exist, they wanted the slave unit to be able to accept any Continue and Clock commands and buffer them while the unit is chasing. This could be made to work, except that a little math will show that a chase time of 30 seconds, with the master tempo set at 120 would mean that the slave would have to buffer over 1400 clock commands during that time: (120 BPM/60 sec.) X 24 MIDI clocks per beat X 30 sec. =1440. This is more storage than any MIDI event buffer I have ever seen. A more reasonable size for a MIDI event buffer is probably about 256 bytes, which would cover about five seconds of chase time.

What would have been nice in the original MIDI Spec would have been some sort of "hand-shake" method of having the MIDI slave unit tell the master unit that it is ready. But how would several slave units tell the master? Via several different MIDI cables going back to the master? How will the master know how many "ready" messages it must wait for? Nothing is perfect, and no one is going to claim an exception from this rule for MIDI. I think the next few months are going to be interesting ones for those dealing with Song Position Pointer.

—Jim Cooper

SYSTEM-EXCLUSIVE FORMAT

Let us now delve into the system-exclusive data format, and see how various manufacturers structure their data dumps through it. (All the notation below is in hexadecimal, or base 16, form in which a two-digit hex number corresponds to one byte.)

In the most basic form, system-exclusive dumps are extremely simple:

September 1986

After the manufacturer's ID code, it is totally up to that manufacturer to decide what format the data will be sent in. There may be a channel sent, there will probably be a model ID, there may be a couple of bytes indicating how many data bytes will follow. The only real requirement is that the whole thing be followed by the F7 byte, which is the EOX (end-of-exclusive) command.

Having this much freedom has led, of course, to a rich assortment of implementations, much to the graying of the hair of the people who write software to handle the bulk storage of these dumps on disk. We'll look at a number of these options. First, one of the simplest forms that I could find is the dump that we use on the Linn Drum MIDI retrofit:

F0 15 08 00 ...(16,192 data bytes)... F7

The command byte says that data is following. If it had been a 1, as in:

F0 15 08 01 F7

it would have been a request for a data dump. A computer would send this string of bytes to the Linn if it wanted to receive the data dump.

The 16,192 (this is in decimal) bytes of data have only a nibble (four bits) of actual data in each byte, this being the low four bits. The upper four bits are set to 0. An eight-bit byte of data is thus sent out as two of these four-bit MIDI bytes. Why not just send the whole byte? You may remember that all MIDI "Data" (as opposed to MIDI commands, such as the F0) must have the high-order bit as a 0. Since the high bit of real data may well be a 1, we must either split the data byte into two nibbles, or do a fancy shift routine that packs seven bytes into eight of these MIDI data bytes. The former is much simpler, and us lazy programmers usually use this method unless there is a good reason (such as massive amounts of data) to do it the other way.

So now we have a way of requesting the data, and a form in which the data is to be sent out. We could take this exact dump data as sent to the computer, and send it back into the Linn, and it would be accepted and stored. Notice that there is no provision for specific drum-machine parameters like pattern number or song number in this straightforward implementation.

A slightly more complex protocol is used by the Oberheim Xpander:

F0 10 01 01 00 pp ...data... F7

The first command byte says that a data dump follows. Oberheim ues 00 here to request a dump. In the second command byte, the 00 means that this is voice data rather than multi-patch data. Finally, Oberheim has no "all-data" dump format; instead, the patches are sent individually. So a number from 00 to 63 (0 to 99 decimal) is put into the program number byte to specify the patch number.

Now we will get into implementations that are more complicated to handle. First, let's look at Roland's JX-8P dump:

F0 41 35 cc 21 20 01 ...data... F7

I'm not really sure what all of the format, level, and group numbers mean, but they had all better be there. One of the real joys of interfacing computer dump software to this instrument is that there is no way of requesting a dump over MIDI. When in the right mode, the JX-8P sends the above packet of bytes whenever a program select is made. So if all the patches are to be saved, the user must press each of the 32 program select buttons in turn. And since the actual program number is not part of the message, you have to make sure you don't press one twice or skip one.

Even more fun is the Roland Super Jupiter MKS-80 format. It consists of a hand-shaking protocol whereby messages are sent and acknowledgements are sent back asking for the next data, or to show that the original message was indeed received. A request for a patch dump looks like this:

F0 41 41 cc 20 [6 bytes that say "MKS-80" in ASCII] cl F7

Certainly the six bytes in the middle don't leave any room for confusion about what unit this message is meant for! (ASCII, in case anybody is wondering is a standard way of converting alphabetical characters into data bytes.) The checksum at the end is a safety device to make sure that a bit or byte wasn't garbled in the middle. Assuming that it checks out, the MKS-80 will respond with:

F0 41 42 cc 20 ...data... ck F7

The data is 248 (decimal) bytes long. Since this isn't nearly enough bytes to dump the unit's entire memory, we must send an acknowledgement (ACK) to request more data:

F0 41 43 cc 20 F7

When the Roland receives this, it will send the next data message, with its 248 bytes of data. We will then send another ACK, it will send more data, and so on until it has sent all of the data, at which time it will respond with:

F0 41 45 cc 20 F7

This is the end-of-file (EOF) message. We must then send one last ACK, or else the MKS-80 will lock up. If an error was detected in the checksum, an error message should be sent instead of an ACK:

F0 41 4E cc 20 F7

Now the Roland will send back a rejection message (sort of a "how dare you!"):

F0 41 4F cc 20 F7

Complicated, isn't it? Something similar is done when you want to send data to the Roland, except you send a "want to send file" message, wait for an ACK, send a chunk of data, wait for an ACK, and so on.

Casio also uses a sort of ACK system, but they break the rules for messages a bit, I'm afraid. The MIDI Bible says that all system-exclusive messages must be ended with the EOX (F7). Casio got started on something of a wrong foot, and haven't been able to get back into the fold. This is sort of okay in most cases, but if another piece of equipment is left hooked up to the computer when a transfer is made, it may get sadly confused. Let's take a look at a dump request for a CZ-101:

F0 44 00 00 7c 10 pp

Notice that there is no F7 at the end? The CZ responds with:

F0 44 00 00 7c 30

This is an "are you sure you want this?" message. Again, there is no F7 at the end. The computer must respond with "yes, I'm sure!" message:

7c 31

The CZ will then send its data in the form:

...data... F7

Finally, an EOX! The computer then responds with:

F7

When the computer wants to send data to the CZ, it sends a request in this form:

F0 44 00 00 7c 20 pp

The CZ responds:

F 44 00 00 7c 30

The computer then sends the data, ending the transmission with an F7, and the CZ responds by sending a final F7 of its own.

That's enough bytes for now. I hope I've conveyed some of the interesting flavor that a programmer tastes when dealing with system-exclusive. You may well ask why there isn't more uniformity. The partial answer is that system-exclusive was meant to be the private domain of individual manufacturers, to do with as they would. I doubt that in the earliest days of MIDI anyone really worried about bulk-dump-handling disk units or computer programs, so no proposal was made. MIDI's designers had their hands full with the things that did get standardized. A couple of tries have been made since then, most notably by *Keyboard* columnist Steve Leonard, who writes dump save programs. But by now most manufacturers are sort of set in their ways, and they probably don't care how gray Steve's hair gets.

—Jim Cooper

MORE SYSTEM-EXCLUSIVE FORMATS

October 1986

One of the first uses manufacturers made of system-exclusive messages was to allow external software to reach in and tweak the value of some parameter, such as filter cutoff frequency. Since parameters such as these would be very specific to a given model and brand of synth, no attempt was made to assign a unique MIDI control change message to each of them. If that had been done, then each time a new synth was introduced with a brand-new function, all of the manufacturers would have had to agree on the assignment of a new control I.D. number for that function. Having been present at a few MMA tech sessions where similar topics were broached, I shudder at the thought!

So instead, the individual manufacturer will normally make the new function control part of the sys-ex parameter control for that instrument. By publishing the specs, they allow any interested software developers or hobbyists a chance to twiddle with all of the internal functions. Let's look first at the omnipresent DX7's parameter controls. The structure (remember that all numbers are in hexadecimal unless otherwise noted) is:

F0, 43, substatus, group, parameter no., parameter value, F7

The substatus has a value between 10 and 1F, corresponding to a channel number when the DX7 is set to receive on MIDI channel 1 through 16. The group is either 0, for common DX voicing parameters, or 2, for DX7 function parameters. Finally, the parameter number is the number of the actual parameter of interest. For instance, a number 0 would be used to set rate 1 of operator 6's envelope generator, and a number 8A would be used to set the LFO delay time. All of these numbers are on the DX7's MIDI implementation chart. Putting it all together, a data stream of—

F0 43 10 00 8A 25 F7

—would send, to a DX7 set on channel 1, an LFO delay time of 25. Just exactly how long a delay a value of 25 will represent has to be determined by experimentation; that is not in the spec sheet.

The above example represents a common DX voice parameter. That is, the same data could be sent to a DX9, a DX5, or even a TX816, and it would do exactly the same thing. The only thing to watch out for is that there are some parameters for the DX7 that have no counterpart in the more limited DX9. For instance, there are no operators 5 and 6 in the DX9, so parameter control messages for these will have no effect.

The DX7 also has certain so-called function parameters, which are not part of an actual patch, and which are handled separately. They include pitch-bend range (parameter 41) and after-touch assignment (53). So sending—

F0 43 10 02 41 06 F7

—would set our synth to have a pitch-bend range of ±6 semitones.

Another example I'll give of sys-ex usage for special control is in the Casio CZ-1. After wading through the 39-page utilization pamphlet, you would find that—

F0 44 00 00 70 41 data F7

—will allow you to transpose any MIDI note data that comes in. The data value is as follows:

data	key	data	key	data	key
45	G	41	B	03	D#
44	G#	00	C	04	E
43	A	01	C#	05	F
42	A#	02	D	06	F#

I've copied the numbers and the keys exactly. Some of you may wonder how the synth is supposed to know just what key things are being played in. I did too. What is happening is that the key of C in the above chart represents no transposition, not an actual key. That is, sending a data value of 41 would result in a downward shift of one semitone of all data coming in.

The CZ-1 has sys-ex commands for about everything imaginable, such as setting the position of the cursor on the LCD display, split points, and the amount of time that the CZ-1 allows between bytes from the computer before giving up (if someone pulls the MIDI plug, for instance). A very impressive implementation.

Aside from bulk dumps and external control of parameter values, sys-ex allows a rich area for expansion of the basic MIDI spec. One area I have mentioned before is sample dumping—that is, a standardized way of dumping sampled data from a unit such as the Sequential Prophet 2000. To review, sometime back, a proposal was made to set aside two so-called manufacturer IDs, 7E and 7F, to be used for certain universal applications. The 7E is to be used for non-real time applications, such as sample dumps. The 7F is to be used for real-time usages, and is yet to be actually used for anything. The MIDI Time Code (MTC) that I mentioned last will be part of the 7F area.

There will usually be at least two steps involved in sample dumping—a set-up data section that lets the receiving equipment know what it is dealing with, and a data section that contains the actual sample in number form. Let's look into it in a little depth. The basic sample dump header takes the form of:

**F0 7E aa 01 bb bb cc dd dd dd ee ee ee
ff ff ff gg gg gg hh F7**

where:

aa=Channel number. Not to be confused with basic MIDI channel numbers. Since this is a seven-bit number, any of 127 logically isolated devices may be serviced over one MIDI wire (theoretically at least).

bb bb=Sample number, with the LSB (least significant byte) first.

cc=Sample format, or number of significant linear bits (LSB) of quantization, from eight to 28.

dd dd dd=Sample period (1/rate) in nanoseconds. LSB comes first.

ee ee ee=Length of the entire sample, in words. If quantization is at 12 bits, one word would be 12 bits.

ff ff ff=Loop start point, LSB first. This would be the number of words into the sample that the loop starts.

gg gg gg=Loop end point. Ditto.

hh=Loop type. 00=forward, 01=backward. More types to come.

This header message would be sent once at the beginning. The actual data would be sent as:

F0 7E aa 02 packet# data checksum F7

where:

aa: Once again, the channel number.

Packet#: A seven-bit number that sequentially numbers the data packet being sent. When the number reaches 7F, it rolls over to 0.

data: 120 bytes of data.

checksum: An error-checking byte sent to insure data integrity.

This data packet is sent as many times as necessary to complete the sample dump. After each one is sent, the destination device will send either a special ACK message to request the next, or a NAK to indicate that the packet was garbled and request a re-transmit of the packet. Several other messages, which we don't have space to go into here, are also defined within this standard.

By using this sort of standardized data form, a sample dump from one brand of instrument can theoretically transfer to another brand. The only trouble is that there are several different types of quantization out there, from non-linear eight-bit to linear 16-bit. In a transfer from an eight-bit non-linear machine, the software must convert as accurately as possible to, say, 12-bit linear. What will this sound like in a 12-bit machine? Not exactly the same, probably.

An area for future exploration is a standard sys-ex dump format for dealing with sequencer (and drum machine?) data. If this comes to pass, it might be feasible to record on one brand of sequencer and transfer the data to another brand which may have, for example, more advanced editing capabilities. It is possible to just plug the MIDI out of one unit into the MIDI in of another and put the first into play and the second into record. But sometimes small alterations are made in the length and position of the notes when this is done (even when the two units are synced). An actual dump definition would be preferable.

—Jim Cooper

READING MIDI IMPLEMENTATION CHARTS

November 1986

MIDI devices, by definition, are all compatible. By this I mean that when you properly connect one to another, neither instrument will melt down when the two are powered up. Furthermore, in the case of MIDI keyboard instruments, you can expect them at least to recognize each other's note-on and note-off messages. However, when you are creating a system of MIDI devices, things aren't always so easy. You need to know whether, and how, your instruments can interact beyond this common level.

A MIDI implementation chart is the most important source of information regarding what dialect of MIDI your instrument speaks. It is usually provided with the instrument's documentation. The MMA (MIDI Manufacturers Association) and JMSC (Japanese MIDI Standards Committee) have standardized the format of this chart so that all manufacturers can present implementation data in a uniform manner.

The chart is not self-explanatory, however, and there are some slight inconsistencies in the way information is displayed. Since we will be looking at the interaction between MIDI devices fairly often in this article, it's worthwhile to spend some time explaining how to interpret these charts. If you own a MIDI device, pull out its implementation chart and refer to it as you read.

You already may be familiar with the chart's layout of four columns and 12 rows. The first column, *function*, identifies a particular MIDI function. Most function headings are split into sub-headings. The next column, (*transmitted*) tells whether the function is transmitted, and in what fashion, when the device is used as a source of MIDI messages, or MIDI master. The *recognized* column indicates whether, and how, the device will respond to that function when it is acting as a MIDI slave, that is, receiving MIDI messages.

The symbols O and X are used to indicate whether or not a message can be transmitted or received. Most charts use O to indicate yes and X to indicate no, but some charts are contrary. (This may be due to the fact that the standard chart in the MMA's Detailed Specification document gives the reverse assignment as a example.) In any case, the bottom right corner of the chart should give a key to the convention used.

The final column, *remarks*, provides further information about how the function is implemented.

Let's go through the functions one at a time:

Basic Channel. There are two subheadings for this funtion. *Default* indicates the transmit and receive channels assigned automatically upon powering up. In most cases, this will be channel 1 for both. The chart should also indicate whether the default channel can be changed by the user; that is, whether you can re-assign the default channel so that, upon powering up, the instrument will automatically be set to channels of your choice. The subhead marked *changed* indicates which MIDI channels can be assigned, by the user.

Mode. There are four MIDI modes: omni-on/poly (mode 1), omni-on/mono (mode 2), omni-off/poly (mode 3), and omni-off/mono (mode 4). The *default* subheading indicates which mode will be active when the unit is first turned on. If the default mode can be re-assigned, that will also be indicated here.

Messages describes which MIDI channel mode messages are transmitted and/or recognized by the unit. The possible messages are *omni-on, omni-off, poly-on,* and *mono-on.* They may also be written as *omni on/off, poly,* and *mono.* Some instruments, such as the Casio CZ-5000 and the Oberheim Xpander, can be set manually to operate in different modes, but they don't recognize the messages for those modes when they arrive through the MIDI in port. This kind of information should be in the *remarks* column.

The *altered* subheading describes how the instrument will respond to a message requesting a mode that is not implemented. For instance, the Roland RD-l000 electronic piano operates in modes 1 and 3 (omni-on/poly and omni-off/poly) only. If it receives a message requesting a change to a mono mode, for example, its response will depend on the specific contents of that message. In order to explain this, we'll have to look more closely at the format of the mono message. The third data byte in this message (which we'll call M) contains a value that tells the receiver how many mono MIDI channels to assign voices to. If the RD-1000 receives a mono message with an M value of 1, it will change to mode 3. Any other M value will set the

Function··········		Transmitted
Basic **Channel**	Default	all ch
	Changed	×
Mode	Default	Mode 3
	Messages	OMNI OFF, POLY
	Altered	**************
Note **Number**		0-127
	True voice	**************
Velocity	Note ON	O
	Note OFF	× 9n v=0
After **Touch**	Key's	O
	Ch's	O
Pitch Bender		O
	0-63	O
	64-121	O

Figure 1. A small portion of a typical MIDI implementation chart.

instrument to mode 1. This is indicated on the chart as follows:

MONO (M=1) 1, (M=1) 3.

Note Number. The range of MIDI note numbers transmitted by the instrument is listed in the *transmitted* column. Usually the range will coincide with the number of keys on the instrument (if it is a keyboard). If the range is greater than the number of keys on the unit, then the unit has some kind of MIDI transpose feature, which you'll find explained in the *remarks* column.

There are two possible ranges of note numbers that can be shown in the *recognized* column. The first range (which is not labelled) indicates which note numbers the instrument will respond to. Note numbers beyond this range will be ignored (that is, they won't be played by the device). The second range, labelled *true pitch*, indicates the actual pitches playable by the device when note number 60 is tuned to Middle *C*. Recognized note numbers outside of the true pitch range will be transposed in octaves until they fall within this range. For example, many instruments recognize note numbers 0 through 127, but the only true pitches they can play correspond to numbers 21 through 108—the 88 notes of a grand piano.

Velocity. The *note-on* subheading tells you how the device deals with attack velocity. A "yes" in the *transmitted* column indicates that the instrument has a dynamic control mechanism (keyboard or otherwise). A "no" means that the device isn't capable of transmitting attack dynamics. A "yes" in the *recognized* column indicates that the voices in the instrument will respond dynamically to incoming attack velocity data, while a "no" means that velocity information will be ignored (all voices will play with the same loudness).

Transmission of and response to release velocity data is indicated in the same manner under the *note-off* subheading.

Valid MIDI not-on velocity values are 1 through 1227. A note-on velocity of 0 often is synonymous with a note-off message. If an instrument transmits "note-on, velocity 0" when it means "note-off," it will be indicated in the *transmitted* column, which usually contains the hex code for that message: 9nv=0.

After-Touch. The *keys* subheading indicates whether or not the device transmits and receives polyphonic key pressure messages, and the *ch* subheading does the same for channel pressure messages (the more common monophonic after-touch).

Pitch-Bend. The *pitch bender* information tells you how the instrument deals with incoming and outgoing pitch-bend data. The *remarks* column may give the bender resolution in bits. On some newer instruments, this row

Figure 2. Moving the pitch-bender on a transmitting master sends not one, but many pitch-bend messages—one for each increment of bending that occurs.

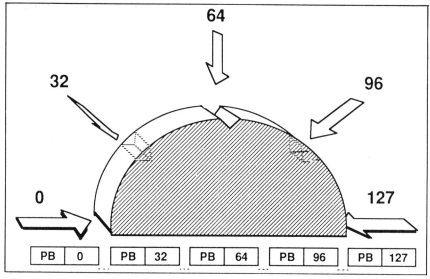

will also tell you whether or not it can transmit or recognize messages setting the bender's range.

Control Change. This is where all of the unit's control facilities and their assignments will be listed. As you may know, there are 64 valid controllers currently allowed by the MIDI Spec. The numbers listed with each controller indicate the code numbers used when a controller message is transmitted, and what numbers the instrument will respond to when a message is received. If the controller numbers are user-selectable, the range of possible selections will be indicated here. This section will also tell you whether transmission and recognition of these messages can be selectively disabled.

Program Change. A "yes" or "no" under this heading tells you whether program change messages are transmitted and/or received. The range of numbers transmitted will appear in the *transmitted* column (the maximum range is 0-127). The ranges shown in the *recognized* column describe what numbers are recognized, and the actual program numbers these will correspond to in the particular device (indicated by the *true #* subhead). This is where you can find out what preset number slave instrument X will change to when you switch programs on master instrument Y.

System-Exclusive. The *remarks* column in this case usually tells you what kinds of messages are transmitted via sys-ex data. This may include patch dumps, sequence dumps, and parameter changes. Other documentation provided with the instrument will give more detailed information about a given instrument's system-exclusive implementation.

System-Common. The unit's ability to recognize and transmit song position pointer, song select, and tune request messages is listed here under the appropriate subheadings. Although the first two of these are not implemented by most keyboard instruments, sequencers and drum machines often deal with these messages.

System Real-Time. Real-time messages handle synchronization functions. In order to act as a timing master, a device must be able to transmit clock messages, and to be clocked by MIDI it must recognize them. These capabilities are noted under *clock*. If your keyboard has a built-in sequencer or arpeggiator, this is where you can find out whether those functions can be synchronized with MIDI drum machines and sequencers.

A "yes" under the *commands* subheading indicates transmission or response to one or more of the following messages: *start, stop,* and *continue.* The remarks column will tell you which.

Aux. This section of the chart covers local control, all-notes-off, active sensing, and reset commands. You may be able to enable/disable local control manually even if the *local control* subheading indicates that this message is neither transmitted nor received. As for all-notes-off commands, there are five ways to specify this message: Each of the four mode messages can be interpreted as an all-notes-off message, and there is also a dedicated command for the purpose. Technically, controller numbers 123 through 127 are reserved for these messages. If "yes" appears in either of the *all notes off* columns, the number(s) of the specific messages (s) will be listed.

Miscellaneous. At the bottom of the chart is an area reserved for any additional comments the manufacturer wishes to make about the instrument's MIDI implementation.

Familiarize yourself with the charts for any MIDI devices you own. You will rely on them more as you add instruments to your system; they can save you a lot of frustration and time spent on trial-and-error experimentation. You'll also find that they prove useful when you're looking for a device to fill a particular slot in your MIDI setup.

—Steve De Furia

SMPTE TIME CODE AND MIDI

July 1986

What is SMPTE? Just so nobody wastes their precious minutes/seconds/frames, I'll go into a little detail.

SMPTE Timecode. In the late '60s the Society of Motion Picture and Television Engineers (SMPTE) decided to bring some order to the chaos of video tape sync systems by establishing a standard, much as synthesizer manufacturers did with MIDI. The idea of this standard was to allow the identification of each frame of a picture on videotape by means of a digital code. (Unlike film, videotape isn't divided into frames. For the sake of convenience, however, a second's worth of tape is divided into several units, and for the sake of convention, these units are called frames.) This allows electronic editing and synchronization among a number of tape machines. The editor simply tells the monitoring or editing electronics which particular frame to switch over on, and lets everything fly. In brief, this is how it works:

Each video frame has 80 digital bits of data associated with it. In Longitudinal SMPTE (probably the most common version), this data is recorded on an audio track running the length of the tape. This recorded data is much the same as what you get when you do a cassette data dump from a synthesizer.

The 80 bits are grouped into ten words of eight bits each. Two of them are used to synchronize the SMPTE reader electronics. The remaining eight words specify an exact frame/second/minute/hour, as shown in Figure 1.

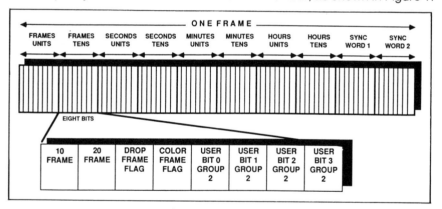

Figure 1. SMPTE timecode for a single video frame. Eighty bits are divided into ten digital words, specifying frame location in hours/minutes/seconds/frames and two synchronization words. Detail of second SMPTE word shows how its eight bits are allocated between frame information, flags, and user-defined bits.

Actually, each word has two parts: Two, three, or four bits are used to describe the given location on tape, and the remaining bits are used either as special flags or as user-assignable bits. The lower part of Figure 1 shows how the second word of the code is broken down. The color frame bit is not relevant to this discussion. The drop frame bit is, though, and I'll explain it in a while. the four user bits can be used for anything: specifying a reel number, the date of recording, or the editor's favorite color.

All of this is recorded over and over again down the length of the tape, whether audio or video, with the tape location numbers changing frame by frame. Assuming that you have the proper equipment, you can wind part-way into a reel, and the electronics will know exactly where you are. The only other information you might need is the starting time of the particular segment of tape, which isn't necessarily 00:00:00:00. (You can set that yourself by entering the location for the top of scene five, or take three, or whatever.) Subtracting the starting time from the location you're interested in yields the elapsed time, right down to the frame. If you add more electronics, you can have one tape transport mechanism sync to another by comparing the SMPTE code played back by each machine, while adjusting the speed of one to keep the codes in alignment. This method, of course, is used in thousands of audio studios to lock together two or more multi-track recorders.

Most SMPTE In the U.S. operates at 30 frames per second, which is the standard frame-rate for our TV system. With 80 bits per frame, bits are passing by at a rate of 2,400 per second. In Europe, where the standard is 25 frames per second, the bit rate is a little lower: 2,000 bits per second. This is known as the EBU (European Broadcasting Union) rate. Aside from the frame rate, the standard is exactly the same. You may also run across SMPTE running at 24 frames per second, which coincides with the motion picture rate of 24 *actual film frames* per second.

There is a special case of the 30 frames per second rate called drop-frame timecode. For reasons that I'm afraid I don't know, color signals are sent out at a rate close to 29.97 frames per second. That's pretty close to 30—but no cigar. Everything will come out right, however, if 108 frames are skipped, or dropped, every hour. This is accomplished by dropping two frames per minute, each minute, except the 10th minute, the 20th minute, and so on in multiples of ten. This makes up the difference. A value of 1 in the drop frame flag bit mentioned above indicates to decoding devices that this is supposed to take place.

So What? You may be wondering what all this has to do with you. After all, few of you work closely with video, and I doubt many of you own large recording studios. Why talk about frames per second when you just want to make music? Well, in just the same way that MIDI has found applications far afield from its original purpose, SMPTE is creeping into the world of music. (That's the wonderful thing about a standard specification: It gives a sense of security to technologists of all stripes.)

One nice thing about SMPTE-locked tape recorders is that they can be synchronized from anywhere in the song. Have you tried that recently with a MIDI sequencer and a drum machine? With most MIDI equipment, you have to start from the beginning each time, since only start, stop, and clock commands are implemented. The most recent devices (I know of fewer than ten) use MIDI Song Position Pointer (SPP) commands to allow a lock from an arbitrary point. This is certainly part of the future, but an SPP by itself won't sync to music that's already on tape. The usual tape sync won't do it (it also needs to hear the beginning of the song). In order to do this, drum machines and sequencers require built-in SMPTE, which is rare indeed, or a SMPTE-to/from-MIDI converter. Off the top of my head, I know of four units that do this job in one way or another: the Roland SPX-80, the Garfield Electronics Master Beat, the FriendChip SRC, and the Fostex 4050. Using these devices, you can set a tempo and the unit will read SMPTE and generate SPP commands, start, stop, and a 24ppq pulse code. In some cases you can enter locations for a tempo change, and it will be accomplished on the fly.

One of the drawbacks of SMPTE is that a chunk of electronics must be devoted to decoding the audio bit stream (from tape) into usable digital numbers. Rather than having this circuitry replicated in each piece of SMPTE-reading gear, why not do the decoding in a stand-alone unit, and have that box send the digital data via an interface more universal to musical instruments? Let's see, what interface could we use? Hmm. I'm still thinking. Wait a minute—it's right on the tip of my frontal lobe. I've got it! Let's use MIDI!

As much as I'd like to take credit for this idea, it was the brainchild of Chris Meyer, who works for Sequential and also heads the MIDI Manufacturers Association (MMA) Technical Board. He reasoned that MIDI could be used to distribute SMPTE code to all interested equipment, and devised a proposal for how to standardize it all. There are two parts to his proposal for what was originally called MSMPTE (MIDI/SMPTE) but is now known as MTC (MIDI Time Code). The first is for real-time distribution of the SMPTE frame time. Each second, a burst of 13 bytes would convey the hour, minute, second, and four bytes worth of user-defined data. What about frame number? In order to cut down on the amount of data that has to go through the MIDI cable, this 13-byte message would only be sent once per second, and we could use one of the unassigned system-common messages either every frame or every 1/4 frame, depending on the desired resolution. Since this system-common frame message would be only two bytes long, we could send it 30 or 120 times per second without using up too much MIDI bandwidth. (It works out to about 2 percent of the bandwidth for full-frame messages, and 7 percent for 1/4 frame messages.)

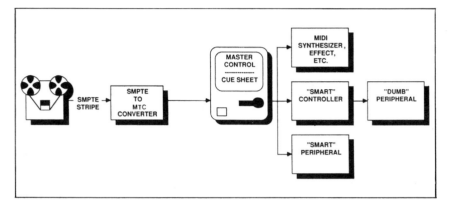

Figure 2. MIDI Time Code in action. The SMPTE time code track recorded on tape is routed to the SMPTE-to-MTC converter, which feeds the master controller (in this case a computer with sequencing software). The master then drives various slave devices.

(For those of you who are new to the subject, MIDI bandwidth refers to the amount of data that can be passed through the interface. The bit rate for MIDI is 31,250 bits per second, and there are ten bits in each MIDI byte—eight data bits, plus two synchronization bits. Thus, MIDI bytes are sent at a rate of 31,250/10 or 1,325 per second. That is the bandwidth of MIDI.)

The other aspect of the proposal concerns MTC setup information. This includes defining punch-in and -out points, cue points, and the like. All of these would be defined in terms of SMPTE frames. A master computer acting as a cue list editor could then download the setup information to intelligent controllers associated with mixdown automation, lighting, tape transports, air conditioning, or anything else you might care to come up with. In the future, these products may well include MTC capability. Figure 2 illustrates one possible arrangement.

After an initial reaction of "That's interesting. What do you use it for?" I've heard some very enthusiastic responses to the MTC spec. The best news is, MTC was ratified in early 1987, and should become a common feature of many MIDI products.

—Jim Cooper

CLEARING THE AIR SURROUNDING THE MIDI SPEC

March 1986

Rumors have been flying for some time now regarding a so-called MIDI 2.0, supposedly a souped-up revision of the original Spec. I'm sure these rumors have been exacerbated by the introduction of the Sequential Prophet 2000, and by the Yamaha MCS (MIDI Communications and Service Controller) chip. I think it's a good use of this space to address the issue of an upgraded MIDI spec, to offer some opinions, and to explain the contributions of the MIDI Manufacturers Association and the Japanese

MIDI Standards Committee.

The Prophet 2000 is capable of dumping its sampled data via MIDI. Simple arithmetic shows that a full dump of the 2000's data would take around three minutes for 256k worth of 12-bit samples. Since the actual number of microporcessor calculations involved in such dumping is minimal, the engineers at Sequential provided an option to speed the whole thing up. The method employed by the 2000 to create its high baud rate makes this easy as well as practical. So, for the purpose of data dumps only (*not* normal note-on commands and so forth), the Prophet 2000 can operate at twice the MIDI rate. I put it this way because MIDI is *only* specified at 31.25 kilobaud. At any other rate, it ceases to be MIDI.

The Yamaha MCS chip is a sort of intelligent MIDI data processor. Much like the Roland MPU-401, it can relieve an instrument's microprocessor of a great many "house-keeping" chores. Let me tell you, when you sit down to design a chip like this, you don't want to leave anything out. A large custom chip is an expensive proposition, and you want to throw in everything possible. This particular chip is capable of operating at four times the MIDI rate. At the same time, it can operate at rates as low as 75 baud (1/4 that of MIDI). I'm sure that Yamaha doesn't expect anyone to use the chip for MIDI at 75 baud—it's just that they've elected to use a more generalized approach to the internal baud-rate generator.

No manufacturer of MIDI equipment is looking to cut its own throat by adopting some sort of unilateral "planned obsolescence" strategy. MIDI equipment that you buy today is not going to be obsolete any time soon for any reason having to do with MIDI speed. I can say this with confidence because of the support manufacturers have shown for the Japanese MIDI Standards Committee (JMSC) and for the MIDI Manufacturers Association (MMA). The memberships of these two organizations include just about every manufacturer of MIDI equipment in the world.

The MMA is a non-profit corporation of about 32 members. Their purpose is to promote the MIDI Spec, and this includes making technical data available to any interested party, providing a forum (through meetings and the Technical Board Bulletin) for proposals regarding extensions of the MIDI Spec, and generally keeping MIDI products as compatible as possible. At the present time there is *no* discussion regarding a MIDI 2.0 specification at the MMA.

Finally, I'd like to add a comment about the so-called MIDI speed problem. It is true that if you send a lot of notes with fast attacks *simultaneously* through a single MIDI cable, the notes will spread out a bit in time. This produces an effect similar to shuffling a deck of cards. The problem is real, but it's easy to solve. The Yamaha QX1 sequencer handles it by providing eight separate MIDI outputs, each of which can connect directly to a receiving instrument. The Southworth and Musicworks interfaces for the Macintosh also have multiple outputs, and I expect we will see more interfaces of this sort in the future.

A more common complaint comes up when keyboardists simply slave one synth to another. This is the simplest kind of MIDI connection and, after all, this is precisely what MIDI was designed to do. The problem is a slight delay between notes produced by the master and those produced by the slave. Such delay is always a result of the slave synth's own internal software. Inevitably, it takes some time to process incoming MIDI information. It's not unusual for five to ten miliseconds to go by *after* the MIDI note has been received, before the note actually sounds. This would be the case even if the MIDI data were travelling through its cable at the speed of light.

Another aspect of the MIDI Spec that draws occasional fire is the five-pin DIN connector. A tangle of MIDI cables is becoming as common as the microphone cables found strewn across the floor of any musical stage or studio, and yet until a couple of years ago few musicians had even touched a DIN connector. Clearly, an explanation is in order.

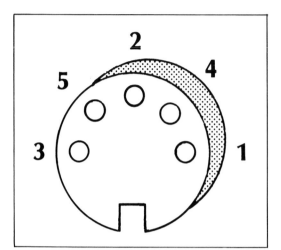

Figure 1. The numbering for each of the DIN plug's five pins, as established by the MIDI Spec, is indicated above. A shielded, twisted pair is connected to pins 4 and 5, while the shield is connected to pin 2 at both ends. For MIDI out jacks only, pin 2 is connected to ground.

When the first meetings were held between various American and Japanese manufacturers to discuss the interfacing specification that was to become MIDI, there were few DIN-plug cables in the United States. Although owners of Roland drum machines might have noticed a DIN connector on the rear panel, the few DIN cables around were mostly used with European and some Japanese audio equipment. Japanese manufacturers requested that the 180-degree, five-pin DIN connector be used for MIDI.

Since suppliers of the DIN connector could be found in the States, American manufacturers agreed to the proposal. It seemed like a good idea for other reasons as well. DIN connectors are reasonably inexpensive, especially compared to something like the XLR-type connector, which is used on low-impedance microphones. They are pretty reliable, too. MIDI requires at least three conductors, and by choosing a five-conductor connector, there were a couple of spare pins for unforeseen future developments.

The MIDI Spec requires that the MIDI cable be a shielded, twisted pair, connected to pins 4 and 5 of a male connector. The shield must be connected to pin 2 on both ends. The maximum length of the cable is supposed to be 50 feet. Let's take these items individually, and examine why they are specified.

Shielded, twisted-pair wire. MIDI transmissions send pulses. These pulses have rise and fall times of a few microseconds, and they are sent at a rate of 31,250 per second. This would create radio interference with near-by equipment were it not for the shielding. Twisted-pair wire is generally favored for this kind of signal transmission.

Use of pins 4 and 5. Roland and Korg drum machines have used the five-pin DIN connector for synchronization purposes for some time, using pins 1 and 3 for the start command and clock outputs respectively. In all likelihood it was considered safer to avoid these pins for use with MIDI.

Shielding. The shield is attached to pin 2 (traditionally the ground pin for DIN connections) on both ends of the cable. You might worry that this could lead to ground loops, but don't fret. The MIDI Spec states that only the MIDI output jacks should have their pin 2 connected to ground. Thus the shield is always attached to ground, and at the same time there is no possibility that the MIDI cable might complete a ground loop.

Maximum Length. Even though it is serial, digital information, the MIDI signal is not unaffected by its passage through a cable. Because of the capacitance between the signal wires, and between them and ground, each MIDI pulse gets a little distorted. The amount of distortion is directly related to the number of feet of cable the signal passes through. Fifty feet is a general, rather than an absolute, maximum. The actual length of cable that you can get away with depends on a number of factors:

(a) The quality of the cable. The less capacitance per foot, the more feet of cable you can use. I try to stay away from Radio Shack cable, although I know of many musicians who use it with no problems.

(b) How many MIDI thru ports you daisy-chain the signal through. Each time you use the thru port of a MIDI device, you distort the pulses. This, of course, is in addition to any distortion introduced by the cable itself.

(c) The opto-isolator. Most MIDI units use the Sharp PC-900 opto-isolator, but there are faster (lower-distortion) and slower (higher-distortion) units available, and some products use those.

(d) The tolerance to this distortion of the receiving instrument. There seems to be a wide variation in the degree of pulse distortion tolerated by different brands of MIDI devices. What works fine with Brand X may not work with Brand Y.

What problems does this distortion cause? If a pulse is misinterpreted, the receiving unit will respond to a different command byte than the one sent. This might simply cause an incorrect velocity value. On the other hand, it could result in a note-off command being supplied to the wrong note, leaving its intended note ringing on indefinitely.

You can find a wide variety of MIDI cables at your local music retailer these days, ranging from downright cheap to outrageously expensive. You will have to look into your own setup—and your own pockets—to decide what is best for you. In general, if the cable runs are short, and if you don't expect to do too much plugging and unplugging, inexpensive cables are probably fine. But if you are pushing the 50-foot limit, or if you are really going to torture those cables, I wouldn't skimp—in the life of a MIDIfied musician, few things are as embarrassing as a stuck note at the end of your climatic closing number.

—Jim Cooper

CIRCUIT CHECKERS, CODE CRACKING, AND CONTINUOUS CLOCK

I thought that I would give you a couple of super-simple projects to play with and then answer a couple of common questions, which may shed some light on problems some of you have encountered.

I saw a MIDI cable tester made by CAE Electronics (1150 E. Santa Inez Ave., San Mateo, CA 94401) at NAMM that got me thinking about simple devices that could be used for MIDI system debugging. I came up with something about as simple that I have been using quite a bit ever since. It is particularly useful when you have to keep your eyes on what you're doing, and need to be able to hear rather than see MIDI data. You'll need a pair of headphones and a 1/4" phone jack. Make the connections shown in Figure 1. How is that for simple? When MIDI data is not being sent, no current flows thru the current loop. When a single MIDI byte is sent, the current pulses on and off for about a third of a millisecond. This will produce a clearly audible click in the head-phone. When more data is being sent, like when a pitch wheel is being moved, the data sounds more like something ripping.

You can make it with either a male or female DIN plug, or even have one of each lying around. To use it, just plug it in—no batteries required. You will not even need to wear the phones in most circumstances. I generally plug the adapter into the thru jack if I want to monitor what is going into an instrument.

If you would like to monitor the MIDI signal as it travels from one instrument to another, use the circuit in Figure 2. By adding a resistor, you can keep the phones from "hogging" too much of the current. This cuts down the signal quite a bit, and you will probably need to actually wear the phones. Those of you who are well acquainted with the MIDI spec might be concerned about using a parallel circuit with MIDI. You are right—it is generally not a good idea, but there is no possibility of damage. There is only a possibility of MIDI bytes getting garbled, and I think the chances of that are extremely slim. In general, I wouldn't leave it attached for anything other than debugging, though.

I thought some of you might find a couple of very simple MIDI switches of interest. The first of these (Figure 3) is just an on/off switch.

The next example (Figure 4) is a circuit that may be used to select either of two MIDI data sources to go to a single slave instrument. This could be

May 1986

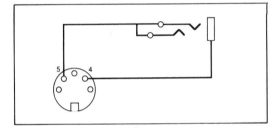

Figure 1. Connecting phone jack to MIDI plug for monitoring data.

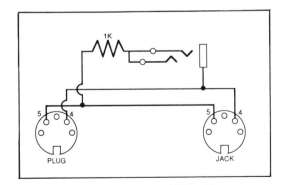

Figure 2. Monitoring data across a MIDI cable.

49

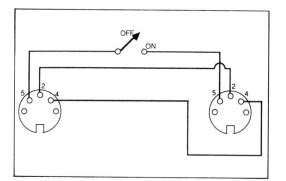

Figure 3. Simple MIDI on/off switch.

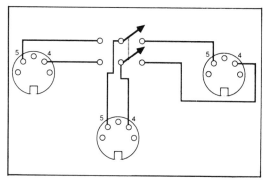

Figure 4. Simple MIDI switch box.

used by a musician who uses both a fixed and a portable keyboard in his act. The switch would select which was connected at a given moment. The switch could either be a toggle type of Double Plus-Double Throw (DPDT) or rotary switch. If you use a rotary, try to get a type known as "Break Before Make." This means that the common terminal disconnects from one side to the other.

Alternately, you could use this same circuit to decide which of two slave devices is connected to a single source. This circuit is too simple to allow you to switch both of the slaves to the master. Why? Because that would mean the two slaves would be hooked in parallel directly to the master. The MIDI spec doesn't allow for this, and data errors will probably result (stuck notes, etc.).

Now for some questions.

I'm using a Dr.T Keyboard Controlled Sequencer (for the Commodore 64 with Sequential interface) and a Roland 707 drum machine. The only way I can get them to start and stop together is to use the MIDI clock (from Dr.T to 707) and start the song from the sequencer. I would like to have the 707 as master, since it is easier to control the tempo with the knob.

I assume the problem you are having syncing the sequencer to the drum machine is that the Dr. T sequencer doesn't stop when the 707 does-it just keeps running, making it essentially impossible to synchronize the starts. I gave a call to the folks at Dr. T and they said that by the time you read this, there will be an update available for a small charge. The main reason I printed this letter is to use it to point out one of the possible problem areas with MIDI synchronization.

The MIDI specification contains within it areas that, while maintaining a degree of flexibility, also allow room for some non-compatibility.

THE MIDI 1.0 detailed spec contains a section that says "There is no objection to sending a timing clock (F8) during the time the sequence is in stop mode." Of course, this allows for two situations: One brand may stop sending the clock data as soon as it stops its sequence (or pattern) with a stop "pulse" (FC), and another brand may continuously send clocks, just sending starts and stops as necessary. The argument for not sending continuous clocks is, "Why send extra, unneeded MIDI data, taking up precious time?" The argument for continuous clocks is that the receiving sequencer or drum machine might be made smart enough by the continuous clocks to know the correct tempo as soon as the start pulse is received.

In any event, both systems are in use out there. No problems arise, however, unless the writer of software that operates one way fails to allow for receiving data that follows the other scheme. In the case of the Dr. T software, the program recognizes the start and clock, but didn't have stop recognition built in, not expecting the clocks to continue.

It might be possible for the opposite problem to exist. The receiving software might need the clocks to continue in order to bring things to an orderly halt (inside housekeeping). In the case of a sequencer, it might not be able to do little things like turn off any notes if the clocks stop before it thinks they should. It seems to me that I have heard of this problem in the dim early days of MIDI, but I'll bet it has been ironed out by now.

I have a CZ-101 slaved to a DX7. How come whenever I operate the data slider on the DX7, the CZ-101 goes out of tune?

When MIDI Spec 1.0 first was published, only the modulation wheel controller command was actually defined. At that time, the others—which were later defined as described in the tutorial above—were just up for grabs. Unfortunately, Yamaha grabbed the controller #6 code for its data slider, and Casio picked the same controller code for its master tune control. Since that time, the Yamaha usage of #6 for data entry and several others have been adopted by the current Detailed MIDI Spec. That is, the Casio usage is now out of spec.

Who's at fault? Casio used #6 in good faith at the time. Their machines don't have EPROMs, which are easily changed—the program that runs the computer is inside the microprocessor chip, so it is difficult to get at. So you are out of luck as things stand. Your only hope is that soon there will be accessory boxes that allow you to translate one controller number to another (i.e., you could play with the mod wheel, and affect volume level).

You might be concerned about this whole issue of undefined controller numbers being used for whatever functions each different manufacturer wants, giving rise to incompatibilities between various instruments. Fortunately, the issue is under pretty good control now. The Japan MIDI Standards Committee (JMSC) and the MIDI Manufacturers Association (MMA) now coordinate the usage of extra controller numbers. The plan is that manufacturers make proposals to their respective organizations, to be passed on to both memberships for comment. The controller code number is permanently assigned if there are no arguments.

I've got a Roland MKB-1000, a Roland MSQ-700, and an Oberheim Xpander. I'm having trouble getting the MKB and MSQ to talk to the Xpander on multiple MIDI channels simultaneously. Do you know what the problem might be?

Apparently, this problem only occurs on early model Xpanders, since Oberheim found the glitch and corrected it on newer models. According to the Oberheim service department, the problem is that the early Xpander only responded to all-notes-off commands on its basic MIDI channel. This meant that notes being played by voices assigned to other MIDI channels would be clipped off, stuck on, and generally screwed up by the information coming in on the basic channel. There are two fixes. The simple one is to set the Xpander's basic channel higher than any channel in use in your system. The not-so-simple-but-simple fix is to get the latest software revisions installed in your unit. For Xpanders still under warranty, software update kits and installation are free. For non-warranty instruments, the kit is free, but installation charges will be determined by the qualified Oberheim service center that installs it. If you want to check to see if your Xpander has these updates or not, the updated software is main processor version 1.2 and voice processor version I.4. Your owner's manual includes instructions on how to check the current software version.

—Jim Cooper

MORE TIPS

Active Sensing

If you've ever noticed that data is coming out of your DX7 almost constantly, what you're seeing is some form of MIDI active sensing. If you have an early DX7 (with serial numbers between 1001 and 24880 and between 25125 and 26005), the data sent was two bytes—F0, 43. It was sent every 80 milliseconds except when a system-exclusive dump was going on. Newer DX7s send one byte, FE, every couple of hundred milliseconds when nothing else is going out of the synth.

The idea with both of these is a good one—if the connection between a master and slave gets broken, then the reception of these active sensing bytes also stops, and the slave should turn off any notes being held. In the slave unit, reception of the first active sensing command "arms" the software to start timing. Each subsequent command (or any other MIDI data)

December 1985

resets the time. If the timer ever times out, the slave knows to perform some sort of reset. With this scheme, attaching a slave that uses this system to a master that doesn't presents no problems, since the "arming" never takes place.

If you're well acquainted with the MIDI spec you might notice a problem with the active sensing used in the earlier DX7s. A command of F0-43 starts like a system-exclusive command with a Yamaha manufacturer's ID, but doesn't have the required end-of-system-exclusive (EOX) byte. This is an example of very early confusion over MIDI usage. It is possible that this code could confuse some slave device or sequencer, although I don't know of any problem off-hand. These early DX7s also used a different after-touch command than is currently used (it was a controller command with a controller number 3). For these two reasons, it might be a good idea to get your software updated. Contact your friendly local Yamaha authorized service center.

Using Y Cords

Here's a common question, "Why can't I just hook up a Y cord between the MIDI out connectors of my two DX7s and the MIDI input of my sequencer? I want to be able to record from both DX7s at the same time. I have tried this, but get less than great results."

The answer is that MIDI digital data is much different than audio signals, which shouldn't be mixed with a Y cord either, by the way. In order for MIDI data to be correctly recognized, each data bit must be received, in turn, separately. If a Y cable is used, the bits from one of the DX7s will collide with the bits from the second, and the result will be unintelligible. It would be like two typists trying to use the same typewriter. The result would be words consisting of letters from both typists, and having no meaning.

What is needed is some sort of MIDI mixer which will accept individual MIDI inputs and mix them by means of a microprocessor into a single data stream. This is a bit tricky for the following reasons. First, the messages from MIDI instruments often take advantage of a shortcut called "running status." In some situations it isn't efficient to send a note-on command each time you send a note. If a quick flurry of notes is played, why not let the subsequent note-ons be assumed after the first one? This note-on running status is then allowed to run until a different command, such as a note-off or a program change, is sent, at which point the new command's status is allowed to run. In this way, one data word for each note in the flurry need not be sent. This in turn makes the whole flurry happen faster, minimizing the "shuffling the deck" effect that happens when too many notes are being sent at once. This means that our MIDI mixer has to have the smarts to recognize a running status situation coming from one input, and to reestablish it if it is interrupted to send some data from the second input.

Another tricky area is data overload. If you are playing, say, a DX7 fairly hard, you send a *lot* of velocity data. If, in addition, you are working the pitch-bend wheel, you will get very close to using up 100 percent of the possible data time that a MIDI cable can handle. What does this mean? In the tutorial above we saw that it takes 1/3,125 second to transmit each MIDI word. A typical note-on message requires three of these words, so it will take up about 1/1000 second, or one millisecond. Nothing else can travel through the MIDI cable during that millisecond. If you flip the pitch-bend wheel rapidly, you can send hundreds of individual pitch-bend commands per second, each also taking about a millisecond. If we send a combination of pitch-bend, velocity, and note messages per second, we have "filled" the MIDI cable.

So where do we put the data from the second DX7? The answer is nowhere—it's impossible. All our MIDI mixer can do is store away the extra data and wait for a period of time when the cable isn't so busy. With two hot and heavy players, this could easily happen too late to be musically useful. (I have this mental picture of the players leaving the stage and the synths playing on!)

One solution is to have a "filter" on this MIDI mixer for each MIDI input. Then if there were an overload, you could filter out, say, the after-touch data, so that it didn't use up any data time. This filter concept could have additional uses, such as perfecting a sequenced musical line one MIDI parameter at a time. I have heard rumors of MIDI mixer devices, but I haven't actually seen any yet.

To answer an unasked question about Y cords, you shouldn't use them to take one MIDI output and split it into two MIDI inputs either. While you might get it to work in a given circumstance, it is definitely going against the MIDI specification and may lead to the dreaded Stuck Note Syndrome. Invest the moderate bucks and get a splitter box.

And while we're on that subject, let me go a little further into the MIDI delay issue. There's a type of MIDI delay that has nothing to do with actual perceived delay, but with the purity of MIDI's electrical signal.

When a MIDI waveform goes through the opto-isolator at the receiving end, the off part of the waveform is delayed about two microseconds more than the on part is (see illustration). This is not a problem in itself, but if the

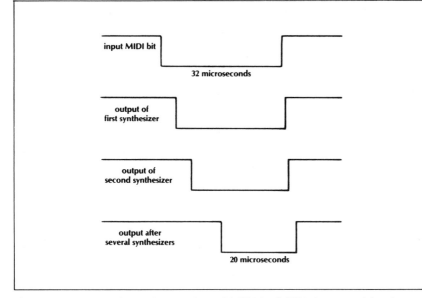

input MIDI bit

32 microseconds

output of
first synthesizer

output of
second synthesizer

output after
several synthesizers

20 microseconds

Figure 1. Cumulative signal distortion from chained MIDI outputs.

signal must pass through a series of MIDI in/MIDI thru combinations, as happens with a chain of synths, this distortion is cumulative. Since the MIDI bit is only about 32 microseconds long to begin with, a significant amount of distortion can happen after only a few synths. If the waveform is distorted enough, the receiving circuitry will not be able to correctly interpret the data, and once again, Stuck Note Syndrome will strike.

This is quite a different matter than perceived delay. In an instrument designed to MIDI specification (and I know of none that aren't in this regard), the MIDI thru is only a re-amplified version of the opto-isolator output data. The output of the MIDI thru follows within a microsecond or so of the MIDI in signal. This is not going to be audible! The distortion-type delay, however, does occur, and becomes exaggerated as the signal passes through successive opto-isolators. It is for this reason that I am not a great fan of the MIDI thru connector, and highly recommend that you use MIDI splitter boxes for all but the very simplest hookups.

—Jim Cooper

4

THE GEAR

KEYBOARD CONTROLLERS

January 1986

MIDI ushered in the rebirth of the component synthesizer system. Where we used to have islands of individual instruments that needed extensive modification in order to be able to talk to each other in the most simplistic ways, we now have the ability to interconnect, synchronize, and control multiple electronic musical instruments of every size and brand.

Along with the flood of MIDIed synthesizers, samplers, drum machines, and what-have-you has come the realization that the more synthesizers you

The Seiler Showmaster electric MIDI grand piano. Aside from an integral pickup system to amplify the piano's acoustic sound, the Showmaster is a full-fledged MIDI controller, with 100 presets available.

buy, the more room you take up with all those black-and-white things—keyboards that are more or less redundant. And so the question arises, why not get one master keyboard to control all your various MIDIed instruments instead of buying the black-and-white part over and over? Granted, you may be in a situation where you need a keyboard on each synthesizer, but if you would like to use MIDI to its fullest, you may want to look into a MIDI keyboard controller or a MIDIed strap-on keyboard.

So what the heck is a MIDI keyboard controller? It's a box from which MIDI devices and many MIDI functions can be manipulated. It does not have sound-generating capabilities of its own. The idea is for the manufacturer to build a keyboard with the best action possible and pair it with electronics that allow you to address many different combinations of synthesizers and synthesizer modules from one central keyboard. With this kind of arrangement, you're left to concentrate on playing your single keyboard, rather than having to worry about dancing around between five or six of them.

Some controllers have full-size piano-like keyboards, with weighted actions and an 88-note range (although some support the full 128 note range of MIDI by being transposable). This type of keyboard may put off players who have gotten used to the typical flaccid synthesizer action, but for those who really want to feel resistance when they slam away at a velocity-sensitive action, these actions can't be beat. Of course, for those who do mind those ultra-heavy piano-like actions because they don't allow their fingers to fly over the keyboard, there are non-weighted keyboard controllers.

One feature you'll find in the full 88-note weighted controllers is that their actions aren't the only things that are weighted. The actual boxes themselves, because they house (in most cases) a lot of moving parts, weigh enough to give anyone but Arnold Schwarzenegger a hernia. Consequently, these larger keyboard controllers are great in the studio, but not so great for the band that doesn't have a full complement of roadies. Unless, of course, you're a masochist at heart.

For those in a live performance situation, or anyone who needs portability in their MIDI keyboard, a strap-on MIDI keyboard could be the answer. Strap-ons have been around for years. Billy Preston and Edgar Winter used to sling Univox electric pianos around their necks in the pre-MIDI days of the early '70s, and Jan Hammer and Roger Powell brought the strap-on into focus as a way for synthesists to get out and get mobile with the best of the guitar players. However, the units played by Hammer and Powell—modified Minimoog keyboards and later Powell's Probe —required extensive modification and a thick multi-pin connector cable, and were generally a pain in the rear compared to the MIDI strap-on keyboards currently available. Best of all, a MIDIed strap-on can drive any instrument with MIDI on it, whereas the older hot-rodded strap-ons could only be hooked into instruments specially modified for them.

The now discontinued Sequential Prophet T8 is still popular with synthesists since it has weighted keys and after-touch.

The larger MIDI keyboard controllers—and some of the strap-ons—can save you a lot of headaches when it comes to hooking your MIDI instruments together, since most offer more than one MIDI out, or a mixed MIDI out/thru. This can take the place of extra MIDI thru boxes, and can in general make your patching arrangements a little less nightmarish. The Roland MKB-1000, for instance, has a MIDI in, a MIDI thru, and four MIDI outs. This lets you have your entire setup controlled by or passing through the MKB.

Besides simplifying your MIDI setup, a MIDI keyboard controller should be able to *control* things. The Yamaha KX88 has the ability to send certain types of system-exclusive information to any brand of synthesizer. This would allow you, for example, to alter the cutoff frequency of a particular preset in your Korg Poly-800 by moving remotely a data entry slider on the KX88. Strong stuff! None of your keyboards have a split function? No problem. MIDI keyboard controllers can usually send more than one channel at a time, and you can assign which channel you play on the upper half and which channel you play on the lower. You will also be able to control parameters such as pitch-bend, modulation, velocity, after-touch (pressure), preset changes, sustain, breath control, and MIDI mode. *Polyphonic* after-touch, a relatively new feature available on some MIDI keyboards, is

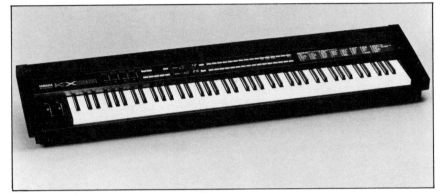

The Yamaha KX88 controller keyboard has piano-like weighted action, and is one of the more popular 88-key controllers.

something you may want to look for in a keyboard controller. With polyphonic after-touch, you can add after-touch-controllable functions to individual notes in a chord by varying the pressure of each of your fingers. The Sequential Prophet-T8 and the Yamaha DX1 are two of the synthesizers that offer polyphonic after-touch, but the T8 is no longer manufactured and the DX1 may be out of your price range. What your synthesizers will or will not be able to do with the after-touch information when they receive it is of course another question.

MIDI controllers may not even have a keyboard. If you play an acoustic instrument (a sax, a trumpet, or even your voice) and you want to double what you play (or sing) on a synthesizer, you'll need a pitch-to-MIDI converter. A pitch-to-MIDI converter turns volume and pitch into velocity and note data. MIDI controllers might be shaped like a guitar. The Roland Guitar Synth, the Octave Plateau MIDI Guitar, and the Synth Axe are all MIDI controllers for the guitar player.

There are even a few companies that will build MIDI controllers into an existing instrument. If you like the feel of your acoustic piano and want to play your synths from it, you can have it MIDIed without changing the action or tone of the piano. These retro-fits include velocity sensitivity, channel select, programmable split, and other features described in the list of products at the end of this article. MIDI add-ons are also available for Hammond organs and accordions.

Strap-on MIDI keyboards give many of the same options as keyboard controllers without the weight. Most strap-on keyboards only have three or four octaves of keys, but allow you to play in a larger range through the use of octave switches. A strap-on keyboard will have its controls arranged either on a panel just behind the keyboard, on a handle or neck to the left of the keyboard, or a combination of the two. Each manufacturer has its own way of arranging the controls. You will need to decide what arrangement is most comfortable and useful for you. The Yamaha KX5, for instance, has a pitch-bend strip and a push-button for sustain. The Roland Axis has a barrel-shaped roller for pitch-bend and a pedal on the floor for sustain.

Several major keyboard manufacturers offer a MIDI controller or MIDI strap-on keyboard. When you choose a MIDI controller, be sure you like the feel of the keyboard. You'll be using that keyboard a lot. If you're looking at a strap-on keyboard you'll have to decide between full-size or half-size keys and AC or battery power. You should also consider the weight of the

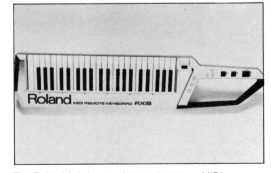

The Roland Axis is one of several strap-on MIDI controllers on the market. The Axis features after-touch, a sustain pedal, and numerous MIDI implementations.

57

instrument. Whether you're looking at controllers or strap-ons, *always* try it with the kind of equipment you plan to use it with. Yes, the MIDI spec is an accepted standard, but functions on one manufacturer's keyboards may not be as easily accessed with a controller made by another manufacturer.

Keyboards

Kurzweil MIDIBoard. The MIDIBoard has an 88-note weighted keyboard with velocity, release velocity, polyphonic pressure, and retrigger sensitivity. It transmits on up to eight channels at once. It has 12 user-definable controllers for MIDI functions and system-exclusive information. $2,200.00

The Kurzweil MIDIBoard controller, pictured at the bottom of the photo. The system shown is one of the student workstations at the Berklee College of Music in Boston.

Oberheim Xk. The Xk offers a 61-note non-weighted keyboard with velocity, release velocity, and pressure sensitivity. It has one MIDI out but can transmit on up to six MIDI channels simultaneously. The keyboard can be split into three programmable zones. The Xk has 100 presets and also offers an arpeggiator. $995.00.

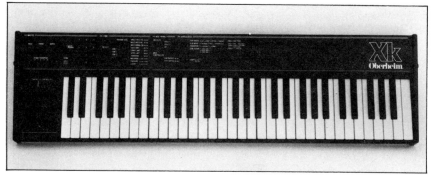

The relatively affordable Oberheim XK controller features an on-board arpeggiator.

PPG PRK-FD. The PRK-FD has a 72-key weighted keyboard which boasts a Steinway piano action and velocity sensitivity that can be programmed for any MIDI function. It has 60 presets that can remember the channel and system-exclusive preset information for up to 64 synthesizers. The PRK-FD has one MIDI in and four independent MIDI outs. It also has a 5¼" disk drive built in for storage of setups and presets. $4,650.00.

Roland MKB-1000. The MKB-1000 has an 88-note weighted-key velocity-sensitive keyboard. It has 128 presets that can remember MIDI channel, MIDI mode, patch numbers, and keyboard split point. The back panel includes one MIDI in, four MIDI outs, and one MIDI thru. Controls include a pitch-bend and modulation lever, damper and soft pedal inputs, and adjustable velocity level. $2,195.00.

Roland MKB-300. The MKB-300 is just like the MKB-1000 except that it has 76 non-weighted keys. $1,295.00.

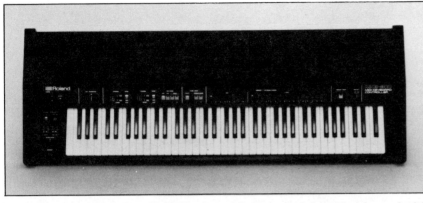

Roland's MKB-300 is the scaled-down version of their MKB-1000 controller keyboard.

Yamaha KX88. The KX88 has an 88-note weighted keyboard with velocity and monophonic pressure sensitivity and an assignable split point. It has 16 presets for patches, channel info, and splits. The KX has a MIDI out/thru which merges outgoing data with incoming MIDI signals. This controller can transmit system-exclusive information to any brand of synthesizer. Reviewed in *Keyboard*, Oct.'85. $1,695.00.

Yamaha KX76. The KX76 has the same features as the KX88 except that it has only 76 unweighted keys. Price not yet available at press time.

Strap-On MIDI Keyboards

Europa Systems Lync. The Lync is a four-channel, four-octave, velocity- and pressure-sensitive keyboard. It has an adjustable head and controls for sustain, hold, patch advance, sustain, pitch-bend, modulation, and one user-definable wheel for any MIDI function. One interesting feature is the chord function. When the user plays a chord and presses the chord button, any notes played after the chord is released will be harmonized with the chord tones. 10 lbs. $1,295.00.

Korg RK100. The RK100 has a 41-note keyboard. Controls include VCO modulation, VCF modulation, program select, volume, and pitch-bend. It is powered by six AA batteries or optional 9V AC. Under 10 lbs. $395.00.

Roland Axis. The Axis is equipped with a 45-note velocity- and pressure-sensitive keyboard. It has a user-definable wheel destination so that MIDI functions and system-exclusives can be controlled. The Axis has chord memory and a remote power supply with a sustain pedal. Presets and MIDI channels are accessed through the keyboard. 7 lbs. $695.00.

Yamaha KX5. The KX5 has a 37-note mini-key keyboard. It has 32 presets and velocity sensitivity, and includes volume, sustain, modulation, octave change, and channel selection controls. The KX5 has a pitch ribbon, which more closely imitates the pitch-bend action of a guitar. Breath control input is also available. Battery power. 7 lbs. $495.00.

MIDI Retro-Fits

Forte Music MIDI-Mod. The MIDI-Mod is a modification to keyboard instruments which adds polyphonic velocity sensitivity, programmable split, and programmable MIDI range. Controls include channel select, transpose, and a MIDI on/off pedal. MIDI-Mod also sends sustain pedal information.

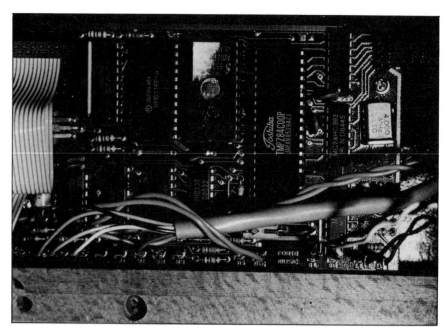

An insider's peek at some of the electronic retrofitting employed by Forte Music for their MIDI-Mod.

MIDI-Mod is available for: acoustic pianos, $1,495.00; Yamaha PF10 and PF15, $475.00; Yamaha CP-70, $1,195.00; Yamaha CP-80, $1,295.00; Kawai EP308, $1,295.00.

Hammond B-3 To MIDI Adaptor. This modification allows you to send note on/off and sustain information from your Hammond B-3 to any MIDI keyboard or module. The kit includes two pedals which are used to turn MIDI on and off, activate sustain, select the range of active MIDI keys, and transpose. Bill Butler installs the kit in the Omaha area, or it can be purchased as a kit. $850.00 installed, $750.00 mail-order.

MIDITEC Accordion Retro-fit. The MIDITEC accordion retro-fit is available for both electronic and acoustic accordions. It sends note-on/off information as is, but MIDITEC will customize the hardware and software to a player's specifications if desired. The prices listed do not include installation. Electronic accordions, $250.00; acoustic accordions, $350.00.

—David Frederick

COMPUTERS

January 1986, May and July 1987, updated September 1987

Microcomputers are great musical tools, and they became well established as valid keyboard "peripherals" almost as soon as the first MIDI synthesizers hit the stores, because the MIDI data stream is exactly the sort of input that computers thrive on. But which is the best computer for the MIDI musician?

Besides the all-important consideration of your budget, there are two main factors that should figure in your choice of a computer for music.

First, the golden rule for buying a computer system: *Choose the software, then select the computer which will best run that software.* Hardware specs are of secondary importance. Most doorstop owners were wooed by computer dealer buzzwords—"it has 2 megs of RAM, an RS-422, SCSI, it's expandable, interfaceable, retractable, reverseable, edible . . ." They later find that the only software for this techno-wonder is a word processor and an accounting package for dentists.

When choosing software, you need to identify your primary use for the computer. Will it be sequencing? Synth programming? Music printing? Record-keeping? See what's available, make a list of what you'd like to do, and then go out and find a good music store where you can get demos on a variety of software.

As the second factor, how good is the computer itself from a musician's point of view? For the most part, the features that make a computer good for general use make it good for music, but there are issues of particular concern for musicians:

Operating Systems. The reason you can't run your preferred software on just any computer is because each type of computer has its own operating system. The operating system (OS) software controls the computer's basic housekeeping functions. In the case of the IBM PC, the OS (DOS 2.0) is loaded from a floppy disk when the computer is turned on ("booted"). Many computers (including the Macintosh and Atari ST) have their operating system software stored inside the computer on ROM (Read-Only Memory) chips.

As far as the user need be concerned, there are two basic types of operating systems: command-based and icon-based. In primarily command-based systems such as the IBM PC, Commodore 64, and Apple II, you must memorize a set of commands that control the computer's basic functions. For example, to run a program, you might have to type "A:load program name." The complexity of these commands can range from simple to mind-boggling.

Icon-based operating systems are generally more user-friendly. Files and functions are represented on the computer's screen by small pictures called icons. Icon-based systems almost always include a hand-held pointing device such as a "mouse." To delete a file, you would typically point (using the mouse) to the file, then "drag" it onto a small on-screen picture of a trash can (the "delete" icon). Icon-based systems are very intuitive and easy to use, but there is one drawback: Quite a bit of computer power is required to manage the onscreen graphics, often slowing the computer down considerably.

Which is better? Icon-based systems are growing in popularity, but many people like command-based systems. However, you should try to get a hands-on demo of a variety of software products that do the kinds of things you want to do, and then decide which system you like best. Don't listen to veteran computer users—they always like the system they have used the longest. Go by your own instincts and pocketbook.

Memory. Theoretically, the more RAM the computer has, the more sophisticated the software can be and the more MIDI data storage you get. But be sure the software you're thinking about using can take advantage of the increased memory. If there is no provision in the sequencer program itself to send data to your optional memory expansion board, the board might as well not be there.

Speed. Disk drive access speed is the big concern, especially if you want to use the computer in performance. You probably don't want to prolong the dramatic silences between your tunes while the drive grinds away loading the next sequence. This is less critical at home or in the studio, but slow drives are always a nuisance. How fast the computer updates its screen display is another consideration. The speed of data processing and transfer isn't likely to be a crucial issue unless you're writing very complex sequences with lots of MIDI controller data. Even then, the interface will probably gag before the computer itself does.

Graphics Capabilities. All the popular computers can display decent graphics, but a truly high-resolution screen is a lot easier to see onstage, and is essential if you want good-quality standard notation. On the other hand, many powerful music programs don't need graphics at all.

Color or B&W? Should you buy a color or monochrome monitor? Again, it's personal preference. Generally, a color screen is harder to read and not necessary for musical applications, but if you intend to run any game software in your spare time or want to do any serious color graphics work, you may consider color essential. In the case of IMB PCs/compatibles and Atari STs, be sure to check whether the software you want to run requires a color or monochrome monitor. Some software operates differently or not at all if the wrong monitor is hooked up.

Built-In Music Capabilities. Almost all of the popular machines can make some sort of sound, but usually it's limited to a monophonic squeak. A few come with respectable internal synthesizers. These may not offer any competition for your main keyboard, but with the right software, they may be enough for roughing out your compositions.

Ergonomics. How big and bulky is the machine, and how easy will it be to lug around? Are there a lot of cables and external components, or can peripherals be added internally? How easy is it to position the keyboard and screen to make the best use of the space you have?

A genuinely portable self-contained computer is great for travelling musicians. But some people think using computers onstage is suicidal, since disk drives aren't particulary noted for their sturdiness, and it's too easy to break a monitor screen. They may be right. The Macintosh is very portable, since it's mostly self-contained. It can be packed in a minute and comfortably carried. However, if the monitor screen gets smashed in transit to a gig, you'll be out your entire computer. In contrast, a full-blown IBM PC is a major moving project, but because of its modularity, if any one component fails, you can still use the rest of the machine, renting a replacement component while yours is being fixed. If you're an IBM person and you need to move the computer frequently, spend a little extra money and buy a Compaq or other portable PC.

There are a couple of companies building rack-mount versions of various computers, including the PC and the Mac. At one point, there were plans for a rack Amiga too. There are also two lap-top Macintosh clones on the drawing board. But these look like they're going to be very expensive when they finally hit the market.

If you decide to buy an Atari ST computer, and portability is an important factor, I'd recommend the 1040ST. Unlike the 520ST, the 1040's power supply and disk drive are built into the main unit. The 520ST has at least five separate pieces that are a major pain to pack and move.

Reliability. There are no accurate statistics on the relative reliability of the various makes and models. Probably your best resource is a repair technician at a shop that services a good range of models.

Interfaces. A computer can't communicate with MIDI unless it has an interface attached to it. Interfaces come in different sizes and shapes, depending on what computer they're designed for, and depending on how much you want to spend. At this point, only the Atari ST and Yamaha CX5M computers have MIDI built right in. Even so, some companies (notably Hybrid Arts) are marketing interfaces that allow the ST to talk to SMPTE. Interfaces for the Commodore 64/128 tend to be the least expensive interfaces (around $100 or so), while Mac MIDI/SMPTE interfaces and Roland MPU-401 interfaces for PCs and compatibles tend to be the most expensive ($100-$500).

Individual Computers

To recap, the most important advice anyone can give is to identify your musical needs and the software you want to run before you decide on which computer is right for you. No matter how fabulous a computer looks on paper, no matter how great its specifications, if it won't run the software that fills your musical needs at a price you can afford, it's not the computer for you.

Let's take a look at several of the most popular personal computers, and examine each machine's strengths and weaknesses for musical applications. The computers are separated into three price categories: inexpensive (under $600), moderate ($600-$1,500), and expensive (over $1,500). These prices are approximate and include only the base computer (central processing unit, monitor, and keyboard). Bear in mind when doing your shopping that prices can vary greatly from dealer to dealer, and that sometimes going with the best deal doesn't always mean going with the lowest price. Ask what kind of after-sales support your dealer can supply. Can they service your computer in their shop or will they need to send it to some service center in Timbuktu? Will you need support with *music* software, and if so, can the store supply it? And don't forget, the computer is only the first step in building a music system, so don't blow your entire budget on the computer alone. You're also going to need disk drives, the software, a MIDI interface (in most cases), floppy disks to store your work on, and whatever peripherals you may fancy (or be able to afford); *i.e.* modem, printer, etc.

With that said, let's take a look at some computers:

Apple Macintosh

Current Models: 512K, 512K enhanced, Mac Plus, Mac SE, and Mac II.
Price range: Moderate (512K) to very expensive (Mac II).
MIDI interfacing: Add-on component. Choices range from simple (one in, a thru, and a couple of outs) to complex (multiple ins and outs, SMPTE generating, etc.). Mac Plus requires self-powered interface.
Comments: Many people consider the Mac to be the best music computer. The existing software base is excellent now (after a slow start) and includes everything from powerful sequencers and the best music printing (using Apple's Laserwriter printer) to advanced sample editing, synth voicing, and more. Despite the fact that it doesn't fold up into a single box, it's fairly portable, although some might complain that because its display screen is in the same box as the CPU, it's less convenient to fix if the screen gets trashed in transit. The recently released Mac SE and Mac II are designed to be fully compatible with existing Mac programs. While there seems to be no problem with the Mac SE (basically an enhanced Mac Plus), in fact the Mac II only runs 50-60 percent of the existing software—the problem is related to copy protection. With luck, this incompatibility will be solved in the future, though it might not matter to you—the introductory price of the Mac II (with color monitor and a hard disk) exceeds $6,000.

Commodore Amiga

Current Models: Amiga 1000, 2000, and 500.
Price range: Moderate.
Interfacing: Outboard. Few choices at this point—simple in, out, and thru. Only one we know of with drum sync capability. There are rumors of a SMPTE-compatible interface in the future.
Comments: The Amiga is a very technologically advanced, impressive, and seductive machine. It features high-quality graphics and internal sampled sounds with eight-bit companded resolution. There are, however, reliable reports that the Amiga does not have a consistent high-speed timing chip. Software developers are working on various ways around this problem, but if you expect good timing resolution from a sequencer it's best to ask exactly what timing reference is being used before you buy the software.

Atari ST

Current Models: 520ST, 1040ST.
Price range: Inexpensive to moderate.
Interfacing: Simple (in, out/thru) MIDI interface is built-in. SMPTE-

Apple Macintosh SE shown with Opcode Studio Plus Two MIDI interface.

Commodore Amiga 1000.

Atari 1040ST.

63

Commodore 64.

Apple IIGS shown with AppleColor RGB Monitor and 800 kilobyte, double-sided Apple 3.5 Drive.

IBM Personal Computer with Monochrome Monitor and Graphics Printer.

generating interface available from one developer as an add-on component.

Comments: The STs are great candidates for becoming the computer of choice for the majority of computer-conscious musicians. The ST offers hardware comparable to the Macintosh's at a much lower price. Judging by the inclusion of MIDI jacks on the ST, Atari appears to be interested in promoting its use as a music computer. Although the ST does not yet have the extensive software base of the Macintosh, many excellent programs have been released for the ST in the past few months. Judging by the number of developers working on ST software, the machine should be very well supported in the coming years. The ST has some advantages over the Mac (faster processor speed), as well as some disadvantages (some users find the ST's operating system, GEM, much clumsier than the Mac's operating system). The ST is Atari's budget alternative to the Mac. Does Atari have an answer to the Mac II up their sleeve? Rumor has it that they are also developing a 68020-based powerhouse, and you can bet it will be less expensive than the Mac II.

Commodore 64

Current Models: Commodore 64, 128, and SX-64 (portable).
Price range: Inexpensive.
Interfacing: Outboard. Choices include a simple in, out, thru box with or without tape sync.
Comments: This is currently the most commonly owned machine for making music, probably because of the great price and the volume of software available. And it's a great machine for the price. The C-64's computing speed and power can't compare with more expensive systems, but some very clever programs make the most of the machine. A good choice if you want to get into computers without spending much money.

Commodores have an internal three-voice multi-timbral analog synthesizer (the SID chip), which can put out a decent range of musically useful timbres. The synthesizer can be controlled with BASIC or machine language, or you can buy non-MIDI software or keyboard interfaces to make it easy to use.

Apple II

Current Models: Apple IIGS (prior models include the Apple II, II+, IIe, and IIc).
Price range: Moderate.
Interfacing: Add-on component. Choices much the same as the Commodore 64 series with addition of a Roland MPU-401 intelligent interface.
Comments: The IIGS, which was only recently introduced, is a good value with an excellent installed software base. It incorporates a faster processor, better graphics, and a built-in Ensoniq sound chip. The IIGS runs existing Apple II software, giving it instant access to the most extensive software library available for any computer.

IBM PC

Current Models: IBM PC, PC XT, PC AT, Personal System/2 Model 30, Model 50, Model 60, and Model 80.
Price range: Moderate to very expensive.
Interfacing: Add-on component. Selection includes two smart interfaces (which manage some data management tasks on their own). The Model 30 offers an add-on board with a simple in, out, thru interface and the guts of a Yamaha FB-01 digital synthesizer.
Comments: The PC or one of the many compatibles is the machine of choice for those who prefer command-based systems over the icon-based systems used by the Mac, ST, and Amiga. The heart of the original IBM PC is

an Intel 8086 microprocessor, while the newly introduced Model 80 (which is probably a lot more computer than anyone will ever need for music, and has a price tag to prove it) uses the more powerful 80386 processor. The PC is a fairly "plain," no-frills computer, but there are tons of hardware peripherals available to enhance the basic system. Excellent sequencing and music printing software is available for the PC, as well as a huge selection of database, word processing, and business software.

Atari 130XE

Current Models: 130XE, (prior model: 800 XL).
Price range: Inexpensive.
Interfacing: Add-on component. From Hybrid Arts, the MIDImate offers MIDI in and out, sync in and out, and more.
Comments: The new low-end Atari is essentially the same computer as its predecessors, such as the 800XL, with a change in packaging and the addition of more memory capacity. It's a powerful, inexpensive computer, but the 130XEs haven't sold too well, and there aren't many music programs available. One notable exception to this is a very complete MIDI package from Hybrid Arts.

Yamaha CX5M

Current Model: CX5M MKII-128.
Price range: Inexpensive.
Interfacing: Simple (in, out) MIDI interface is built-in. Sync-to-tape facility available with outboard Yamaha components.
Comments: The CX5M is comparable in power and features to the Commodore 64 series and the less expensive Ataris, with the significant difference that the computer has built-in MIDI ports and an eight-voice multi-timbral FM synthesizer. Yamaha markets sequencing and DX voicing software on cartridges, and there are two optional external keyboards. The CX5M uses the MSK operating system, introduced in 1984 by several Japanese manufacturers. MSX hasn't been well received in North America, and as a result, little third-party software exists for the CX5M. The MKII version includes a disk drive.

Yamaha CX5M Music Computer.

Others

Now that there are RS-232-to-MIDI conversion interfaces, any computer that supports this standard for serial data communications can theoretically serve as a MIDI controller/computer. There are a great many CP/M and other oddball computers out there with RS-232 ports, and you can get great deals on used but perfectly functional computers that were big sellers a year or two ago. There's just one catch—you're probably going to have to write your own software.

— Peter Gotcher and Steve Cummings

COMPUTER-TO-MIDI INTERFACES

Unless your computer has on-board MIDI ports, you'll need an interface device to get the computer to talk to your synthesizers. At a bare minimum, a MIDI interface simply passes the MIDI data to and from the computer in a form the latter can digest. A somewhat fancier interface might also have timing circuitry, drum machine or tape sync capabilities, or a footswitch jack. Programmable units that can store and process MIDI data so the computer

January 1986, updated September 1987

doesn't have to work as hard are at the sophisticated end of the interface spectrum.

Simple Interfaces. MIDI transfers data serially, meaning that data bits are sent and received one at a time. The heart of any MIDI interface is a UART (universal asynchronous receiver/transmitter), a chip that can read incoming serial data and send it out again. If the computer also uses a serial communications format, the only requirement for proper interfacing is that the computer transfer the data at the proper speed.

Many computers use a parallel data transmission format (eight or more bits are sent and received at once), but this presents no real problem in interface design—a UART that can temporarily store all eight bits is simply used. When the computer is sending data, the UART stores each eight-bit "word" and reads through the data bits one by one, sending them along serially. When the computer is on the receiving end, the UART accepts data over its MIDI port and assembles each group of eight successive bits into a word, which the computer then reads. Since MIDI bytes are ten bits long, the interface must also add and strip off the start and stop bits, but this isn't difficult for it to do.

Simple interfaces that don't have any on-board data processing can still have a variety of supplementary features. Extra MIDI in or out jacks are often provided. Sync functions are very common, and almost all of the interfaces sold commercially let you drive a drum machine (with a 5-volt clock pulse) or sync to a tape deck (with FSK or some other sync tone system).

All of the so-called Passport-compatible interfaces for the Commodore 64 (those by Syntech, Sequential, Yamaha, Korg, Mimetics, Siel, and so on) fit the above description of simple interfaces. The main differences between these different brands are often only their price and the inclusion or exclusion of tape sync capability. For the most part, software written for one Passport-compatible interface will run on any other Passport-compatible interface.

Roland's MPU-41: one of the most powerful "smart" interfaces.

The interfaces marketed for the Apple II+/e by Passport, Syntech, Mimetics, Lemi, Steinberg, and so on, are also simple interfaces which don't feature any on-board processing. Their features are much the same as those offered by their Commodore-interface counterparts, although they may connect to the computer in totally different ways (via expansion slots rather than game cartridge ports).

Aside from the necessary MIDI in and out ports, other features to look for—depending on your needs—include:
● MIDI thru.
● Clock in and out.
● Extra MIDI outs.
● Drum machine trigger outs.
● SMPTE Time Code in and out.
Macintosh interfaces fall into the simple interface category. Since the

Mac transmits over a serial port, all the interface has to do is read the incoming data and send it on its way again. The only real difficulty in designing a Mac-to-MIDI interface is getting the computer's serial port to function at the correct speed. The Mac's serial ports normally operate under control of the internal clock, which can only operate at speeds about half as fast as MIDI. To bring the ports up to speed, it's necessary to include a clock that controls the serial port's speed.

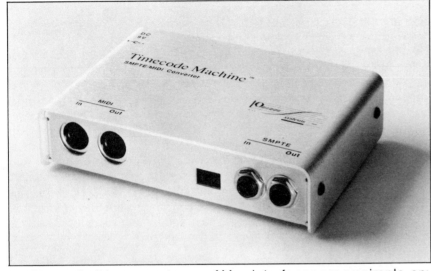

A SMPTE-to-MIDI converter from Opcode Systems.

Since all of the current crop of Mac interfaces are so simple, any interface can be used with any Mac software (as long as it can select the proper communications speed, usually 500kHz, 1MHz, or 2MHz). The exception to this is the Southworth. The company goes to great lengths to copy-protect their Total Music software by tying its operation to their interface. Check the listing for the specific features of the various Mac-to-MIDI interfaces.

Rumors of MIDI interfaces causing Macs to blow up have been circulating recently, but according to Evan Brooks of Digidesign (designers of the Assimilation interface), the problem is a result of a defective transformer on the Mac's power supply board. When a computer with one of these bad boards is left on for long periods of time, the transformer may short out and disable the monitor. A spokesperson for Apple confirmed that on some Macs the tolerances of one component on the power supply board were not as tight as they needed to be. On most of the units shipped, however, the actual performance of this component is within specified limits, and no problems should occur. If you encounter a problem, check with your Apple dealer or service center. It should be noted that these problems have nothing to do with connecting a MIDI interface to your Mac.

One of the most comprehensive interfaces available—and sure to be a portent of future interfaces—is the Southworth JamBox/4. This unit (designed for use with the Mac, the Atari STs, or the Apple IIGS) features:
- 4 MIDI ins and 4 MIDI outs.
- Clock in and out.
- SMPTE time code in and out.
- MIDI time code in and out.

MIDI and SMPTE time code reading and generation will continue to having a growing importance to musicians, since it allows precise sequencing to video or multitrack recorders (see page 44).

Smart Interfaces. MIDI interfaces with built-in microprocessors and ROM software are often called "smart," because they can carry out fairly complicated MIDI functions with only simple short commands from the main computer. On-board RAM further frees up the host computer by allowing the interface to store MIDI data being recorded or played while the computer performs other tasks. Roland's MPU-40 is the most visible example of a smart interface, though microprocessor-equipped units are also sold by Voyetra Technologies, System Design Assoc., RMD & Assoc., and Hinton.

When the features of a smart interface are taken advantage of, it can be easier to program complicated MIDI operations. For example, the host computer can scroll the monitor display while the interface keeps track of the MIDI data stream. Real-time operations on the data, such as transposition, are often much easier for the programmer to implement too, because they're handled with a simple command to the interface.

The MPU-401 provides clock sync facilities and does a lot of filtering and buffering, which takes the load off the programmer, enabling him or her to concentrate on higher levels of the program. For the end user, this often means that programs that run on an MPU-based system are able to offer features that are difficult or impossible to implement on non-smart interface systems. On the other hand, the MPU isn't without its limitations. The designers apparently made the assumption that you wouldn't want more than eight tracks, and so only eight tracks are supported on the unit, although some people have come up with tricks to get around this limitation. In fact, in spite of the enthusiasm of some software developers, there is still real controversy about whether the smart interfaces are really better than the simple pass-through interfaces. The programming solutions chosen by the designers of the interface are locked in, and may not work well for every situation.

The MPU can theoretically be connected to any computer with the necessary interface; however, Roland only markets interface cards currently for the Apple II and the IBM PC. They also make an equivalent of the MPU-401 and Apple interface on a single cirucit card for the Apple only (the MPU-APR).

According to the MPU manual, up to four of the units can be used simultaneously to send or receive up to 64 discrete channels of MIDI data

The British-built MIDIC by Hinton Instruments can function as a MIDI to RS-232/422 interface.

(16 channels per unit). Roland doesn't currently support this feature, but programmer Andy Voekel, formerly with UC San Diego's CARL (Computer Audio Research Lab) says he's found a way to do it. According to Voekel, only a single interface card is necessary since the circuits for alternate ports are already present on the card, but are cut, and just have to be recon-

nected. You then have to make a cable that will split the output of the card to as many MPUs as you're going to use. Voekel has written a series of public-domain software utilities that support multiple MPUs. For a copy, check Bytenet at (603) 924-9820 or the local public-access bulletin board at (714) 642-4408. These are both modem-access numbers.

Aside from the MPU, there are a number of other smart interfaces available for a wide variety of computers. Octave Plateau offers the OP-4001, a single circuit card with both interface and processing circuitry which should make it especially useful for portable PC compatibles like the Compaq. Passport's MIDI Pro interfaces feature on-board software and are currently available for the Apple IIc. Versions of the device are also available for the Mac and IBM PC. Hinton and RMD & Assoc. both offer MIDI-to-RS-232/422 boxes. J.L. Cooper also has a IIc interface. RMD tells us they've sold many of their IDAL interfaces to universities, which are using the box on Apple II, IBM, Radio Shack, Microvax, Vax, and Apple Lisa computers. Both the RMD and Hinton boxes buffer data, storing it up and sending it out in bursts so baud rates of the slower RS-232 (300 to 19.2k baud) can be used with the much faster MIDI baud rate (31.25k baud). The Hinton MIDIC unit can also stand alone without a host computer for processing data in live performance (filtering unwanted MIDI data if desired). Of course, you may have to write your own software for these devices.

Interface Devices

Austin Developments. MIDIFace II for Macintosh; uses modem or printer port. Ports: Two MIDI in, six MIDI out.

Decillionix. MIDI interface for Apple II+ or IIe; uses expansion slot. Ports: MIDI in, MIDI out.

Greengate Productions Inc. MIDI Interface for Apple IIe; uses expansion slot. Ports: MIDI in, MIDI out, MIDI thru.

Hinton. MIDIC, a MIDI to RS-232/422 interface. Ports: MIDI in, MIDI out, RS-232/422 in/out. Optional battery backup.

Hybrid Arts. MIDIMate for Atari 130XW, 800XL, and other similar Ataris (ST not included), plugs into disk drive. Ports: MIDI in, MIDI out, sync in, sync out (read and write click track), Roland-type sync at joystick port #1, TTL clock at joystick port #2. SMPTE-Mate for Atari ST; plugs into RS-232 and 2nd joystick ports. Ports: MIDI in, MIDI out, SMPTE/EBU time code/tape in and out, aux. in and out.

IBM. PC Music Feature for IBM PC, XT, AT Model 30, or compatibles; uses expansion slot. Ports: MIDI in, MIDI out, MIDI thru. Music Feature consists of interface and FM synthesis sound-generating card.

J.L. Cooper Electronics. MPU-401 to IIc interface for Apple IIc; installed internally. Makes the MPU-401, IIc compatible.

JMS (Jellinghaus Musik Systeme) 86504 Interface for Commodore 64, 128, and SX-64; uses game cartridge slot. Ports: MIDI in, three MIDI outs, MIDI thru, 5V clock in.

Korg. MH-01C for Commodore 64, 128, or SX-64; uses game cartridge slot. Ports: MIDI in, MIDI out, Korg sync out. MH-01A for Apple II+, IIe, uses expansion slot #2. Ports: MIDI in, MIDI out, Korg sync out. MH-02A for Apple II+, IIe, uses expansion slot #2. Ports: MIDI in, MIDI out, Korg sync out, tone sync in, tone sync out.

LEMI. MIDI interface for Apple II+ and IIe; uses expansion slot. Ports: MIDI in, MIDI out, 5V drum sync out. Bundled with Future Shock Sequencing software.

Micro Music. MIDI II interface for Commodore 64, 128, and SX-64; uses game cartridge port. Ports: MIDI in, MIDI outs. MIF V64 for Commodore; uses user port to interface an MPU-401 to Commodore.

Mimetics. MetaMIDI interface for Commodore 64, 128, and SX-64; uses game cartridge port. Ports: MIDI in, MIDI out, 5V drum sync out. MetaMIDI interface for the Apple II+ and IIe; uses expansion slot. Ports: MIDI in, MIDI out, 5V Drum sync out. MetaMIDI interface for IBM; uses expansion port. Ports: MIDI in, MIDI out, 5V drum sync in 5V drum sync out. Soundscape MIDI interface for Amiga; uses serial port. Ports: MIDI in, out, and thru.

Musicworks. MacMIDI Star for Macintosh; uses modem or printer port. Ports: MIDI in, three MIDI outs. MacMIDI 32 for Macintosh; uses modem or printer ports. Ports: Two MIDI ins, two MIDI outs. MacMIDI Sync for Macintosh; uses modem or printer ports. Ports: Same as MacMIDI 32 plus 5V drum sync in and out, and FSK tape sync in and out. MacMIDI SMPTE for Macintosh; uses printer or modem ports. Ports: Same as MacMIDI Sync plus SMPTE in and out.

Opcode. Professional Plus for Macintosh 512K or Plus; uses printer or modem port. Ports: MIDI in, three MIDI out. Studio Plus Two for Macintosh 512K, Plus, or SE; uses printer or modem port. Ports: two MIDI in, six MIDI out, modem and printer "thru" ports and switches.

Passport. MH-01A for Apple II+, IIe, uses slot #2. Ports: MIDI in, MIDI out, 5V drum sync out. MH-02A for Apple II+, IIe, uses slot #2. Ports: MIDI in, MIDI out, 5V drum sync out, tape sync tone in, tape sync tone out. MH-01C for Commodore 64, 128, SX-64; uses game cartridge slot. Ports: Same as MH-01A. MH-02C for Commodore. Ports: Same as MH-02A. MH-01X for Apple IIc, uses serial port. Ports: MIDI in, MIDI out, 5V drum sync in, 5V sync out, tape sync in, tape sync out, RS-232 in/out. MH-01P for IMB PC, uses serial port. Ports: Same as MH-01X. MH-02M for Macintosh, uses serial port. Ports: Same as MH-01X.

RMD & Associates. IDAL (It Does A Lot) MIDI for *any* computer with an RS-232 port. Ports: Two MIDI in, MIDI out, tape sync tone in, tape sync tone out. Includes handshake software and EPROM ZIF socket.

Roland. MPU-401 MIDI processing unit with MIF-APL for Apple II+ or IIe, or MIF-IPC for IBM PC. MIF plugs into expansion slot and connects to MPU-401. Ports: MIDI in, two MIDI outs, Roland sync out, FSK tape sync in, FSK out, metronome audio out. MPU-APL for Apple II+ or IIe, plugs into expansion slot. Ports: MIDI in, MIDI out, Roland sync out.

Siel. MCI MIDI Computer Interface for Commodore 64, 128, SX-64; uses game cartridge port. Ports: MIDI in, three MIDI outs, MIDI thru, 5V clock in, 5V clock out.

Sonus. Apple MIDI Interface for Apple IIe, II+, and IIGS; uses expansion slot. Ports: MIDI in, two MIDI out, (optional tape in and out). Commodore MIDI Interface for Commodore 64, 128, and SX-64; uses game cartridge port. Ports: MIDI in, two MIDI out (optional tape in and out). Amiga interface for Commodore Amiga; uses serial port. Ports: MIDI in, two MIDI out, serial "thru" port and switch. MacFace for Macintosh; uses printer or modem port. Ports: Two MIDI in, six MIDI out, modem and printer "thru" ports.

Southworth. Southworth interface for Macintosh; uses modem or printer port. Ports: two MIDI in, four MIDI out, self-powered. Price: Bundled with Southworth Total Music sequencing software. JamBox/4 for Macintosh, Apple IIGS, or Atari ST (1040 minimum RAM); uses modem port. Ports: Four MIDI in, four MIDI out, time code in and out, click in and out, sync out, two RS-422.

Steinberg Research. MSI (MIDI Sync Interface) for Commodore 64, 128, or SX-64; uses game cartridge port. Ports: MIDI in, three MIDI out, drum sync, tape in and out. Also available is the Card 32, which is an MSI interface with Pro16 sequencer and TNS notation programs in ROM. Time Lock for Atari ST; uses RS-232 port. Ports: SMPTE/EBU time code in and out, DIN clock in/out. Bundled with Pro24 sequencing software. SMP 24 for Atari ST; uses parallel port. Ports: Two MIDI in, four MIDI out, tape in and out, SMPTE/EBU time code in and out, DIN clock in/out.

System Design Associates Inc. MIDI card interface for IBM PC and compatibles. Ports: MIDI in, MIDI out or thru, tape sync in, tape sync out, metronome out, auxiliary power out, auxiliary ground out. Bundled with ProMIDI System Sequencing Software.

Voyetra Technologies. OP-4001 interface fot the IBM PC or compatibles; uses short expansion slot. Ports: MIDI in, MIDI out, FSK in/out, 5V drum sync in/out.

Other hardware & software resources are listed on page 108.

Steve Cummings and Dominic Milano

SOFTWARE

Sequencers

It wasn't too long ago that a sequencer was just one more knob-laden panel on a modular synthesizer, the one that stored a few predetermined analog voltages and spit them out, two or three at a time, when supplied with a clock pulse. With the advent of digital technology, this concept evolved into a flexible tool for storing information generated in real time, and in the Age Of MIDI that information can drive practically any instrument on the market.

Since MIDI data is digital, it can be recorded, copied, edited, manipulated in any number of ways, and transferred from one medium to another an infinite number of times, and still remain exactly the same. These processes, if carried out properly, introduce no distortion or errors. And since MIDI data is not actually sonic information, but rather directions that tell a MIDI-equipped instrument what sounds to make, the performance of the instrument will be "live" every time the MIDI data is played back into the instrument's input. In this way, MIDI is to synthesizers what a piano roll—one that records the actual *feel* of the performance rather than the notes alone—is to a player piano.

By recording MIDI data instead of actual sounds, the new generation of sequencers can record and manipulate musical information without the sonic degradation associated with analog tape recording. Today, multi-track MIDI sequencing threatens to replace the recording of electronic instruments on audio tape altogether. With the ability to manage musical works of truly orchestral proportions, from composition to revision to final performance, the sequencer has come into its own.

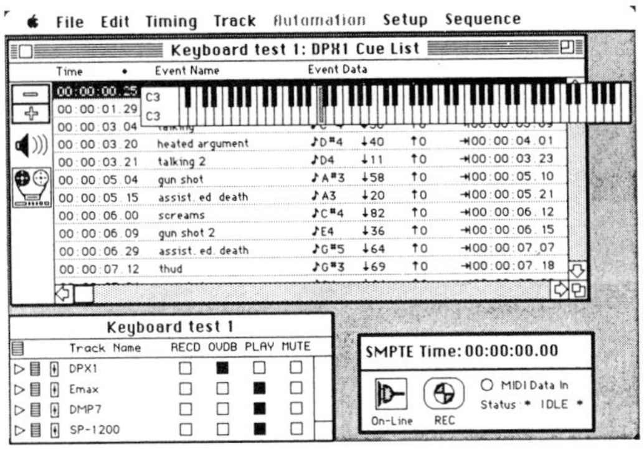

There's just one hitch. Alongside these growing capabilities has come a diversity of products, guaranteed to further baffle musicians already mystified by recent technological leaps and bounds. Sorting out the plethora of features and styles of operation offered by the new sequencers is no mean feat, and deciding which particular product best suits your needs will take some effort.

The bewildering array of products can come to look more like an advantage, however, if you remember that their designers had in mind the very same concerns that you do; the differences lie chiefly in their priorities and methods of implementation. The chances are that if you look carefully enough, you'll find a sequencer that suits your budget, your computer, your general manner of creating or performing, and the style of music you work with most often, and even exhibits some unexpected idiosyncrasies that happen to fit your own quirks like a glove.

There are two major strains of sequencer on the market, each offering its own benefits and limitations: software and hardware. Of the two, the software products are by far the more diverse and plentiful. Nonetheless,

January 1986

Figure 1. Digidesign's Q-Sheet is a MIDI/SMPTE automation program and a MIDI-event sequencer.

dedicated hardware sequencers seem to be the ones musicians feel most comfortable with—at least for the time being. For one thing, a hardware panel is generally less intimidating than a CRT screen display, as it suggests its own operation by providing buttons with familiar labels (like "on" and "off," for example). At this point, most keyboardists working in popular styles are familiar with drum machines, and the operation of most dedicated sequencers is similar enough to drum machine conventions not to be too intimidating. A dedicated sequencer is also much more portable, as well as more rugged, and can be carried into the studio or to a gig as easily as a little Casio keyboard. A small sequencer box fits easily onto a stand, and looks pretty hip in your setup, too.

Software, however, also offers distinct advantages, perhaps the most striking of which is that it is easily updated. Basic technological changes can be made simply by rewriting the program disk. Most software companies offer updates periodically, as new features are invented or implemented, at a fraction of the price of the original program. Along the same lines, software functions can be divided into modular sub-programs, each of which can be purchased separately as the need (or the cash) arises. All they require, in order to become an integral part of your system, is that you boot them up. Thus, you could buy a module implementing real-time input capabilities first, and perhaps later add step input capabilities without upsetting your basic *modus operandi*.

Software is also many times cheaper to produce than hardware, if you disregard the amount of time and effort involved in creating it. (On the down side, the cost of a computer, printer, and disk drives can more than offset the savings.) Costly switches and circuit boards are replaced by a screen display that can incorporate as many switching functions as the disk can hold. And with the trend toward software-dependent hardware devices, which use a few assignable toggles, knobs, or sliders to perform any number of tasks, a computer screen displaying one "knob" for each function can seem downright user-friendly. Besides, many sequencing operations are best understood in graphic terms, which computer screens are particularly good at providing. Hardware sequencers, with their limited data displays, don't always give you the kind of visual feedback you'd prefer.

Disk storage, still the province of computer-based systems (though not for long), is notably quicker, easier, and more reliable than other forms of memory, such as cassettes and RAM cartridges. And software only takes up the space of a single disk (along with a screen and a disk drive or two).

This suggests a major disadvantage: a software sequencer is dependent on a computer. The computer system may not lend itself to use onstage, or in the studio, or to being lugged around between the two.

Software can be configured in any way imaginable. The only constraint is the genius of the programmer himself, and as you may have heard, most geniuses are pretty idiosyncratic. This makes for enormous differences in the operating styles of software sequencers. Some are intended to emulate a multi-track tape recorder, and forego some of the advantages of software technology in order to do so. Others introduce powerful functions that, being software-inspired and software-oriented, will prove difficult for many musicians to grasp. Some programs try to pack the greatest note-memory into the smallest RAM-space. Others sacrifice memory in the name of more "musical" input procedures.

No sequencer, software or hardware, can do everything, and if one that will is ever devised, you probably won't want to pay for it. Real-time input capability is not inherently better than step input, nor is the reverse true. A rock and roll player probably won't be interested in programming *rubato* tempi, and a mad-scientist electro-noisemaker doesn't require a programmable tempo with the same urgency that a live performer does.

A sequencer's usefulness depends a great deal on the user's needs, the particular combination of features available, and the operating style implicit

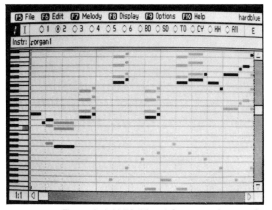

Figure 2. Ad Lib's Visual Composer is a music composition and editing package.

in its command architecture.

To further cloud the water, there are as many ways to implement a given function as there are ways to report your taxable income. Anyone who understands the difference between analog filtering and digital FM "filter" effects is familiar with this idea, and it's even more true of software than hardware.

For example, if a manufacturer reports that a given sequencer incorporates an edit buffer, allowing the user to save an unchanged version of his or her sequence while auditioning some global operation such as quantization, it may mean several things. It may mean that the user can go through a cumbersome process in order to copy the old sequence, then perform the quantization, file away the quantized version, and finally call up the original for comparison; or it may mean that the sequencer automatically saves previous versions, which can be called up in one keystroke for A/B comparison. The latter, of course, is the intended meaning of the "edit buffer" designation.

Software sequencers featuring user-definable macro-keys, especially, should be evaluated carefully for what functions they can and cannot implement. Macro-key definitions, by which a set of multi-keystroke commands can be assigned to a single button, may enable you to do all kinds of things not directly implemented in the software.

Which gives rise to another problem: The terminology used to describe sequencer functions is far from standardized, so there's some potential for misinformation and misunderstanding.

In some cases, the information you'll see in advertising copy applies to updates that aren't on the market yet. The version you find in a music store may have been on the shelf for a few months, during which time the product may have been through any number of versions. Revision fever knows no seasons, although it does tend to heat up a bit as the NAMM show approaches; suffice it to say that few software products ever achieve a stable definition, and many hardware products depend on internal software. In order to counter this effect, be sure to check revision numbers.

Any questions regarding the current capabilities of a product are best answered by the manufacturer itself. A directory of their addresses and phone numbers begins on page 108.

Choosing The Right Sequencer

Most sequencers are designed to facilitate the composition of song-like music—that is, pieces made up of a number of strophic sections which repeat from time to time. The music is divided into segments (corresponding to "verses" and "choruses"), most often of a user-defined length, which are constructed in an input mode. Then the segments are called up for playback (or "chained"), one by one, in a song mode. This makes effective use of memory space, since each repeated segment only needs to be stored once. The song structure, however, often governs other functions, such as the points at which you can begin playing the sequence back (often only at the beginnings of segments) and how often you can change time-signature (usually only one time-signature per segment).

What if you wish to produce through-composed music? It might be more useful to own a program that encourages you to compose, note by note, on the staves of a displayed score, and allows you to edit minute alterations in tempo and dynamics for each note as well. Alternatively, if you perform improvised music, note-by-note editing is much less important than real-time recording of tempo, dynamics, and articulation. Maybe all you want is a computerized scratch-pad for roughing out spontaneous ideas, in which case editing features aren't that important. And if you're interested in creating minimalist phase music, extensive track-by-track, phrase-by-

73

phrase looping would assist your compositional process as well as conserve memory. The style of music you're interested in, and also your personal approach to music composition, are important considerations in deciding what features to look for.

Number Of Tracks. Those interested in multi-track sequencing—that is, using their sequencer as a multi-track tape machine—might start by looking for a usable number of tracks. Generally, those software sequencers offering an unlimited, or at any rate outrageous, number of tracks are not really track-oriented in their operation. Such programs usually allow you to create "files," which can be treated as tracks (that is, they can be played back synchronously, or in a number of other ways as well). In some cases the number of tracks a sequencer can actually play *at one time* is significantly smaller than the number reported in the manufacturer's promotional literature; with these sequencers, the extra tracks allow you to make large numbers of alternate takes or arrangements, and then to mix and match in playback.

There are two basic relationships between tracks and MIDI channels. The first is very straightforward: Some sequencers simply require that each track be assigned to a MIDI channel. Any information that is recorded on this track *is transmitted only on the assigned channel.* If two tracks are merged to a third track (an operation analogous to bouncing, or ping-ponging, two tracks of audio tape to a third), then the information from those two tracks, originally transmitted on separate MIDI channels, will be transmitted only on the channel to which the third track is assigned. Such sequencers don't *record* MIDI channel information, since channelization is taken care of by the track-to-channel assignments.

(Incidentally, some sequencers have functions on which recorded channel data can later be edited, then MIDI data may be loaded on any MIDI channel that happens to be convenient, and then edited to transmit on the desired channel. In this way, such a sequencer is just as useful with a DX7, which only transmits on channel 1, as with an instrument offering selectable channel transmission.)

The second relationship is more complicated. In sequencers that do record MIDI channel data, any track can usually transmit on any number of channels simultaneously. The tracks only *hold* information, and bear no direct relationship to MIDI channel transmission. In this case, if you merge two tracks into a third the results are quite different. Each of the two tracks may be coded to transmit on separate MIDI channels. When merged to a third track, they will retain their channel data, and, even though they're occupying the same track, will continue to transmit on their own respective channels.

According to this scheme, theoretically only two tracks are necessary: one to begin the recording process on, and another to merge to. This way, incoming data can be merged with the first track, and each successive input/merge operation will maintain a discrete MIDI channel. Each will transmit on its own channel when the sequence is played back. If you use your sequencer simply to rough out ideas, or if your music doesn't get too elaborate, two tracks may well be enough. However, there are limits to the amount of MIDI data a single track can hold before the processing of all that information begins to cause audible delays. Continuous controllers like pitch-bend and after-touch add lots of data to the MIDI signal, and it takes a little time to address each bit. Of course, a two-track sequencer that doesn't record continuous controllers in the first place will be less prone to such problems, not to mention potentially less expressive.

In addition, there are any number of processing operations that are more commonly performed track by track than MIDI channel by MIDI channel. These include transposition, looping, delay, quantization, and punching in and out. For nearly every sequencer currently on the market, once two tracks are merged, there is no way to apply such operations to one set of data without affecting the other.

Simultaneous MIDI Channels. The number of simultaneous MIDI channels the sequencer transmits is also relevant. If you only have four sound-generating instruments, none of which is multi-timbral, do you really need to have a program that transmits on all 16 channels? Probably not—if the one you get reads sync codes. If it does, you can allow a sync code recorded on multi-track tape to drive the sequencer, and make as many passes as the tape recorder will permit. (This, of course, negates the first-generation advantage of recording MIDI rather than audio, but most of us are on a budget.) Otherwise you might want to put your money into some spare sound-generators, or consider scaling your compositions to the number of instruments and MIDI channels available to you.

Input Modes. There are three basic ways of feeding information into a sequencer. Real-time input refers to the ability to record exactly what you play, as you play it, in much the same way a tape recorder does. Step input usually involves one note at a time. This is for musicians who make up stories about how their hands got sucked up by a vacuum cleaner when they were young whenever they're called upon to play keyboards. Some features aren't relevant to a sequencer that records only by step: quantization and metronome, for example. The third input method is drum machine-style looping, in which a segment of predetermined length automatically plays back over and over, allowing additional input in real time with each successive pass.

Note Capacity. This number is the great bugaboo of MIDI sequencing. The figure given here is the manufacturer's estimate, using the minimum amount of memory required of the computer. This number is not directly proportional to the number of bytes of memory; two times the number of bytes usually gives you more than double the number of notes. But, naturally, it's not that simple. What defines a note? Some manufacturers count *MIDI events*. Generally it takes at least two MIDI events to make an actual, sounding note—a note-on command and a note-off command. (In other words, it is conceivable that some of these ratings must be halved in order to approximate accuracy.) But if you make use of any of the MIDI continuous controllers, like after-touch or pitch-bend, and if the sequencer records them, you are adding a huge number of MIDI events to the definition of each note. In fact, the more data it takes to define a note, the more MIDI events it requires, and the more computer memory is necessary to store it. So how many notes can you record? That's between you and the machine. The note capacity figure should be regarded as a relative, rather than an absolute, measure.

Keep in mind, as well, that material looped in playback does not require additional memory space. If the same ten-note phrase loops 30 times, you've still only made a ten-note dent on your sequencer's note capacity. The specific looping options offered by each sequencer will determine just how clever you can get in using this method to conserve note-memory.

Recording & Filtering. Once again, if the sequencer doesn't remember after-touch data in the first place, then after-touch data won't use up available MIDI events or computer memory. When reading the specs on any sequencer, you should check to see what MIDI parameters are recorded on input, and then look to see if that parameter data can be edited, individually, later. This capability can be used either to alter a note (to change the after-touch data if you originally hit the note too hard, for instance), or to remove that information from the data stream entirely, note by note (in order to conserve memory or unclog the data stream). MIDI parameters you may want to record and independently edit include pitch-bend, program change, velocity, modulation wheel, sustain pedal, channel assignment, and system-exclusive. Incidentally, reasons for recording system-exclusive data include recording real-time patch adjustments as part of the sequence, and using the sequencer's memory as a dumping ground for patches. The

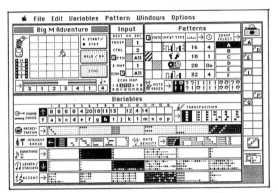

Figure 3. The principal screen for M; an automated randomization and systematic variation package made by Intelligent Music.

editing of system-exclusive data is a more esoteric operation, and one that most users probably won't want to mess around with.

The ability to remove a given MIDI parameter from the data stream entirely, in a global fashion rather than one note at a time, is called filtering. If you know ahead of time that you won't be needing after-touch data, you can filter it out at the input stage so as not to waste memory with it. If you find out later in the recording process that you're running out of memory, or find that an overloaded MIDI data stream is resulting in delays, then you might want to eliminate less important data from tracks that you've already recorded, as an edit. Some sequencers allow different parameters to be filtered independently of one another, but in other sequencers a number of parameters can be filtered only as a group. Keep in mind that if a program doesn't record a particular type of data in the first place, filtering it is not an issue.

A few sequencers allow filtering to be applied in a more flexible fashion—measure by measure, or by eliminating every third or every fourth value ("density filtering").

Editing Functions: Punching. The ability to punch in and punch out, in the style of multi-track recording, is included on many sequencers, some of which feature automated punch-in and out (so that the machine does the punching while you keep your hands on the keyboard). Some sequencers don't implement automated punching directly, requiring an additional step: that you record the "punch" on a separate track or in a separate file, and then insert it where it belongs. "Smart" punch-out, means that the program will make sure that there is a note-off command for every note-on command, in the event that you punch out in the middle of a note. If the punch-out function is not smart, there's a possibility that the scourge of MIDI Land, Stuck Note Syndrome, will strike.

Mute, Solo & Merge. Mute and solo are analogous to the same functions on an audio mixer, and a merge is basically same as a bounce in multi-track terminology, combining several tracks into one. Merging is implemented directly in some sequencers, while others require a bit of patching to make it work. Merged data, of course, becomes subject to any commands globally affecting a given track.

If a sequencer offers extensive filtering but lacks independent editing of MIDI parameters, resourceful use of the merge function and careful track allocation can make up for its deficiencies. You might record *only* note-on and -off data on one track, pitch-bend data on another, and modulation on a third. This way you can edit each of them, independently, to your heart's content. When each is exactly as you want it, then notes, pitch-bend, modulation, and anything else can be merged together into a (simulated) single performance.

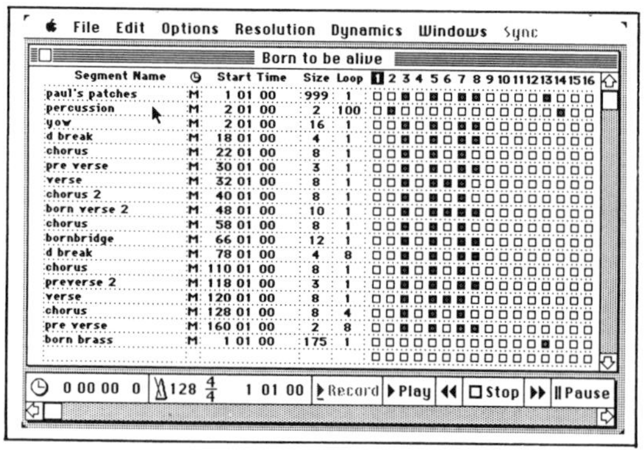

Track Shift. This function moves individual tracks, in time, in relation to one another by increments of a fraction of a second (or a fraction of a beat) in either direction. Track shifting can be useful in compensating for MIDI delay. For this purpose, the delay function should be applicable to each track separately, and should offer delay times ranging from around five to 25 milliseconds. Some sequencers allow the MIDI clock output to be delayed as well. Delays can also be applied to copied tracks or files in order to produce conventional delay effects. (As with any MIDI processing function, it is the MIDI signal that is delayed, rather than the actual audio signal coming from the sound source.) The "limited" designation, in this case, usually refers to a track shift operation based on common divisions of a quarter-note, such as a 32nd-note or a 16th-note. This may be useful in a number of musical situations, but it won't solve MIDI delay problems or induce delay effects.

Quantization. A number of types of quantization, or error-correction, are commonly encountered. There is a great deal of ambiguity, however, regarding what these types should be called, what choices should be offered, and how they should be used. The lack of precise terminology is

Figure 4. MidiPaint, by Southworth, is a 16-track sequencer.

regrettable, though perhaps inevitable at this stage of MIDI product development. One issue that is both relevant and relatively easily discussed is how a given quantization function treats note-on and note-off commands. There appear to be four basic approaches.

If note-on commands *only* are corrected, the attacks of all notes affected by quantization will be brought into line with their nearest quantization value, while their release points will remain precisely as they were originally performed. This may change the note's duration slightly. Note-on-only quantization also permits the possibility that note-on commands moved backward in time will overlap note-off commands from previous notes, a situation which might cause some cacophonous confusion in MIDI Land. Different sequencers will probably react differently to this situation. A "Smart" implementation will avoid overlap problems, usually by chopping note-endings short in order to make way for advancing note-on commands.

Alternatively, each *entire note* may be moved so that its attack is in line with the quantization value; that is, the note-off moves in the same direction and by the same amount as the note-on, maintaining the integrity of the entire note-event. At the risk of losing some readers, two variations on this "note coherent" approach are worth mentioning. All information generated between the note-on and note-off commands can either be moved along with them, or retained in its original position. This includes pitch-bend and modulation introduced as part of the note: it may either be moved, along with the note, toward the quantization value, or left as it was originally performed. The relative merits of these two methods are staunchly defended by manufacturers that implement them; which one is preferable probably varies with each specific situation.

In another type of quantization, which we refer to as B-type (for *both*), each note-on command is moved to its nearest quantization value, while each corresponding note-off command is moved to *its* nearest quantization value. That is, the note either spreads itself out, or squeezes itself together, depending on the quantization values nearest to the beginning and end of the note. This is the most common type of quantization, and probably works best for players who have the least control over their fingers. It may make the music sound a little more mechanical.

Quantization of duration is noted as well. This feature corrects the duration of all notes to a predetermined value, without necessarily quantizing the note-on or note-off commands. This evens out the distance, in time, between note-on and note-off commands. If duration is corrected to values shorter than the shortest note played, such a function may also be useful in fixing note-on/note-off overlap problems of the kind mentioned above. On the other hand, depending on how the function is implemented, duration-quantizing to long note-values could cause the notes you played with such care to spread out over each other like aural peanut butter and jelly.

In all types of quantization, the flexibility with which the function can be applied is dependent on some maximum number of clock-pulse divisions, and the choices allowed regarding how division of the clock-pulse is calibrated. Naturally, the more divisions of the clock, the higher resolution is possible. (Sequencers with an extremely high upper metronome limit are likely to have a high clock resolution, although the reverse is not necessarily true.) This can be crucial if you're working with B-type (both note-on and note-off) quantization: If you've played a *staccato* note, and the quantization is too grossly adjusted, then the note-on and note-off commands may both be closest to the *same* quantization value. This would quantize the note right out of existence. What fun.

Some sequencers offer variations such as "progressive quantization," with which you can correct timing by percentages other than 100 percent, in order to make a passage "more correct" rather than "completely correct." The idea is that this retains some of the original "live" feel. Clumsier quantization functions affect an entire sequence. Most perform the

77

operation track by track; some, measure by measure. An additional feature is called "real-time quantization," in which quantization does not affect recorded data at all; rather, the operation is performed *as your sequence plays back.* This way you don't need an edit buffer (not, at least, to preview the effects quantization), and there's no chance you'd ever damage a track irreversibly by quantizing it. Keep in mind, that quantization is not an issue when considering sequencers that offer step input only.

Looping & Transposition. Some sequencers allow individual tracks to be looped while others play on normally. A looped track one measure long, for instance, would repeat four times if the other tracks were four bars long. Often the same effect can be simulated by copying the "looped" track material enough times that it plays over and over continuously, while the other tracks are playing beneath it, although this requires more memory. Segment looping is a very basic capability for sequencers that build larger sequences from smaller segments. It is a much more sophisticated function in a real-time-oriented system, where the segment must be defined, after the fact, within a larger sequence.

Metronome. A metronome (or click) establishes a steady tempo for real-time input. Some sequencers display the metronome visually. The metronome range is usually given in beats per minute. If a sequencer you're interested in doesn't have a metronome, one can usually be rigged by syncing the sequencer to a drum machine.

Programmable Tempo. A few sequencers will not memorize a tempo setting, requiring that tempo be set at the time of playback, or determined by some external device such as a drum machine. Of those that do remember a tempo setting, some will remember only a single tempo per sequence (or segment), while others permit abrupt changes in tempo. A few sequencers will allow programming of a *rubato* tempo, or one that varies gradually. As usual, there is a variety of ways in which this can be accomplished (some more practical than others). In a few cases, any kind of tempo can be entered in real time at the input stage, and sometimes as an edit (say, by tapping the space bar in time). A more cumbersome method requires editing in a new tempo for each beat, or for each measure, to achieve gradual changes. Of course, for most popular music the entire question of a varying tempo is moot.

Time Signature. Sequencers which permit a varying time-signature are noted. While a sequencer that merely records whatever notes you play has no need to recognize time signatures, some allow punch-ins or track playback to begin only on a bar line. If this is the case, then you might care whether the machine thinks you're in 3/4 or 4/4.

Edit Buffer. An edit buffer function allows edits to be auditioned before they're written into the sequence you're working on, so that you can try them out before you decide to keep them. This is particularly useful with a global, or track-by-track, edit such as quantization. If quantization options are offered, you might want to try them out before deciding which sounds best, or at least make sure that quantization won't totally destroy your work. This can usually be accomplished without an edit buffer *per se*, by copying the segment to be quantized to a free track and trying the operation out on the copy first. The "limited" designation usually refers to this. Depending on the program's architecture, though, this can be an arduous process. A/B comparison between the edited and unedited versions generally requires a buffer, unless the sequencer has track-copy and track-mute functions, or implements real-time quantization.

Locator. The multi-track tape recorder analogy is common enough that many sequencers include tape-transport-style rewind and fast-forward functions. These can range from audible and visual scrolling at an adjustable speed, to visual scrolling only, to measure-by-measure paging. Most sequencers allow you to locate points in a sequence (a "go to" function), usually measure by measure. Some offer several programmable cue points, to be located at the touch of a button, so you don't have to keep a list in front of you noting where each chorus begins. Very few include no location functions whatsoever, requiring that you begin always at the beginning of the sequence and play through to the point you need to access.

Synchronization To External Codes. Synchronization codes that sequencers may be able to read include FSK; SMPTE; MIDI clock; Roland DIN-plug; 24, 48, or 96 ppq; all standard pulse rates; any click; and so on. These can be used to drive the sequencer from an external sync generator, or from a tape which has been striped with code. If a sequencer reads (or puts out) any sync code at all, it can be synced with virtually any other code, given the proper hardware. Such hardware includes sync converters and rhythm controllers; any such devices which sync to MIDI clock are mentioned in the MIDI accessories section.

Memory Counter. A memory counter function displays how much memory is still available, or how much has been used. Keeping an eye on this display will help you decide when to consider turning on filters, if you aren't already in the habit of using them as a memory-conservation measure. In some cases available memory is counted in notes, sometimes in events, or in percentages of capacity. On some products, the counter is part of the main display; on others this information must be called up.

Thru-On-Input. Not all MIDI keyboards make sounds—some only generate MIDI data, leaving the noisemaking for a separate sound-generator module. In order for you to actually hear the notes as you enter them from this kind of keyboard, your sequencer must echo (MIDI-speak for "pass along") the MIDI input signal at a MIDI thru port. If MIDI-thru-on-input isn't provided, it will be necessary to use a thru, or splitter, box in order to route the MIDI signal to a sound-generating device as well. Thru boxes are catalogued on page 94.

Many sequencers offering MIDI-thru-on-input allow the thru signal to be transmitted selectively on any MIDI channel. Without this capability, the signal available at the thru port will be transmitted on its original channel—that is, the channel on which it is transmitted to the sequencer's input. Selectivity of the thru channel might be important if you're sending input from a DX7, which only transmits on MIDI channel 1, in order to send the thru to a sound-generator that is set to receive on some other channel. Once again, if the thru is not channel-selectable, you could use a channel-selector box to perform this function. Channel-selector boxes are also covered in the MIDI accessory.

Display. Generally, there are three basic kinds of screen display: notational, graphic, and alphanumeric. Most software sequencers make use of one of these types, although many employ a combination. Players accustomed to reading or scoring music will probably prefer a software sequencer that generates standard notation. Many of these programs are actually oriented more toward notation-based editing and printing than they are toward sequencing. A number of sequencers can accommodate modular software add-on programs that will convert sequencer files into notation, but by themselves can't generate a notational display.

Graphic displays come in many different forms ranging from circle and bar graphs to piano-roll-style displays to pseudo-notation. Such displays attempt to present recorded information in pictorial terms on the theory that this is easier to read and understand.

Another type of display is the alphanumeric display. This is usually a table of numbers representing the values of various MIDI parameters, and cataloguing various sequences and segments. While some musicians regard this form of information as inherently unmusical, others prefer it as more clearly representative of the stored data. An alphanumeric display might well be preferable in programs that offer extensive note-by-note editing of various MIDI parameters.

Special Features. One special feature of particular interest is the

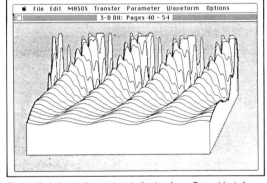

Figure 5. A three dimensional display from Sound Lab for the Ensoniq Mirage Digital Sampler.

79

implementation of the MIDI Song Pointer. Song Pointer is used by the sequencer to tell (or be told by) other devices that read the MIDI clock precisely where in a sequence one or another of them is to start (or stop). The pointer function is, in a way, MIDI's answer to SMPTE, which defines time as a succession of unique points. Without this function, an external device synced to the MIDI clock won't know where to begin when it's asked to start anywhere but at the beginning of the sequence.

Modular Add-Ons. These are software "modules" designed to work in conjunction with the sequencer, but not included along with it. These include voicing programs, librarians, MIDI-to-notation conversion programs, notation editing and printing software, and performance setup utilities.

Patch Voicing And Librarian Programs

One of the main design innovations contributing to the ongoing drop in synthesizer prices is single-potentiometer data entry. According to this scheme, which is becoming more popular every day among instrument manufacturers (if not among synthesists), a single knob, slider, or button is assignable to a number of different functions of the instrument, setting the values for virtually every parameter of the patch. This makes for less expensive instruments because one little knob replaces ten or 20 buttons, toggles, switches, dials, sliders, and what-have-you. It makes for more convenient setting of patch parameters as well, since all values are set from one location on the instrument's panel. At least that's what the salesperson told you when you bought the instrument.

Voicing. The problems with single-pot design only became an issue when everyone and his brother went out and bought the mysterious, new DX7 a few years back. After proud DX-owners awoke from the sonic stupor brought on by the instrument's wondrously bell-like Rhodes preset, they discovered that the front panel bore no discernible relationship to the patch they were listening to. And things didn't get any less murky when they tried to program their own sounds. Despite the tremendous power and flexibility of its six-operator FM voice, the DX7 quickly gained a reputation for being basically incomprehensible.

Admittedly, the difficulty of DX programming stems as much from the differences between analog and FM synthesis, and between ADSR and rate/level envelopes, but there was clearly a need for a front panel that related, in graphic terms, to the structure of any given patch. While manufacturers such as Roland addressed this problem by offering an optional hardware panel for their single-pot synthesizers, the computer hacker's underground quietly went to work, dissecting MIDI system-exclusive data in order to get at the guts of the machine. The so-called voicing programs they devised will probably alter the shape of synthesizer programming for all time to come.

Display. A voicing program, at its most basic, provides a simultaneous display of parameter values. Parameters are either given all at once on a single screen, or grouped by function on separate screen pages. Common screen displays provided by DX7 programs of this kind include envelope generator settings, algorithm, and keyboard scaling pages.

Some programs take a graphic approach, presenting an alternate "front panel," while others simply show you a table of numbers. Graphics are particularly effective, because for many functions a picture can convey more information more quickly than numbers. For example, a graphic envelope display can translate DX-style envelope generator settings into ADSR-like graphs. The actual graphic design itself can also contribute to a program's effectiveness; Data/7 by Mimetics, for instance, simultaneously displays all eight DX7 envelopes clearly by using three dimensions. A

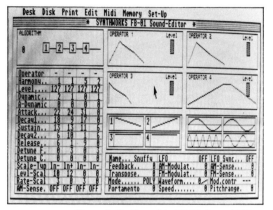

Figure 6. Southworth's FB-01 Sound Editor.

two-dimensional display of all eight envelopes can get too crowded to be readable. Graphics generally take up more space, requiring several separate screens, though, and those who wish to see the entire patch at a glance might be happier with a single-screen, numeric table approach.

An integration of the multi-page and single-screen approaches might be called "window" style. Such programs provide a single master screen, giving an overview of the patch, and then allow the user to zoom in on particular sections, or windows, for more detailed information. Window-style DX voicing programs usually configure the master screen to look like the algorithm of the patch at hand; a box representing each operator contains basic values such as frequency and level. The user can then choose to view each operator's window separately, for envelope data, feedback values, and the like. This ability to zoom in, unique to computer-generated graphics, offers exciting possibilities for graphic representation of instrument functions.

Editing. There are two ways of editing patch data. One is from the computer keyboard; in this case, as whenever you're dealing with a computer, it's nice if the program's commands relate in mnemonic fashion to the functions they control, and are arranged logically on the computer keyboard. The other method of data entry is from the instrument's panel, as though you weren't using a voicing program. Some programs offer one or the other, while others allow both. Which you prefer is a matter of personal taste. The important thing is that any data entered shows up on the screen display, in real time.

Conversely, some programs make it possible to control the software from the instrument keyboard. The lowest C on your DX7, for instance, may switch the voicing program to its algorithm page. This might be convenient, as your hands would never have to leave the instrument while programming. Another convenient feature is an edit buffer, or several of them, allowing you to work on more than one patch at a time without either losing your edits or having to write them to disk. In addition, some programs offer printing options, for making hard copy data-sheets of edited patches.

While most of the voicing software currently available is written for the DX7, programs for other instruments are becoming more common. There isn't an instrument on the market that couldn't be programmed more effectively with the aid of an intelligently designed utility program, since no synthesizer can have, onboard, the graphics power of a personal computer. Besides the plethora of Yamaha DX/TX programs, voicing software now exists for the Casio CZ series, Oberheim Matrix-12, Sequential Prophet series, Yamaha GS series, Voyetra, SIEL DK80, Roland Juno-106 and Juno-10, and Korg DW-8000. Such programs promise to be even more useful with sampling instruments, in which complex waveforms are manipulated directly, as indicated by software packages for the E-mu Emulator II, Ensoniq Mirage, Akai S900, Prophet 2000, Korg DSS-1, and so on. The field, clearly, is growing.

Librarian Functions. For as long as synthesizers have been equipped with RAM, musicians have been demanding greater and greater memory capacity for patch storage. Disk memory offers potentially unlimited storage for patches, and has the additional benefit of being simpler, more reliable, faster, and often less expensive than such common forms of data storage as cassette tapes and RAM cartridges. For software already designed to access and manipulate patch information, storing that information to disk is a simple matter.

Although virtually all voicing programs are capable of storing patches, programs designed primarily for this purpose are becoming quite common. These programs are known as librarians, and often include various utilities for convenient management of patch information. Some librarians can store information not stored in the patch locations of the instrument itself, such as DX7 function parameters. In some cases these are stored with each

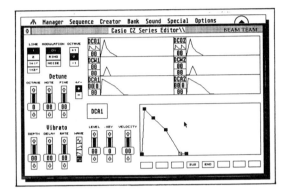
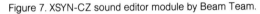

Figure 7. XSYN-CZ sound editor module by Beam Team.

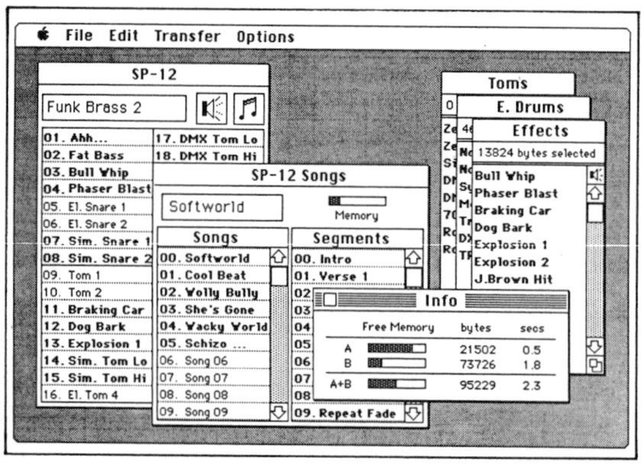

individual patch, though in others they may be stored separately as function patches, and called up in conjunction with individual patches.

It's important to be able to name your programs so that they can be identified later. Most programs organize these names into banks, for easy transferral to and from the instrument. Some go so far as to differentiate between banks of related patches (all plucked-type sounds) and banks properly ordered for a live performance. There's no technical difference between the two, but they suggest the need for convenient bank-assembly procedures. Does the program allow individual patches to be moved from bank to bank, and to and from the instrument? Can patches be transferred in blocks? Or must they be moved one bank at a time?

Banks and voices can be called up in one of two ways: either by typing the desired bank number or patch name directly at the computer keyboard, or by calling up a list and pointing to the item you're interested in. The program may also allow you to print out bank directories, and even the parameter data for individual patches.

Transcription, Scoring, And Notation

Many of us can appreciate the differences between writing in longhand and composing text with a word processor. Those readers who haven't yet entered the computer age can, at least, compare the awkwardness of scribbling quickly and legibly enough to get a point across with the comparative speed, ease, and elegance of even the most outdated manual typewriter. And yet those of us who do our composing of music straight to paper still suffer the tedium of pen and ink. In many ways, music production is relegated to a dank, monastic cell, and technologies that revolutionize fields like business and communications are rarely provided with R&D money to upgrade the day-to-day operations of composers. Music copying is one of the arcane arts, like the Biblical transcription performed by monks during the Dark Ages, practiced with proficiency by the few, the elect. The fact that this is a special issue on MIDI should alert you that things are changing. Whether you regard it as fortunate or unfortunate, an Enlightenment of sorts is upon us.

What music notation processing means, in practical terms, is an end to ruler-guided stemming and beaming; an end to unerasable ink copying, to copying redundant measures, phrases, and even sequential patterns that repeat identical pitch relationships through a succession of different keys; an end to recopying concert pitch and transposed versions of the score; an end, even, to that monstrous injustice of concerted noisemaking, the copying of parts. Add to this the possibility of changing your mind about anything from phrasing to key signature to barring, and being able to see how it looks (and, depending on the program, how it sounds). Or consider not having to make up your mind at all: many programs will notate whatever you play on your keyboard, as you play it.

Rudimentary music notation processing software first appeared on the heels of the galloping microcomputer invasion, but it is only within the past year that such programs have begun to take advantage of MIDI. The MIDI spec provides score processors with a standardized data entry format, making file transfer to and from sequencer programs, as well as real-time entry and transcription, more convenient.

With or without MIDI, however, devising a program that will make, at the touch of a button, all of the judgments that an expert copyist would is pretty tricky. Some programs make a number of decisions for you (for example, if you choose to compose on two staves, that the lower staff should contain a bass clef and the upper one a treble clef), and with some programs those decisions are final. Others, particularly those with macro-key assignments (which activate, with one key, a user-defined sequence of commands) allow

Figure 8. Drum File is a song/sound management package from Blank Software.

you to configure complex operations a bit more flexibly. Many programs make no pretense to intelligence, relying upon the user's agility with the editing commands. The following paragraphs will cover some of the relevant issues in music notation processing.

Input. The considerations regarding input style are much the same as those associated with sequencing. Improvisers will probably want to see their extemporaneous prestidigitations realized in print, which requires that the program accept data from a MIDI keyboard. Given keyboard input, there is the possibility of actually watching the program generate notation in real time, as you play. There are profound implications in this capability for improvising composers with particularly strong reading and analytic skills. A more common arrangement involves the conversion of MIDI information, recorded in real time, into a notation file afterward. This implies that the program includes sequencing functions; these range from the rudimentary to the comprehensive.

Sequencer files, in themselves, don't contain explicit guidelines for their representation in a score. A keyboard improvisation performed in a single pass, for instance, implicitly would be notated on two staves, as a piano part. But it could conceivably be written on ten staves as well (given ten possible voices of polyphony, one for each finger), or, depending on the arrangement, for any smaller number. How much choice, regarding the score-formatting of transcriptions, does a given program offer? And can the sequence be reformatted for new arrangements? The conventions determining which notes are assigned to each staff are also worth looking into.

Most programs provide note-by-note entry, analogous to step-entry in a sequencer. The input device may be a MIDI keyboard, or a computer keyboard, or, in the case of Macintosh programs and a few others, a mouse. In this case, the most relevant concerns are probably the number of staves and measures visible on the screen at once, the ease of getting to other parts of the file, and the accuracy of control over the cursor. Cursor control that is too gross will make it very difficult to place that # symbol next to the proper note. And what symbols are available in the first place? All programs will provide the ubiquitous ♮, ♭, and #, but beyond that nothing is for sure. At least one program, Standard Productions' Personal Composer, allows you to make up your own symbols—a must for notating avant-garde techniques.

There is also the page setup to consider. How many staves are allowed? Can they be joined by braces or brackets? What instrument names can be assigned to them, or will the program set up a page in standard orchestral score order, and allow the user to alter it? What clefs are available, and can they be applied freely? What time-signatures are available? (Most of us would be happy with up to 12 beats per measure, dividing the measure by

Jim Miller's Personal Composer (distributed by Standard Productions) is one of the most advanced musical transcription programs available, and runs on the IBM PC.

note-values from a half to a sixteenth. Frank Zappa, or Pierre Boulez for that matter, would be satisfied with nothing less than the ability to baffle players with signatures such as 17/64.)

Editing. Regardless of which input method you use, you will have some need to edit your score. Accidentals assigned by the software may not communicate your musical intentions; note stems may point in the wrong direction; stems may not be beamed properly; the program may have interpreted the triplet eighths you played as an eighth and two sixteenths. You may have played a few wrong notes. Or you may simply change your mind: The flute line should be doubled an octave lower in the horns, and the B section should modulate to the dominant. Can these operations be performed in a single command? Or will it take several keystrokes? Are the commands themselves mnemonic, or otherwise related to the functions they represent?

Developed by Stanford University professor Leland Smith, Passport Designs' Score is another powerful transcription program designed for the IBM PC (or compatible). Passport Design's experience with note-transcription programs dates back to the days of pre-MIDI, with their Apple II-run SoundChaser synthesizer.

Cut-and-paste style editing allows you to clone passages within a staff, or from one staff to another. Within the cut-and-paste operation, the segment you're working on may or may not be deleted from its original location (the difference between "copy" and "move"), and the utility may or may not allow for additional operations, such as transposition. The way the program deals with bar lines is relevant here: If you transfer a nine-beat phrase into two 4/4 bars, will the program alert you to the fact that you've crammed too many beats into one bar? Will it automatically rebar the ninth note outside of the two measures, so that you may not even realize it's there? Or can cut-and-paste operations only take place in measure-length units, so that you would have to transfer the ninth note separately?

Note-by-note editing is generally available as well, though it, too, may be limited in ways that don't suit your way of making music. In some cases, it's easy to change an accidental, but impossible to extend a note's duration by adding a dot. Find out what aspects of each note can be manipulated.

Some programs will merge staves, and some will later unmerge them. But what happens to the stem direction and beaming of the merged parts? Are you given options, for example, between stems-up/stems-down or chordal stemming? And, regardless of whether two staves have been merged, if a chord contains a wrong note, can that note be corrected, or must the entire chord be deleted and reentered?

Output. Besides the CRT display, score editing software usually provides printed music and some audible representation of your score. Printing options may include concert or transposed scores, transposed parts, reduced or enlarged size, and printing of selected measures. Some software will support high-quality printers only; others provide some latitude. While there's little use in printing notes of such low resolution that they're difficult to read, keep in mind that the kind of printer a program requires can add quite a bit to the cost of owning it.

Programs with sequencing capability generally provide the most extensive score-playback capabilities (consult the sequencer chart). Most important, perhaps, is the ability to hear your work during the editing process. It is also convenient to be able to start the playback from any point in the score, rather than having to start from the beginning each time. A MIDI thru-on-input function makes it possible to hear notes as they are entered, although if a program you're interested in lacks this feature, a splitter box will serve the same purpose.

System Integration. One attractive possibility, already realized in such high-end instruments as New England Digital's Synclavier and the Fairlight CMI but becoming more affordable and more practical all the time, is the integrated MIDI music production system. Such a system could incorporate separate software modules—to handle such diverse tasks as scoring, notation printing, sequencing, voicing, patch storage, automated mixing, and timing your microwave oven—all munching on the same MIDI data stream.

The beginnings of such a system already exist in the Personal Composer program, which, with its DX7 voicing and librarian functions, is a natural for use with a MIDI keyboard controller and Yamaha's TX rack. There are many programs, though, which will handle notation functions alone, and even those with multiple functions may be used for notation processing only, if more useful software can be found to handle the other tasks.

There's a whole world of software products out there that take advantage of the fact that your instrument sends out a constant stream of MIDI data. While sequencers are king of the MIDI mountain, flanked on either side by voicing/librarian and notation programs, an unruly rabble of products that put MIDI to even more imaginative use threatens to march off with the banner. This motley group serves to perform no single function other than to push at the outer limits of MIDI technology.

Many are modular utility programs, for use in conjunction with the sequencer, notation, and voicing software mentioned elsewhere in this book. As system modules they serve, most often, to organize sequences in a convenient fashion for live performance. There are also a few sampling programs, which record, store, and edit samples to be played back under MIDI control. Some companies specialize in retrofits to permit MIDI control of outboard effects such as digital delays and reverb units. As MIDI data manipulation becomes easier and more instrument-independent, the need for transmitting MIDI over the telephone will become more compelling; one product makes this procedure more accessible to musicians. There are also a couple of ingenious programs designed to create delay, flanging, and other effects by processing MIDI, rather than audio, signals.

The full potential for processing MIDI with personal computers won't be realized for a long time. Meanwhile, we can look forward to the continuing proliferation of exciting, creative applications.

—Ted Greenwald

SYSTEMS

January 1986

Gathered together here are discussions of an incredible variety of musical instruments and related devices. The common thread that binds them all together is that they can talk to one another using MIDI. MIDI is changing the way we create, perform, and produce music, making it possible for the first time to combine a collection of synthesizers, keyboards, sequencers, and so on into a single integrated system that can be oriented toward your individual musical requirements.

I will try to provide some guidelines that can help you define what you will need in your own personal MIDI-based music system. I'm not going to explain how to use the individual components of the system. Rather, I'm going to point out some of the most important things that you must consider in order to put a system together intelligently.

An article of this sort is bound to be very incomplete, not only because the existing hardware and software offers so many diverse possibilities but because rapid developments are changing what music systems can do, and what we ask them to do. There is a feedback loop between musicians and musical instrument designers, in which the musicians envision a new possibility and the engineers then set out to make it a reality. In the process, the engineers may create devices that will do things not foreseen by anybody. We have reached a point at which this feedback loop leads to exponential growth, with new musical possibilities coming into being at an accelerating rate. As you ponder what sort of MIDI system you will need, remember that an important attribute of such a system is *open-endedness.* In working with one generation of your system, you will begin to see much more clearly what its next generation ought to look like.

Few of us have the luxury of buying all the items we need at once. Your system may take years to assume its final form. This is another reason for thinking things through ahead of time. A well-planned system need never go out of date; it can be added to whenever you are ready or able. At each stage, you should be able to make music with it. And the components you buy now should be chosen not only because you can use them now but because they will fit smoothly into the larger system you plan to have someday.

So where do you start? There are three steps that you must take: First, learn the basic system concepts. Second, decide what you want your system to do. And third, decide what elements you will need in the system in order to meet your goals. The steps are in this order for a reason. Taking them out of order—for example, deciding to base your system around a particular computer or multi-track tape deck before you have analyzed your musical needs—is a virtual guarantee that you will end up with some sort of tangled nightmare, with redundant hardware (meaning wasted money), devices that can't communicate with one another, or other headaches.

The advantage of beginning with general concepts and then moving on to specifics, which is called a *top-down* approach, is not only that it will save you money and headaches. It may also provide you with a clearer insight into your musical goals. Often we get so immersed in the day-to-day process of making music that we lose sight of what we want ultimately to accomplish. Use this article as an opportunity to take stock of where you are and where you want to be.

Basic Concepts

A system is a group of components that works together to generate, route, receive, and process musical information. Music systems today must manage the flow of three distinct kinds of information signals—audio, MIDI data, and timing. When you design your system, you must equate your musical needs with devices that perform these four tasks on these three kinds of information.

The most important general aspect of a system is *interfacing*. Several individual components (many of them handling more than one kind of information signal) must be interconnected in an efficient yet flexible manner. Your goal when it comes to system interfacing should be to connect everything together and then leave it that way. You shouldn't have to rewire the system every time you do something different with it. A good interface scheme will allow you to route and reroute audio, MIDI, and timing signals without having to crawl around on the floor in search of inputs and outputs.

The specifics of audio, MIDI, and timing interfacing are beyond the scope of this article. However, there are some factors you will need to consider:

Audio. The audio requirements of a music system can be as simple as a single synthesizer connected to a guitar amp with a single cord, or they can be as sophisticated as a recording studio control room. If you have more than one signal source, the heart of your audio interface will undoubtedly be a mixer. You will need enough inputs to handle all of your instruments (and other audio sources). The output configuration will depend on the focus of your system. For live performance, a single output may be sufficient. If you are using a multi-track recorder, on the other hand, you will need, at the very least, an individual input for each tape track, plus a stereo output for monitoring. If you are using audio effects, you will need one or more effects sends on the mixer, which spells additional ins and outs. With systems of any complexity, you'll find that a patch bay will provide the most versatile and efficient method for routing audio signals.

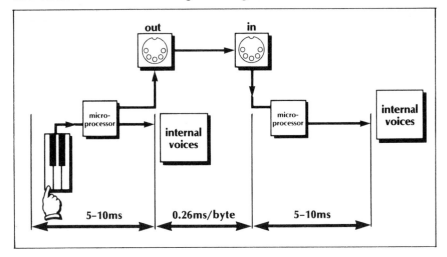

Figure 1. The source of time delays in MIDI systems is not usually the MIDI message transmission itself, but the delays that occur within the master and slave instruments. Typically, there is a lag of five to ten milliseconds between the receipt of a note-on message and the beginning of the note. MIDI messages, however, travel at a rate of 0.32 milliseconds per byte. A note-on command is three bytes long, so it is transmitted in 0.96ms. an entire 16-note chord can be transmitted in only 15.3ms.

Timing. If you are planning on using sequencers and/or drum machines, you must acquaint yourself with the nuts and bolts of synchronization. You will probably find yourself dealing with several different types of synchronization signals. These include MIDI clock bytes, DIN sync, click tracks, FSK sync tones, SMPTE, and electronic pulse clocks with various beat divisions.

These clock signals are all mutually incompatible. That is, if you plug the FSK output of an Oberheim sequencer into the sync input of an E-mu drum machine, which is looking for a pulse signal, the two devices will not sync. In addition, some devices will read one kind of sync and simultaneously generate another that locks with the first, while other devices will refuse to put out a sync signal of any kind while slaved to a master clock elsewhere in the system. You will need to know the differences between these timing

87

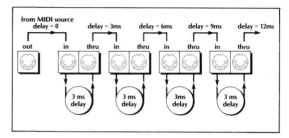

Figure 2. Daisy-chaining, in which each instrument receives its input from the previous instrument's thru port, causes time delays to add up, resulting in an audible lag between key-down and note-on for the last instruments in the chain.

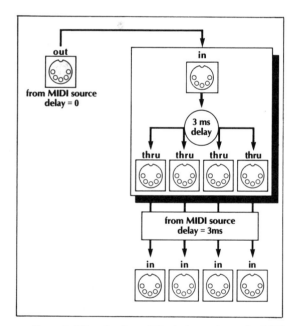

Figure 3. With a thru box, all the instruments receive MIDI signals delayed by the same amount. Time lags, if any, will be caused only by differences in how the various instruments respond to incoming signals.

signals and what is needed to interface mismatched clock types together. For complex systems, a specialized clock translation device may become indispensable. For example, such a device might convert MIDI clock signals to a 96-per-quarter-note pulse clock. The more sophisticated clock converters provide a selection from among several formats and beat subdivisions.

Each type of clock has its own advantages and drawbacks. For example, if you are working with film and video scoring, or if your music depends on free-flowing changes in tempo, I strongly recommend looking into SMPTE as your master timing reference. Most musical instruments can't read SMPTE, however, so installing it would be a pointless expense if you don't need it. To make full use of SMPTE, you will need a special device to read the SMPTE timing code and translate it into MIDI and other types of clock signals.

MIDI. MIDI is the glue that will hold your system together. A solid understanding of MIDI functions, as well as an open-minded view of their potential implications, is essential. In terms of the system, we are concerned mostly with routing MIDI signals rather than using them for specific musical tasks. MIDI interfacing must not only connect the MIDI instruments in a flexible way, it must also route the signals in a manner that minimizes or eliminates MIDI-related time delays.

The method you use for routing MIDI signals through your system will have an enormous impact on its flexibility and usefulness. The four basic tools that are used, the thru box, the A/B switcher, the matrix switcher, and the merge unit.

MIDI Delays. Much has been written about MIDI-associated time delays. Delays of some type are inevitable whenever digital signals are transferred from one device to another. MIDI has taken some pretty hard knocks from certain corners because its transmission rate (31.25 kilobaud) is considered too slow by some people. This is not necessarily true, however. There are several factors other than baud rate that cause delays between when a MIDI command is sent out and when the receiving device begins to act on it. If you are aware of these factors, you can use the routing tools just described to help you minimize their effect.

MIDI messages are transmitted one bit at a time. While MIDI does not employ the world's fastest method of moving bits from one place to another, it does move them fast enough to keep up with any mortal musician. To my knowledge, no one needs to play faster than 20 or 30 notes per second. Even if someone did, we wouldn't hear the result as rhythm anyway, since our lower threshold of pitch perception is about 20Hz. The MIDI transmission rate can transmit more than 1,000 single note events (either note-ons or note-offs) per second! Chords are transmitted one note at a time, so it takes more time to transmit a 16-note chord than it does to transmit a single note, even though all the keys in the chord are played at the same time. Even so, MIDI can transmit more than 65 16-note chords per second. A complete chord can be sent every .0154 second. The time between the notes in a given chord is .00096 seconds, which is *not* humanly perceptible. If this were the only source of delay, and only one performer's messages were being sent over a MIDI cable at a time, I doubt that anyone would ever hear a delay.

If you've been working with several MIDI synthesizers and a sequencer, however, you may have heard some quite noticeable delays. Does this mean you possess super-human ears? No. It means that there are other factors affecting the time it takes for your actions as a keyboard performer to be converted into sounds by a MIDI slave instrument.

One very significant source of delays can be your instruments themselves. When you strike a key, it can easily take between five and ten milliseconds (ms) for that action to be sent to the synthesizer's internal sound-generating circuitry and converted to a sound. It takes about the same amount of time for the instrument to convert that action into a MIDI message and send it to the MIDI out port. When you play a chord, you may think you are playing notes at the same time, but your synthesizer scans its keys sequentially, one at a time. As a result, there is a slight built-in delay between the notes in a chord. This is significantly greater than the MIDI delay for a chord. Normally, we don't hear these delays, but they are there. When the notes in the chord arrive at a new instrument (via its MIDI in port), another 5-10ms passes while the receiving instrument is translating the messages into a form that its voices can understand and sending them to the voices. Only then will you hear a sound. It is quite possible that you will notice the effect caused by the accumulation of these delays. There is not much you can do about this particular situation if it occurs. You should understand, however, that the main source of the problem is not MIDI *per se*. It is the internal processing time of the instruments.

Delay problems are more likely to be caused by the way you are routing MIDI signals in your system and/or the number of simultaneous polyphonic performances you are sending through a single set of MIDI cables. Both of these problems can easily be minimized by the proper use of MIDI routing tools.

Whenever the output of a MIDI source is routed simultaneously to more than one destination, it must be transferred via a thru port. The transfer is not instantaneous, but may as well be, since it's only about three *micro*seconds. Still, if you must connect several instruments to one source, avoid daisy-chaining. Each instrument in the chain adds its own delay to the MIDI signal, which can create a noticeable lag between when you strike a key and when the last instrument in the chain begins playing a note. If you use a thru box, only a single delay is added, and it is the same for all the instruments receiving their signals from the box.

Delays can also be caused by trying to send more messages than MIDI is capable of sending in a given amount of time. As I mentioned above, this is virtually impossible for a single player to do. However, if you are using a multi-channel sequencer to control several polyphonic synthesizers at the same time, you can cause a digital logjam. The messages can only be sent one at a time, and each occupies a fixed amount of time, so some must be delayed longer than others.

To avoid this, you'll want to use a sequencer that has several channel-assignable outputs. Each output should carry the information for only a single channel or a small number of channels. Use a matrix switcher to interface the sequencer's outputs with your instruments. This will allow you to assign any sequencer channel to any MIDI destination, while at the same time the parallel routing will eliminate logjam-type delays.

Applications

I've given a lot of details on MIDI configurations, because I want to make sure you have access to this information. But don't lose sight of the forest while you're staring at the trees. The key to designing a flexible system is your ability to evaluate how each element is to interact with the others. This depends, in turn, on two things: your understanding of system interfacing, and your understanding of your own needs.

Figuring out what you want to do with your system can be the hardest part of putting it together, but it is the most important step. For many of us, the urge to go out and buy new equipment often overwhelms the calm, detached process of defining our objectives. There are several things you must consider before giving in to the temptation to buy a bunch of new toys. Unless you have unlimited funds, your system should be focussed on a specific area of musical applications—the ones that are most important to you. If you are not sure what you want to concentrate on, take the time to

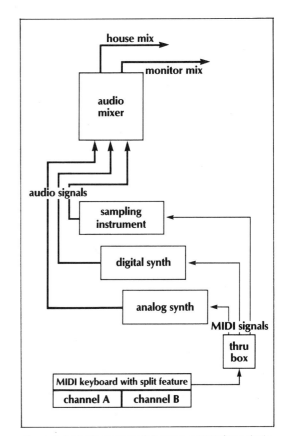

Figure 4. A simple stage performance system for a single player. This player's main requirements are that he needs to be able to play two independent sets of sounds simultaneously, and that he needs to play multi-layered sounds. Several different control combinations are made possible by changing the MIDI modes and channel assignments of the three instruments. For example, the digital synthesizer could be played from one half of the keyboard controller and the analog synthesizer from the other half, while the sampling machine, set to omni mode, is doubling the entire keyboard. The keyboard is shown here as a separate controller, but it could easily be the built-in keyboard on one of the instruments. (In this case, it would be preferable to use as the master keyboard an instrument that has a local-off switching feature, allowing it to play the other instruments without making any sound itself.)

figure it out. You'll be glad you did.

In order to help you with this process, I've taken the somewhat arbitrary step of breaking down the broad panorama of musical activities into four areas: performance, composition, sound design, and production. Each of these areas encompasses any number of branches and subdisciplines, and they overlap to some extent. Most of us work in more than one musical territory, and sometimes it is not possible to draw a line between two or more of these applications. However, each of us usually focuses on a particular musical interest, and our other activities help support that central goal. Do you have such a center? Spend some time thinking about what you would like to accomplish in each of the four areas. The questions below should help you to do this.

Also, consider the way you work in each area. Do you approach things in an intuitive, improvisational manner, or are you analytical and methodical? This is the time, too, to make note of any special requirements. For example, you may have to travel in the course of your work. Or your equipment may have to fit in with a particular stage concept.

Performance. For now, let's not make a distinction between playing onstage, in the studio, and at home. By 'performance' I mean playing your instrument in real time.

● Do you play because it is a convenient way to hear and record your compositional ideas, or is the act of performance an end in itself?

● How important are keyboard dynamics and other types of expression control to your playing style?

● Would you like to relieve yourself of some of the performance responsibilities?

● Would you like to be able to execute musical ideas that are beyond your skills as a player?

Composition. Even if you are a jazz-oriented musician playing tunes written by others, at some point your own creative input will assume a more or less definite form. This is a type of composition. And while we have yet to hear any classical music synthesis that uses MIDI, it's only a matter of time. If you're moving in this direction, your approach to orchestration can be pinpointed by the questions below.

● How much emphasis do you place on doing original compositions and arrangements?

● Are your ideas based on keyboard improvisations, or do you compose with a pencil and score paper?

● Do you approach composition from the top down, starting with an overall sketch and filling it in section by section, or do you start with small motifs and phrases and build them into bigger sections until you arrive at a finished piece?

● Does your writing require any special techniques or skills, such as those used in scoring for film or choreography?

Sound Design. This relatively new field is an especially fertile one for MIDI studio exploration, because of the system-exclusive data dump feature that makes possible the use of voicing and patch librarian software.

● Do you like to create your own sounds, or do you only bother with it when you can't find an appropriate preset?

● Do you consider yourself an expert with a particular type of synthesis, or with a particular synthesizer?

● Do you approach sound design intuitively, or do you thoroughly understand all the parameters at your disposal?

● Do you often use more than one instrument at a time to make composite sounds?

● Would you be more involved with sound design if the instruments were easier to understand?

Production. Again, I'm using this term loosely. You need to think about the kind of finished results you're after.

- Do you want to record demo versions of your compositions at home?
- Do you want to go into the studio and come out with a finished two-track mix or a dubbed video/film?
- Do you want to create a library of synthesizer or sampler sounds that you can sell to others?
- Do you want to create sounds on demand, as in a studio situation?

By now you should have a better idea of what musical areas you intend to concentrate on. You may find it helpful in establishing your priorities to make four vertical columns on a sheet of paper. Label each column with one of the four categories above. Feel free to add other categories if you need to. Number the columns in their order of importance to you. Next, in each column make a list of your needs for that application, using the questions above as guidelines. For each category, number your requirements in the order of their importance. With this list in hand, you will be able to tell which elements of the system to buy first.

Hardware

Many products incorporate several system-related features in their design. This is especially true when it comes to MIDI and synchronization functions. For example, you may find that two drum machines are essentially the same when compared on the basis of price, sounds, and ease of programming. However, one unit may offer more complete synchronization features than the other. This might eliminate the need for you to purchase a separate clock interface, which would make a clear difference in the real cost. If you understand your system requirements, you will have a better idea which unit to buy.

In the same way, if you want to program your own sounds, buying a given computer simply because of the sequencer software it will run is probably short-sighted. You also need to consider whether voicing software will be part of your system, and if so, which computer will run this type of program for the synthesizer(s) you own.

I've listed the major hardware elements of MIDI systems below. For each, I've raised several questions relating to how this unit will interact with the system.

Performance Controllers. These include not only keyboards but pedals, breath controllers, and even pitch-to-MIDI converters, which some of you may find very useful for doubling a vocal line on synthesizer.
- Do you need to play more than one independent part at a time?
- Do you need to alternate between two or more controllers (for instance, to play a strap-on keyboard for some numbers)?
- Which expression controllers (pitch-bend, modulation, footpedals) are important to you?
- Are you committed to a particular type of keyboard or other instrument as your main performance controller?

Synthesizers & Samplers. Obviously, these boxes will be the heart of your MIDI studio. Without them, MIDI has nothing to talk to. Probably the neatest thing about MIDI is that it allows you to buy several instruments by different manufacturers, which typically have very different types of sounds, and control them all from a single source. When considering which sound sources to buy, avoid getting locked into three devices from the same manufacturer if three are all you can afford. While they'll look pretty sitting next to one another, you'll probably find that they have a similar character, robbing your music of depth.
- How many elements of an orchestration do you need to provide simultaneously in real time?

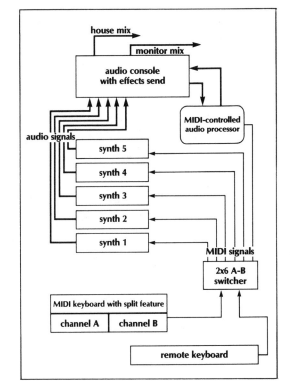

Figure 5. A more complex live performance system than that shown in Figure 4. Here we have added several new requirements: the creation of more sophisticated sounds and the control of more instruments per keyboard zone; control of all instruments from a remote strap-on keyboard; addition of audio effects to the house mix; and control of effects device parameter settings from the remote keyboard. The addition of more synthesizer modules makes it possible to produce more densely layered sounds. The A/B switcher allows either keyboard to control the instrument stack. The effects send from the console is routed through a MIDI-controllable audio processor, probably a reverb or delay line. The programs of the processor can be switched from either keyboard.

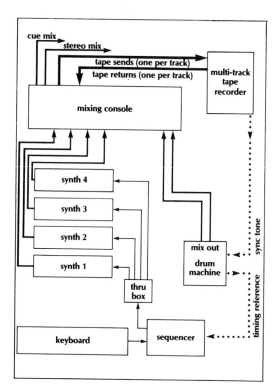

Figure 6. An overdub-oriented studio system. The requirements: synchronizing sequencers and drum machines with a multi-track tape deck; listening to multiple sequencer tracks live without having to record them to tape; creating multi-layered orchestrations from a single sequencer part; and mixing down the finished composition. This system is an expansion of the stage system shown in Figure 4. Several new components have been added to focus the system on multi-track recording. These include the tape deck itself, a stereo recorder (now shown) for mixdown, a mixing console with multi-track recording functions and several more ins and outs than the original stage mixer, a drum machine, and a sequencer. MIDI routing is accomplished as before. There are enough synthesizers to make it possible to listen to several independent sequencer parts at once, without having to record them as tape tracks. The drum machine is synchronized with the tape recorder using its sync-to-tape function, and provides a timing reference to the sequencer so that all overdubs will remain in sync with what has already been recorded. If the sequencer and drum machine have a compatible synchronization protocol, there is no need for a clock interface device.

- Do you need quick access to a large number of preset sounds?
- Do you need to make complex changes in instrument settings between songs or sets?
- If you use a sampling instrument, what type of inputs (microphone, tape, other recordings) do you need for it?

Computers, Sequencers, & Software. This category continues to expand at a rapid rate, making it difficult to know which items to purchase. To date, the big computers for musical applications have been the Commodore 64, the Apple IIe, the IBM PC, and the Macintosh. Newer entries on the market, however—such as the Commodore Amiga and the Atari ST series—are gaining ground. The STs, in particular, may prove to be *the* musician's computer through to the 1990s.

- How many independent parts must your sequencer be able to play at the same time?
- How large, in terms of number of notes, are the largest pieces of music that you plan to play back on one pass in real time?
- Do you want the sequencer to record performance messages such as pitch-bend, after-touch, and so on?
- Will the sequencer have to synchronize with a drum machine, tape recorder, VCR, or other sequencer?
- Will you perform live on a keyboard at the same time that the sequencer is playing back?
- Does your music demand the ability to change tempos and/or bar length during a single piece?
- What synthesizers and samplers do you plan to accessorize with voicing and librarian software?
- Do you need a computer sturdy enough to take on the road?

Drum Machines. In small systems, the drum machine will often serve as the master synchronization device as well as providing percussion sounds.

- Will you need to process the audio of individual drum sounds separately, or will you use only the drum machine's mix output(s)?
- Will the drum machine need to synchronize with tape, sequencers, or other drum machines?
- Do you plan to play the drum sounds from a MIDI keyboard, or use the drum machine to control a MIDI synthesizer?
- If you are using the drum machine and/or sequencer in live performance, how will they be started and stopped, and what will they be synchronized to?

Tape Recorders. For all systems except those dedicated strictly to live performance, some sort of tape deck is a necessity.

- Will a tape deck be part of your system? If so, will you use it simply to capture performances, or do you plan on building music with a series of overdubs?
- After you have made your master tape, will you need to make copies? What sort of format do you want the copies to be in (reel-to-reel, cassette)?
- Do you need master tapes of professional audio quality?
- When overdubbing, will you lay the parts down "on the fly," or must they be synchronized to the music that is already recorded?
- Will any of your synthesizers use tape cassettes for data storage?

Audio Effects. We are only beginning to see MIDI-controlled programmable effects devices, and the prices are still higher than musicians would prefer. But we can look forward to cost declines, coupled with innovative programming applications.

- Do you dedicate particular audio processors to individual instruments? If so, do you need to change the effect's settings when you change the instrument's presets?
- Will you be recording the effects as part of each tape track, or do you plan to record the tracks dry and add the ambience later?

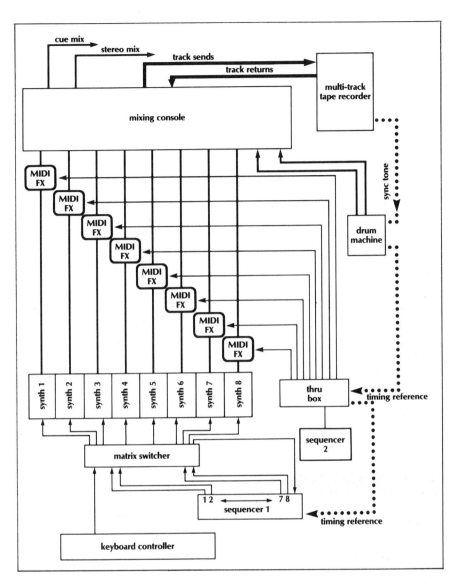

Figure 7. A studio system for recording complex sequencer-based compositions in real time. The requirements: to play a finished sequencer piece without overdubbing; to allow individual audio processing for each synthesizer; to synchronize changes in audio effects with the performance; and to play synthesizers live from a keyboard while the sequence is playing. Two additions have been made to the system shown in Figure 6, in addition to the expanded rack of synthesizers and MIDI-controlled audio effects devices. The 10 x 10 matrix switcher allows the sequencer's multiple outputs to control various synthesizers. Parallel routing of MIDI signals is used for synthesizer control to minimize time delays. A second sequencer is used as an automation tool for controlling the effects devices. This keeps the amount of data on the main sequencer down to a manageable size. With a system like this, the synthesizers don't have to be recorded on multiple tracks at all. They can be laid down live during the final mix, which gives the cleanest possible sound and also frees the tape tracks for recording other instruments or voices.

• Do you need to be able to get at the front panels of your effects during performance, or can they be installed elsewhere?

Mixing & Monitoring. You do want to listen to what you're playing, don't you? Ultimately, your system can sound no better than its mixer and speakers.

• How many simultaneous audio signals will your mixer need to handle?
• How many effects sends/returns are required by the individual synthesizers and effects devices in your system?
• How loud are the loudest sounds your speakers must handle?
• Will your stage monitoring be separate from the house P.A. system?

These questions, remember, address system-related functions. You will also have to evaluate each component in terms of its individual merits as a synthesizer, sequencer, keyboard controller, computer, and so on. Sound, reliability, roadworthiness, and other factors will then be important.

Conclusion

It may be possible for you to design and put together a simple, trouble-free MIDI system that will satisfy all your musical needs for a long time. On the other hand, as you travel further along this particular Yellow Brick Road, you may discover more exotic possibilities that will keep your system in a state of flux. This poses two dangers. One is the constant frustration of never being able to afford all the equipment you'd like to own. So don't forget: You'd still have that same feeling no matter *how* much stuff you owned. At a certain point, you have to take a deep breath, relax, and be thankful for what you have. Ultimately, the greatness of the music you make depends on your musical taste, not on your hardware. And remember—almost none of it existed in any form five years ago.

The second danger, which we have been optimistically ignoring throughout this article, is that when you get your components together and hook them up, they won't work the way they're supposed to. The more elements you're working with, the more chance there is that something will go wrong. Maybe it's something as simple as sending on channel 1 when the slave instrument is set to receive on channel 2. If that's the biggest headache you ever face, you're doing well. We've heard of cases where sequencer software that works perfectly on the machine for which it was written has just been adapted for another type of computer, but locks up on units whose memory expansion boards are configured in a particular way. This kind of thing does happen once in a while, and unfortunately, when you phone the manufacturers, they may be as much in the dark as you are. In order to get the most out of MIDI, you'll find it helpful to adopt a patient, professional attitude. Do your homework so you'll understand the basic concepts. Read your owner's manuals. Make sure all your devices are in the right mode to talk to and understand all the others. Check your connector cables. Treat your disks with tender loving care. Oh, and one more thing. I almost forgot. Mama, get down those rock and roll shoes!

—Steve De Furia

ACCESSORIES

January 1986

The basic idea behind MIDI is a model of simplicity: standardized communication between instruments designed by different manufacturers. So why is it so complicated getting all of your machines to speak to one another? There are two reasons. First, many of your synthesizers, sequencers, and drum machines were built back in the days of control voltages, before the MIDI specification became all the rage. These dinosaurs don't know MIDI from 60-cycle hum. And secondly, musicians are still finding out precisely how to coax MIDI instruments into realizing their full potential.

Even some instrument manufacturers don't have the clearest idea regarding what uses the MIDI data stream might be put to. MIDI was invented on paper, not in a laboratory; a certain period of research and development is necessary not only to iron out the bugs, but to figure out exactly what MIDI is all about in the first place. In addition, it appears that product development and market research—usually two separate stages of production—have been combined in the case of MIDI. For better or for worse, we're all guinea pigs.

As musicians have run into more and more difficulty in harnessing MIDI, a new category of hardware products has sprung up to fill the R&D vacuum: MIDI-processing accessory boxes. Accessory devices range from the simplest on/off switch (allowing you either to send MIDI or not, in one fell swoop) to synchronizers from Garfield and Friend-Chip which can match a MIDI input with any sync code in existence. At first these were designed by enterprising technicians to handle special cases, often at the behest of big-name rock and roll artists. But with MIDI on the rise and much of the confusion still with us, instrument manufacturers have joined in to help musicians step gingerly through the tangle of cables between analog and MIDI instruments, and between MIDI instruments of various makes.

The problem of interfacing between voltage-controlled and MIDI instruments has been addressed by a number of companies. Analog-to-MIDI converters must translate both pitch and trigger/gate voltages into their MIDI counterparts, and vice-versa. The most elaborate of these can be set to send only the highest or lowest note played at any given moment on a polyphonic MIDI synthesizer to a monophonic analog synthesizer. (That is, the analog instrument automatically plays along with either the top line or the bass line.) The simplest, designed for use with drum machines and Simmons-type percussion pads, converts only triggers. A few of these converters are designed to interface between MIDI and a specific model of synthesizer or sequencer.

An additional non-MIDI-to-MIDI interfacing issue is presented by the need to synchronize time-base devices like drum machines, sequencers, and video players. Garfield's original Doctor Click set the comprehensive standard for "rhythm controllers" a couple of years before the MIDI explosion, but now FSK, SMPTE, Roland DIN-plug, and various pulse-rate synchronization codes must be locked up with the MIDI clock. There are a number of accessories today that will handle such functions.

Once you've got your old instruments stepping to MIDI's tune, it's time to get the MIDIfied ones doing what you bought them to do in the first place. Simple master-slave arrangements, in which one instrument's MIDI output controls another, generally go pretty smoothly. It's only when you go beyond basic applications that the problems start to crop up like weeds. Loads of accessories have been developed to make things easier, and they fall into several general categories: thru boxes, switchers, mergers, rechannelizers, and filters. These devices all act on the master MIDI signal in various ways to make it more usable with slave instruments, and are explained in their simplest forms below.

Keep in mind that various models may incorporate any number of useful features too multifarious to go into here, such as programmable memory that can be accessed by MIDI program change commands. In addition, while they are often housed in separate boxes and sold as separate units, many of the accessories listed below combine several of these functions into one multi-purpose device.

A thru box, also called a splitter, is used to route the MIDI messages from a single source to multiple destinations. This simple device minimizes the delay caused by sending a MIDI signal down a daisy-chain of synthesizers through several successive thru ports. This is because the MIDI data stream is subjected to only one opto-isolator (the component that induces distortion-type MIDI delay) and then routed to multiple outputs, instead of passing through one opto-isolator for each thru port. A thru box is a necessity if more than one of your instruments is not equipped with a thru port.

An A/B switcher allows your slaves to be controlled by one of two MIDI sources. This makes it possible to change controllers with the flip of a switch, instead of having to unplug one and plug in another. Matrix switching is a useful alternative to A/B switching. Each output of a matrix switcher can be assigned to send out signals from any one of its inputs. This routing tool combines the advantages of the thru box and the A/B switcher, as well as providing a degree of flexibility not available in any other way.

Perhaps you'd like a single slave to respond to signals from two control sources at once. Or maybe your sequencer can accept input only from one source at a time. You want to mix two MIDI signals. Despite the fact that five-pin DIN plug Y-cables can be found in music stores, MIDI signals can't be combined with a simple Y-cable. Trying to do this, is like asking two typists to use the same keyboard at the same time. The letters from words typed by each one would combine at random, resulting in gibberish. This is what happens to MIDI signals as well if they are improperly combined. A

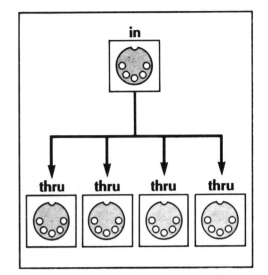

Figure 1. A MIDI thru box, which allows one output from a keyboard controller or sequencer to be sent simultaneously to several instrument inputs.

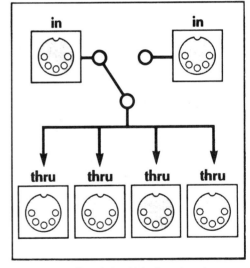

Figure 2. An A/B switch, which allows four slave instruments to be controlled from either of two source controllers.

95

special function known as merging is required, in which a microprocessor keeps track of which signal is which. The microprocessor is able to combine the two MIDI signals without garbling the digital messages they contain.

Some instruments, most notoriously the DX7, transmit only on MIDI channel 1. This is fine for simple master-slave applications, but it can cause problems in other situations. Suppose you're loading a sequencer that records channel information, but doesn't allow you to edit that information. In this case, your entire sequence, no matter how complex it is and no matter how many tracks it combines, will be sent out—in one amorphous mass of MIDI data—on channel 1. If you want to be able to direct different tracks to separate sound-generators, you must have some way of reassigning the channel you're transmitting to the sequencer. You need a rechannelizer. This device changes the transmission channel assignment, otherwise leaving your data stream intact. A rechannelizer is useful in any situation requiring that you transmit on some channel for which your instrument is not equipped.

By now nearly everyone has heard, at least, about MIDI delay. The problem is that it takes time for MIDI information to travel from the master instrument, through the cable, and into the slave—a very tiny amount of time, but time nonetheless. The more data sent over the cable, the more time it takes. And, if you're taking advantage of all of the continuous controllers, so thoughtfully provided by the MIDI spec, to add some life to your music, pretty soon it takes a significant amount of time. One way to combat this problem is to strip irrelevant data out of the stream entirely. If you're using velocity data, but after-touch isn't so important to your patch, for example, you may be able to use a filter to eliminate after-touch data only. This way there's less data travelling through the cable, and less delay in the transmission of relevant data. Filters are relatively new, and are sure to become more plentiful and more flexible in the future.

The term "filter" is also used by J.L. Cooper Electronics to describe a device that rechannelizes the *receive* assignment on instruments designed to receive MIDI on all channels simultaneously (omni-on mode).

Because the MIDI spec provides for system-exclusive as well as performance data, and because the data stream can be recorded in magnetic flux, a host of accessories has arisen to store MIDI to disk and tape. Both media are less expensive than RAM cartridges (the storage method popularized by the DX7); floppy disk boasts the advantages of speed and reliability. These devices can provide bulk memory for instruments lacking conventional cassette and RAM interfaces and additional memory for those with limited capacity, as well as speeding up data transfer for live performance situations. Since instruments from different manufactures require various protocols in order to dump MIDI in bulk, there is no guarantee that the memory-dump/load accessory you buy will work properly with your machine. There are a few "smart" storage units on the market that recognize the instrument they're interfacing with and respond accordingly, but others aren't so bright. It's best to test any unit you're interested in with your instruments before buying.

The final category of MIDI accessories has less to do with inter-instrument interfacing than with taking advantage of the fact that MIDI is being generated as you play. These include programmable switchers that will respond to MIDI program change commands, for configuring outboard effects devices; MIDI-activated stage lighting controllers; MIDI clock-reading autolocators for controlling tape decks; and other devices too diverse to mention. The future is sure to bring so many goodies that any speculation, at this point, is likely to appear short-sighted by the time this appears in print.

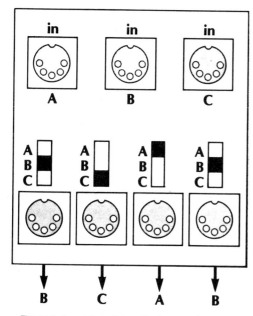

Figure 3. A matrix switcher. Each output has its own selector switch, allowing it to receive the signal from any one of the inputs.

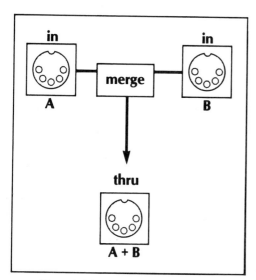

Figure 4. A MIDI mege unit. This device, which incorporates a micro-processor with some data processing capability is required in order to mix two incoming MIDI signals into a single data stream.

—Ted Greenwald

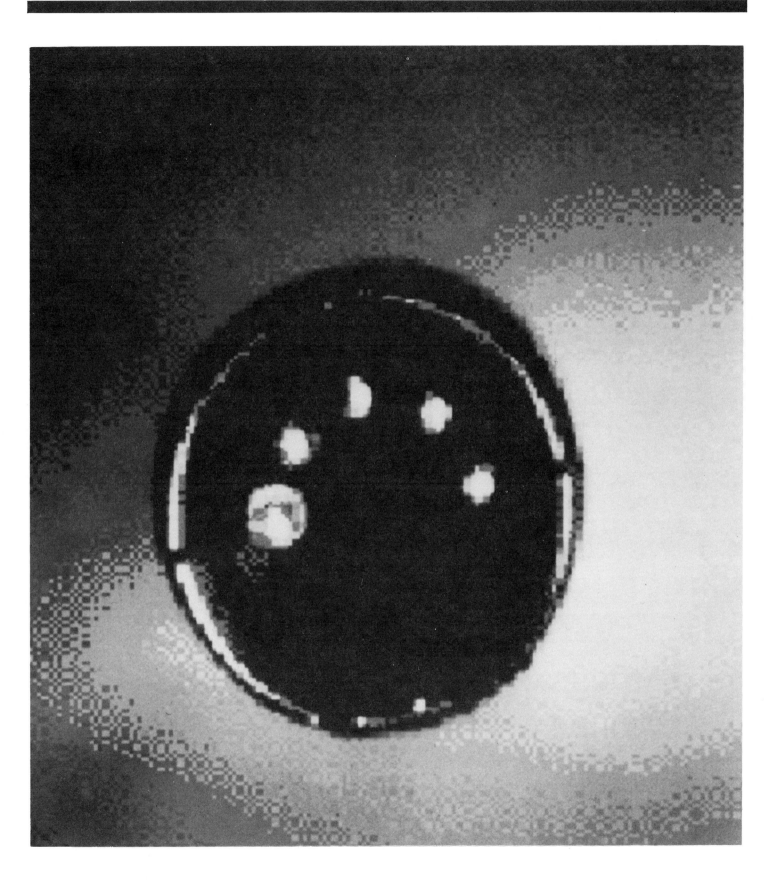

5 APPENDIX

GLOSSARY

A

AD: Abbreviation for Attack/Decay, one of the simplest types of envelope generator. An AD generator produces a rising voltage followed by a falling voltage, but unlike an AR generator, has no sustain segment. Thus the output of an AD generator typically lasts for a fixed amount of time, regardless of whether or not the key that triggered it is still being held down.

additive synthesis: The technique of creating complex tones (for example, a fundamental with a specified series of harmonics) by combining simpler tones, traditionally sine waves. The opposite of subtractive synthesis.

ADSR: Abbreviation for Attack/Decay/Sustain/Release, the four controls found on the most common type of envelope generator. These controls determine the duration or (in the case of sustain) the height of the segments of the envelope.

aftertouch: A type of touch sensitivity in which the keyboard senses how hard the key is being pressed down after it has reached and is resting on the keybed. Also called force sensitivity and pressure sensitivity. Aftertouch can be either monophonic (one pressure-sensing device runs under the entire length of the keyboard, and only one control signal is sent out, representing the total amount of pressure on the keyboard at any given moment) or polyphonic (each key has its own pressure sensor). Monophonic and polyphonic aftertouch are defined separately in the MIDI Specification.

algorithm: A set of procedures for solving a problem or implementing a specific task. The term 'algorithm' is used by Yamaha to refer to the specific configuration of a group of software oscillator/envelope/amplifier sets (called 'operators') whose values are added to or modulate one another in ways specified by the algorithm. The configuration is called an algorithm rather than a patch because the oscillators don't exist as discrete hardware components, only as mathematical functions within a microprocessor. Manufacturers of other software-based devices use the term in a similar way.

aliasing: Undesired frequencies, usually but not always faint and high-pitched, which are produced when the signal being sampled by or generated within a digital sound source is greater than half the sampling rate. Aliasing differs from some other types of noise in that its pitch changes when the pitch of the intended sound changes.

all-notes-off: A MIDI command, recognized by some, but not all, synthesizers and other sound-generating modules, which causes any notes that are currently sounding to be shut off.

amplitude: The amount of a signal, measured by determining the amount of fluctuation in air pressure (of a sound), voltage (of an electrical signal), or numerical data (in a digital medium). When the signal is in the audio range, amplitude is perceived as loudness.

amplitude modulation (AM): A change in the amplitude or loudness of the signal, for example by passing it through a VCA and applying a fluctuating voltage to the VCA's control input. When the modulating signal is below the audio frequency range, periodic amplitude modulation is called tremolo.

analog: Capable of exhibiting continuous electrical fluctuations that correspond in a one-to-one fashion to the audio input or output; the opposite of digital. In analog synthesizers, both control signals and audio signals may take on any voltage value in a continuous spectrum within an allowed range (for example, between –5 and +5 volts). See digital.

analog/digital hybrid: A synthesizer or sampler that makes use of both analog and digital technology, usually in the form of analog tone-generating or tone-shaping circuitry (voltage-controlled oscillators or filters) combined with digital tone-generating circuitry (sampling memory or wavetables) or digital control circuitry (programmable memory).

analog sequencer: A sequencer in which the control voltages to be played back are specified mechanically using a bank of analog pots rather than stored in digital memory.

analog-to-digital (A/D) converter: A device that changes the continuous fluctuations in voltage put out by an analog device into bits of digital information for processing or storage in a digital sampler, delay line, or other digital device.

AR: Abbreviation for Attack/Release, the two parameters controlled by a simple envelope generator. In an AR generator, the sustain level is fixed at 100%, and the release segment begins when the gate signal ends (that is, when the key gating the envelope is lifted).

arpeggiator: A device that automatically steps one at a time through a group of notes specified by keys which are held down (or latched). The notes may be stepped through in ascending order, descending order, or both; or, more rarely, in the order in which they were pressed. Unlike a sequencer, however, an arpeggiator cannot usually play irregular rhythms or chords.

assignment priority: The routing scheme in a polyphonic synthesizer that determines which key will activate which voice. See first-note, last-note, top-note priority.

attack: The first part of the sound of a note. On an envelope generator, the attack control is used to determine the amount of time it takes after the key is depressed for the envelope voltage or equivalent control signal to rise to its maximum value.

attenuator: A potentiometer (pot) that is used to set the amplitude of the signal passing through it at some value between its full value (no attenuation) and zero (full attenuation). Pots can be either rotary or linear (sliders).

auto-correct: A function (also called quantization) found on most sequencers and drum machines, which causes notes played during real-time data entry to be assigned to the nearest available rhythmic value (such as sixteenth-notes). Notes which have been auto-corrected are more rhythmically precise than notes that have not.

auto-bend: A simple attack envelope, usually dedicated to controlling pitch. Auto-bend (also called glide and auto-glide) causes each note to begin with an upward or downward pitch slide of variable length and depth.

auto-glide: A type of glide (portamento) in which there is a pitch slide between notes only when the new key is depressed while the previous key is still being held down. Also called fingered portamento. Playing with a staccato touch produces discrete pitches with no glide. Also see auto-bend.

auto-tune: A button or switch that causes an instrument to automatically tune (and perhaps calibrate the scaling of) its oscillators and other tunable circuits.

B

bandpass filter: A filter designed to allow only the frequencies within a specified range to pass through.

band-reject filter: Also called notch filter. A filter designed to eliminate frequencies within a specified range and pass all others through.

bank: (1) A set of patches that can be called up with a related set of commands. (2) Any related set of items, e.g. filter bank (a set of filters that work together to process a single audio signal).

baud rate: The number of digital bits transmitted per second. MIDI transmissions have a baud rate of 31,250 (31.25 kilobaud), while modems typically have a much lower rate of 300 or 1,200 baud.

bend: To change pitch in a continuous sliding manner using a pitch-bend wheel, lever, or ribbon.

binary: The representation of numbers in powers of two. Computers use this form of numbering because the values 0 and 1 can easily be used to represent on and off states such as a dot being black or white on the display screen.

bit: One binary digit (0 or 1)—the smallest possible amount of information. This gives a simple test of conditions like on or off, true or false, yes or no.

boot: Starting up the computer, usually by bringing in a small program from a disk so that the computer can run a larger program. The term is derived from "bootstrapping," where the computer "pulls itself up by the its own bootstraps" (computer programmers are weird people!).

bpm: Beats per minute.

break point: (1) The third setting in Korg's six-stage envelope generator. The break point and slope occur after the decay segment and before the sustain segment of the envelope; the break point is the level to which the decay segment falls before the envelope begins rising or falling further to the sustain segment. (2) In Yamaha DX/TX synthesizers, the point of reference for an operator's keyboard level scaling curves.

bulk dump: See data dump.

byte: One unit of information, usually comprising eight bits.

C

capacitance sensing: A type of touch sensitivity in that the amount of key surface covered by a fingertip is sensed, and a corresponding output voltage generated.

carrier: A signal (usually an audio signal) which is being modulated by some other signal, as in FM.

cartridge: A plug-in memory storage device. Cartridges may be either RAM or ROM, and are normally usable only on devices built by a single manufacturer.

cassette storage: Digital information about patch programs or sequencer or drum machine patterns stored on cassette tape.

catalog: A list of all the files stored on a disk. Also referred to as a directory.

center detent: A notch in the operation of a controller (especially a pitch-bend wheel) that allows the user to return the controller precisely to its original position.

chain: An ordered series. For example, a program chain is a set of patch programs that the user can step through in order with a footswitch. A song chain in a drum machine is a series of songs, each song consisting in turn of a series of patterns.

channel: In analog audio, a channel is a separate electrical signal path. In MIDI, however, the 16 channels are numerical data designations, all of which share a single cable.

channel pressure: A type of MIDI data that contains monophonic aftertouch information.

chorusing: A type of signal processing built into some synthesizers. Chorusing is a type of flanging in which a time-delayed signal is mixed with the original signal and the length of the delay is modulated by an LFO, which changes the relative strengths and phase relationships of the overtones and thereby creates a fatter, more animated sound. The effect of a true chorus unit can be approximated more simply by detuning one oscillator slightly relative to another oscillator, producing a slow beating between the two.

clamping: The limitation of a voltage to a specified level. Oscillator clamping is a complex type of synchronization in which, when it receives a command pulse, the slave oscillator resets not to the beginning of its cycle (as in normal sync) but to whatever point in its cycle corresponds to the clamping level.

clangorous: Containing partials that are not part of the normal harmonic series. Clangorous tones are more or less bell-like.

click track: A timing reference signal recorded on tape that contains a single click for each basic beat (such as a quarter-note) of a song. Compare with sync track.

clock: Any of several types of timing control devices, or the periodic signals generated by them. A low-frequency pulse clock normally puts out one gate and/or trigger signal for each event to be initiated, and may be used as an adjustable-speed automatic trigger for a sample-and-hold, analog sequencer, envelope generator, etc. An audio-rate sync clock puts out a pulse with which various digitally controlled devices can be synced to one another, or to a tape track containing the sync clock signal.

coarse tune: A control that is used for making large changes in the pitch of an oscillator. Usually used in conjunction with a fine-tune control.

code: (1) A system of representing some piece of information (2) The instructions or statements that make up a program.

companded: Compressed and expanded. Companding is used in analog signal processing to increase the dynamic range and smooth out sharp peaks. In digital audio, data companding allows more dynamic range to be expressed in fewer bits of data.

contour amount: A control that regulates the amount of envelope voltage that enters (usually) the VCF or VCA. Note that the sustain control is a level control *within* the envelope generator that sets the sustain level relative to the peak found at the end of the attack portion of the envelope, while the contour amount control increases or reduces the entire envelope, including the peak, proportionately.

contour generator: See envelope generator.

control input: An input to a signal source or modifier that accepts the signal telling the circuitry what to do.

controller: A device that is capable of producing a change in some aspect of the sound by altering the action of some other device. Examples of controllers include keyboards, pitch-bend devices, and envelope generators.

controller number: One of the standard data designations of the MIDI Specification. The modulation wheel, for example, is controller number 1.

control voltage: An electrical signal that tells a voltage-controlled device or module (such as a VCO or VCF) what levels to go to or changes to make in the settings of any voltage-controlled parameter. A control voltage is an analog signal —that is, the changes in the behavior of the controlled module will be in proportion to the amount of voltage received.

CPU: Abbreviation for Central Processing Unit. The heart of the microcomputer, which performs the calculations and executes the instructions contained in a program.

cross-fade looping: A feature found in some digital samplers in which some portion of the end of a loop is mixed with some portion of the beginning of the same loop so as to produce a smoother loop.

cross-modulation: A term used by some manufacturers to refer to a type of patch in which one of the audio oscillators in each voice is being modulated by another, or by an envelope generator. Also called poly-mod.

CRT: Cathode Ray Tube. See display.

cursor: The symbol on the screen that marks where the next character will be typed in from the computer's keyboard.

cutoff frequency: The point in the frequency spectrum beyond which a filter attenuates the audio signal being put through it. On most synthesizers, the cutoff frequency is both manually adjustable and voltage-controllable.

D

DAC: See digital-to-analog converter.

data: Information, especially that used by a computer when running a program.

data dump: The process of sending memory contents (usually in the form of MIDI system-exclusive messages) to a computer or other storage medium.

DCO: Digitally controlled oscillator. This term is used principally on Korg and Roland synghesizers, whose oscillators can be directly controlled digitally because they are digital oscillators. The analog oscillators on other analog/digital hybrid instruments are controlled digitally as well, but the control signals are often sent through a DAC and converted to analog voltages before arriving at the oscillators' control inputs.

dead band: An area at the center of travel of a controller such as a pitch-bend wheel within which movement of the controller has no effect. A dead band is usually provided to allow a pitch controller to be returned reliably to concert pitch.

decay: The second of the four segments controlled by an ADSR envelope generator. The decay control determines the amount of time it takes for the envelope to fall from the peak reached at the end of the attack portion to the sustain level.

delay: (1) The first stage on a five-stage (DADSR) envelope generator. The delay control determines the amount of time after the trigger signal is received during which the envelope voltage remains at zero before beginning to rise toward its peak during the attack portion. (2) A control function that allows one of the elements in a layered sound to start later than another element. (3) A digital delay line (DDL) used for flanging, doubling, and echo.

detune: A detune control is generally found on instruments that have two (or more) oscillators per voice. It is used to make changes in the pitch of one oscillator within a voice relative to the pitch of another. Small amounts of detuning (from .5Hz to 3Hz) are used to add a chorusing effect to a patch. Larger amounts allow each key to sound an interval or chord rather than a unison.

digital: Using computer-type binary operations; the opposite of analog. Digital equipment uses microprocessors to store and retrieve information about sound in the form of numbers, and typically divides potentially continuous fluctuations in value (such as amplitude or control settings) into discrete quantized steps.

digital oscillator: An oscillator (a source of a periodically repeating waveform) in which the specific waveshape to be generated exists in the form of a series of numbers (the wavetable) that describe the height of the waveshape at various points in time.

digital-to-analog converter (DAC): A device that changes the bits of digital information put out by a digital device into analog fluctuations in voltage. All digital synthesizers and samplers have DACs at their output to create audio signals that can be sent to an amplifier to emerge as sound.

digital/analog hybrid: See analog/digital hybrid.

digital sequencer: A sequencer in which the signals to be played back are stored as numbers in a digital memory.

disk: A small, flat, circular surface used for storing information in the form of magnetic pulses, somewhat the same way sound is recorded onto tape. See floppy disk.

disk drive: A device used to read and write information onto a disk.

display: A device used to visually display information. Also referred to as a monitor, VDT, or CRT.

DOS: The Disk Operating System. A software system that allows a computer to exchange information with disk drives.

double mode: See layering.

duophonic: Possessing two voices, one sounding the highest note depressed on the keyboard and the other the lowest. A duophonic synthesizer (now obsolete) was a simplified polyphonic synthesizer in which the two voices shared a single VCF and VCA.

duty cycle: The percentage of a complete cycle of a pulse wave that it spends in the up portion of its cycle. In the case of audio-rate pulse waves, there is no functional difference between two waves that have duty cycles of 50% + X and 50% - X, as their harmonic spectra will be identical. Also called pulse width.

dynamic voice allocation: A system found on some sampling keyboards and a few synthesizers, in which all available voices can be switched very quickly to sound notes using any of the patches or samples currently resident in memory.

E

edit: To change or modify information.

edit mode: A mode of operation of a programmable synthesizer in which front-panel controls can be used to make temporary changes in the values stored in memory. In the case of a digital sequencer, edit mode is a mode in which the notes stored in the sequence can be changed.

editor/librarian: A piece of computer software that allows the user both to store and retrieve and to edit the data in synthesizer patch programs.

EG: Envelope generator.

eight-bit: A term used to refer to digital audio systems in which sound data is manipulated and stored in the form of eight-bit words. Each bit is equivalent to about 6dB of signal-to-noise ratio, so eight-bit systems typically have more inherent noise than 12-bit and 16-bit systems.

emphasis: See resonance.

envelope: A shape that changes non-periodically as a function of time. The envelope shape, governed by a set of one or more *rate* and *level* controls, appears as a control signal that can be applied to an internal amplifier to control amplitude, to a filter to control timbre, or to any other controllable parameter of the sound, to give shape to a note.

envelope follower: An AC-to-DC converter coupled with a lag processor to produce a DC envelope proportional to the amplitude of the AC input.

envelope generator: The device that generates the envelope (see ADSR, AR, envelope). Also known as a contour generator or transient generator, because the envelope is a contour (shape) that is used to create the transient (changing) characteristics of the sound.

envelope tracking: A function (also called keyboard tracking, key follow, or keyboard rate scaling) that changes the shape of the envelope depending on which key on a keyboard is being played. Envelope tracking is most often used to give the higher notes on the keyboard proportionately shorter envelopes and the lower notes longer envelopes, mimicking the response characteristics of percussion-activated acoustic systems such as the piano.

EPROM: Erasable Programmable Read-Only Memory; a memory module (integrated circuit chip) that can be plugged into a synthesizer or other computer-related device to alter the programming of that instrument. An EEPROM is an *electrically* erasable PROM.

error message: Generally, a message shown on the display to tell the user that some type of error has occurred.

exponential: A relationship between two quantities such that a change in the amount of one is associated with a change in ratio of the other. When a VCA is being exponentially controlled, for example, each increase of one volt in the control voltage might double the amplitude of the output signal. The opposite of exponential is linear.

F

fc: Center frequency or cutoff frequency. In the case of a resonant filter, the fc is the center frequency of the resonant peak.

feedback: A cycle in which the output of a device is fed back into its own input. The term feedback is sometimes used to refer to filter resonance, which is created using a feedback process within the instrument's circuitry. Multiple echoes are produced in a digital delay line using feedback.

file: A collection of data, usually stored on a disk.

file name: The name assigned to a file when it is stored to disk, later used to recall the data into the computer.

filter: A device for eliminating selected frequencies from the sound spectrum of an incoming signal. In addition, synthesizer filters are generally capable of emphasizing certain frequencies in the region of the cutoff frequency, creating a resonant peak (see resonance). For more on filters, see highpass, lowpass, bandpass, and band-reject filter.

fine-tune: A control that is used for making small, precise changes in the pitch of an oscillator.

floating split: A type of keyboard logic in which the instrument attempts to follow the player's performance and intelligently determine which notes should be sounded using which tone color.

floppy disk: A thin, portable disk, either 8″, 5¼″, or 3½″ in diameter, used to store and retrieve programs and files.

FM synthesis: A technique in which frequency modulation (FM) is used to create complex audio waveforms. See frequency modulation.

footage: A way of designating which octave an oscillator will sound when a given note on the keyboard is played. Borrowed from organ pipe terminology, footage settings range from 2′ (high pitch) through 4′, 8′, and 16′ to 32′ (low pitch).

force sensitivity: See pressure sensitivity.

format: (1) The method in which data is organized. (2) To prepare a blank disk to receive information by dividing the magnetic material into tracks and sectors, also called initializing.

formant: A resonant peak in a frequency spectrum. The formants produced by the human vocal tract are what give vowels their characteristic sound.

Fourier analysis: A technique that allows complex, dynamically changing audio waveforms to be described mathematically as sums of sine waves at various frequencies and amplitudes.

four-pole: See rolloff slope.

frequency modulation (FM): A change in the frequency or pitch of a signal. At low speeds, frequency modulation is perceived as vibrato or some type of trill, depending on the shape of the modulating waveform. When the modulating wave is in the audio range (above 16Hz or so), frequency modulation is perceived as a change in tone quality, coupled in some cases with an overall change in pitch.

FSK: Frequency Shift Keying; a type of synchronization signal that consists of a rapid periodic alternation between two pitched audio tones, usually an octave or more apart. FSK is more reliable than an LFO clock when recording a sync tone on tape.

G

gain: The amount of boost or attenuation of a signal.

gate: A control signal put out by the keyboard that tells the envelope generators that a key is now depressed, or an equivalent signal put out by a manual switch, sequencer, or some other module. A gate signal is put out continuously until a moment when no key is depressed (compare trigger).

glide: A function, also called portamento, in which the pitch slides smoothly from one note to the next instead of jumping over the intervening part of the frequency spectrum. Also see auto-bend, auto-glide.

H

hard disk: A storage medium, usually a set of several fixed aluminum platters, which is built onto a computer or its own housing. A hard disk holds more and is faster to use than a floppy disk, but is more expensive and less portable.

hard sync: The standard type of oscillator sync. See sync.

hard-wired: An electrical connection that is built into the instrument's circuitry; the opposite of patchable. Some hard-wired connections can be overridden by patching or defeat switches, while others are a permanent part of the instrument's operation.

hexadecimal: A method of representing numbers in base 16 using the digits 0 to 9 and A to F. Used most often by programmers to facilitate de-bug procedures instead of dealing with binary numbers (example: 100[base 10] = 64[base 16] = 0110 0100[base 2].

high-note priority: A type of keyboard logic found on some monophonic synthesizers and on some polyphonics when they are in unison mode, in which the highest key depressed is the one whose control signal is sent to the oscillators.

highpass filter: A filter that attenuates the frequencies below its cutoff frequency.

hold: See latching.

Hz: Abbreviation for Hertz, the unit measurement of frequency. One Hertz equals one cycle per second.

I

Initialize: (1) To prepare a disk to receive data (see format). (2) To reset all the variables in a program to some initial value.

input: A signal entering a device, or the point at which it enters.

interface: A device used to transfer data from one device to another.

inverter: A device that changes positive voltages into negative voltages and vice versa, thus reversing the phase on periodic signals, causing an envelope to descend instead of rising, and so on.

I/O: Abbreviation for Input/Output. The method of transferring data in and out of the computer to an external device such as a printer or disk drive.

J

joystick: A controller not unlike a small, freely moving gearshift lever, which puts out two independent control voltages simultaneously, one determined by its left-right position (the X-axis) and the other by its toward-away position (the Y-axis).

K

K: An abbreviation for kilobytes. A kilobyte is 1,024 bytes of data, so a 64K computer has 65,536 bytes of memory (64 x 1,024 = 65,536).

keyboard: A controller used primarily for playing traditional melodic and harmonic patterns; on an analog synthesizer, the keyboard sends a control voltage to the oscillators, and gate and trigger signals to the envelope generators.

keyboard amount: See keyboard tracking.

keyboard level scaling: A function in which oscillators or the equivalent can be made louder or softer as a function of which key is pressed. See keyboard scaling (2).

keyboard logic: The system that determines what signals are sent out from the keyboard, and where they are routed. For more on keyboard logic, see assignment priority, high-note priority, low-note priority, last-note priority, single trigger, multiple trigger, split keyboard, layering.

keyboard rate scaling: See envelope tracking.

keyboard scaling: (1) The calibration of an oscillator so that moving from any key to an adjacent key produces the required pitch change, conventionally an equal-tempered half-step. (2) The smooth variation in amplitude of a sound or some component of a sound over the range of the keyboard.

keyboard tracking: Controlling some element of the sound, usually the cutoff frequency of the filter, with a voltage or equivalent pitch information from the keyboard. On some synthesizers the keyboard tracking amount is continuously variable, while on others it can be controlled only by a two-position (on/off) or three-position (on/half/off) switch.

key follow: See envelope tracking.

kHz: KiloHertz (thousands of Hertz). See Hz.

L

lag processor: A device that smooths out sudden changes in voltage. The glide (portamento) control on most analog synthesizers is actually a hard-wired lag processor acting on the control voltage output of the keyboard. A lag processor that will handle audio-rate inputs can be used to smooth out the sharp peaks and dips in a waveform, acting in effect as a crude lowpass filter.

language: The set of rules used to write a program for a computer.

last-note priority: A type of keyboard logic in which each new key as it is depressed activates a voice, taking over if necessary a voice that had previously been sounding the pitch of another key.

latching: A simplified memory system in which the synthesizer continues to operate according to whatever latchable pattern (for example, a set of keys sounding a chord or an arpeggio) was in effect at the moment the latching switch was cued in, until it is released.

layering: Sounding two or more voices, each of which generally has its own timbre, from each key depression.

LFO: Low-frequency oscillator. An oscillator especially devoted to sub-audio applications, and generally used as a control source for producing vibrato, tremolo, trills, and automatically repeating triggers.

librarian: A piece of computer software used to store and retrieve synthesizer patch data. See editor/librarian.

linear: A relationship between two quantities such that a change in the amount of one causes an equivalent change in the amount of the other. A linear pot produces the same amount of change in sound per amount of physical motion throughout its operating range. Compare with exponential and companded.

linear FM: A type of frequency modulation in which the center frequency of the carrier oscillator is not altered by a change in the amount of modulation.

load: To transfer information from an external device (usually the disk drive) to the computer.

lock: To prevent a file (usually on disk) from being changed or erased. The file must first be unlocked before it can be re-written or deleted.

loop: A piece of material that plays repetitively. In sequencers, a loop normally plays a musical phrase. In a sampler, a loop is used to allow samples of a fixed length to be sustained indefinitely while a key is held down.

low-note priority: A type of keyboard logic found on some monophonic synthesizers and on some polyphonics when they are in unison mode, in which the lowest key depressed is the one whose control signal is sent to the oscillators.

lowpass filter: A filter that attenuates the frequencies above its cutoff frequency.

M

master: Any device that controls the operation of other components. For example, a master oscillator is one to which another oscillator is synced, while a master clock is one that controls the timing of other (usually external) devices. See slave.

matrix panel: A patching system, as on the old ARP 2500 synthesizer, in which inputs and outputs for all modules are brought to a central grid and connected to one another using switches or pins.

matrix switching: A type of signal routing in which signals (often MIDI data signals) can be routed from any input to any output.

memory: A system of storage. Synthesizer memories are generally digital, and are used for storing patches, keyboard split points, sequences of notes, and so on.

memory location: A single unit of memory that is identified by a unique address and can hold a piece of information, usually one byte (eight bits).

menu: A list of choices that the computer presents to the user when a program is running.

merge: A device that allows two separate digital streams of MIDI data to be combined.

MG: Modulation generator. A term used by Korg to refer to the LFO section on their instruments.

microcomputer: A small computer whose central processing unit is a microprocessor.

microprocessor: A computer processor that is contained on a single chip (6502, Z-80, 8086, and 6809 are micro-processors commonly found in synthesizers, drum machines, and sequencers).

MIDI: Musical Instrument Digital Interface; this is a specification for the manner in which digital information is transmitted from one synthesizer to another, or between synthesizers, sequencers, drum machines, and computers.

MIDI mode: See mode.

mixer: A device that adds two or more signals together.

mode: The manner in which a device is currently operating. The basic MIDI modes, which describe how devices respond to incoming MIDI data, are omni-on poly (mode 1), which is generally known as omni mode, omni-on mono (2), which is rarely used, omni-off poly (3), which is known as poly mode, and omni-off mono (4), known as mono mode.

modifier: A device (such as a VCF or VCA) that acts on an audio signal to change it in some way.

modular: A type of synthesizer design in which the various sound sources, modifiers, and controllers are semi-independent pieces of hardware that must be hooked together with patch chords or some other patching system.

modulation: The process of introducing a control voltage to a sound source or modifier so as to change the character of the audio signal.

module: A hardware device, either physically separate or integrated into a larger unit, that is designed to make some particular contribution to the overall process of creating electronic sound.

mono mode: One of the three basic operating modes of MIDI (see mode). In mono mode, an instrument responds monophonically to all note information arriving over a specific MIDI channel. The terms "mono mode" and "multi mode" are also used to refer to a multi-timbral type of operation in which the instrument's voices may each be assigned to be played by a different MIDI channel.

monophonic: Capable of producing only one independently moving pitch line at a time. On a typical monophonic synthesizer, only one key on the keyboard will have an effect at any given time.

mouse: A device, moved by hand, which positions a cursor on a screen and can tribber commands by switches.

multi mode: See mono mode.

multi-mode filter: A filter that has more than one mode of operation—both lowpass and highpass, for example, or lowpass, bandpass, band-reject, and highpass. Outputs for each mode may be available simultaneously, or a single switchable output may be provided.

multiple trigger: A type of keyboard logic in which a new trigger signal is sent to the envelope generators every time a new key is depressed, whether or not a legato touch is used. The opposite of single trigger. Polyphonic synthesizers always operate in multiple trigger mode except (perhaps) when in unison mode.

multi-timbral: Capable of generating notes using two or more patches at the same time. The simplest multi-timbral synthesizers are those with a split keyboard feature. On more complex multi-timbral instruments, each voice can be assigned its own tone color.

musique concrete: A type of electronic music produced by the electronic processing and manual splicing of natural acoustic sounds recorded on tape.

N

nibble: Four of the eight bits in a byte.

noise generator: A source for random or quasi-random fluctuations in voltage, which are perceived by the ear as hiss. See white noise, pink noise.

non-volatile memory: A type of memory in which the information is retained when the instrument is unplugged, usually through use of a built-in rechargeable battery. See memory, volatile memory.

notch filter: See band-reject filter.

Nyquist limit: The frequency (1/2 of the sampling rate) above which aliasing will be introduced into a digitally generated sound.

O

omni mode: One of the four basic operating modes of MIDI (see mode). In omni mode (also known as omni-on poly), an instrument responds to note information received over any of MIDI's sixteen channels.

operating system: The set of software instructions that tells a device how to respond to commands from the user.

operator: A term used in Yamaha's DX series synthesizers to refer to a set of software operations that are equivalent in effect to a combination of an oscillator, an envelope generator, and a VCA.

oscillator: A device that creates a repeating electrical wave. In most synthesizer applications, the frequency of this wave can be controlled by various control sources such as keyboards and LFOs.

oscillator drift: The tendency of an oscillator to vary slightly in frequency over long periods of time.

oscillator sync: See sync.

output: A signal leaving a module; also, information transferred from the computer to an external device such as a display, printer, or disk.

overdrive: Intentional distortion of an audio waveform, created by overloading an amplifier. Overdrive is used internally on a few synthesizers to fatten the sound.

overflow mode: A mode of operation in which a MIDI keyboard directs all notes played simultaneously up to some maximum (usually eight) to one sound-generating module (usually its own internal synthesizer) and sends any notes in excess of the maximum out over MIDI. Using overflow mode with two identical sound-generating modules set to produce the same sound allows chords to be played that have more notes than either module could produce by itself.

P

page: One of a group of control-panel configurations in a digitally controlled synthesizer or computer program. While remaining physically the same, the front-panel controls of a synthesizer may assume completely different functions depending on what page has been called up.

parallel interface: A connection between two or more pieces of hardware in which an entire byte of information can be sent simultaneously by routing each of its bits down a separate wire. Compare with serial interface.

patch: To connect together, as the inputs and outputs of various modules, generally with patch cords. Also, the configuration of hookups and settings that results from the process of patching; and, by extension, the tone color that such a configuration creates. Now often used to denote a tone color ('brass patch,' 'string patch') even on an instrument that requires no physical patching.

patch cord: An electrical cord used to connect the output of one module to the input of another.

peripheral device: A device (such as a display, disk drive, or printer) which is physically separate from the computer and connected by cables, usually through an interface card.

phase-locking: An extreme form of oscillator sync in which a special circuit measures the difference in frequency between the master and slave oscillators and actually changes the frequency of the slave so that they match.

pink noise: Random fluctuations in sound, weighted in such a way that there is equal energy

101

present in every octave of the pitch range. Pink noise sounds lower in pitch than white noise.

pitch-bending: See bend.

pitch-to-voltage converter: A device that determines the frequency of an audio waveform (such as that put out by a microphone or electric guitar string) and creates a control voltage that, when applied to the control input of a properly calibrated oscillator, will cause the oscillator to put out its own signal at the same frequency.

pitch-to-MIDI converter: A device that determines the frequency of an audio waveform and puts out the corresponding MIDI note data and pitch-bend data.

pole: A portion of a filter circuit. The more poles a lowpass filter has, the more abrupt the cutoff slope will be.

poly-mod: Polyphonic modulation. A term used by some manufacturers to refer to a type of patch in which one audio oscillator is modulated by another, or by an envelope generator. Same as cross-mod.

poly mode: One of the four basic operating modes of MIDI (see mode). In poly mode (also known as omni-off poly), an instrument responds to information arriving on whatever specific numbered channel it is currently assigned to.

polyphonic: Capable of producing more than one independently moving pitch line simultaneously. On organs and a few polyphonic synthesizers, all the keys can be sounded at once, but on most instruments only a limited number of voices (four, or eight, or twelve, for example) are available.

polyphonic sequencer: A digital sequencer capable of storing and playing back several independent musical lines simultaneously. See sequencer, digital sequencer, sequence.

port: (1) An electrical connector (socket) of some specialized type. (2) To translate one type of computer code into another.

portamento: See glide.

pot: Potentiometer. A device (commonly attached to a knob or slider) that is used to adjust some aspect of the signal being passed through it, or to send out a control signal corresponding to its position. Most pots are used to adjust the amplitude of a single signal, but other types, such as the pan pot (which adjusts the amplitudes of two signals in a reciprocal fashion, thus controlling where a signal will appear to be in the stereo space between two speakers) are also found.

PPQ: Pulses per quarter-note. Usually, timing clock signals are sent out at a rate of 24, 48, or 96 PPQ.

preset: A single button that, when pushed, sets up most or all of an entire patch instantly. Also, a synthesizer equipped with presets. At one time a preset instrument was one that had buttons labelled 'trumpet,' 'violin,' and so on, but today the term 'preset' is being used synonymously with 'patch' in user-programmable instruments.

pressure sensitivity: See aftertouch.

priority: See assignment priority.

program chain: See chain.

program: (1) One of the sets of information about front-panel settings in a programmable synthesizer (see patch). (2) An input to a signal processor that causes the processor to act on another input in a way specified by the program. (3) To create a new sound for such a synthesizer. (4) A set of instructions needed by a computer to perform a particular task. The program must conform to the rules of the language that it was written in.

program change: A command, either generated at the front panel or received via MIDI, that causes an instrument to change from one sound configuration (patch) to another.

programmable: A programmable synthesizer

contains a computer memory that allows the user to store a number of aspects of a patch and recall them all simultaneously to active status by touching not the patch controls themselves but a separate memory control section. Individual controls are said to be programmable if their settings can be stored in memory with separate settings for each patch.

PROM: Programmable Read-Only Memory. A computer chip on which information (such as the digitally encoded sound of a drum) can be encoded only once, and never erased.

prompt: A symbol on the screen that indicates that the computer is ready to receive input.

pulse wave: A signal put out by an oscillator in which a higher steady-state voltage alternates with a lower steady-state voltage. Audio-rate pulse waves are missing every nth harmonic from their spectra, where the duty cycle is $1/n$. Pulse waves with a 50% duty cycle (square waves) sound rich and hollow, while narrow pulses sound thin and reedy.

pulse width: See duty cycle.

pulse-width modulation: A voltage-controlled change in the width of a pulse wave—a special case of waveform modulation. In the case of an audio wave, pulse-width modulation has the effect of changing the tone color, and in extreme cases the perceived pitch.

Q

Q: See resonance.

quantization: The process of adjusting a continuous input so as to produce an output in discrete steps. Rhythmic quantization is often called auto-correct. Quantization of an audio signal is called digitization or digital-to-analog conversion. See quantized, auto-correct, digital-to-analog converter.

quantization noise: One of the types of error introduced into an analog audio signal by encoding it in digital form.

quantized: Set up to produce an output in discrete steps. A quantized tuning pot is an analog pot whose output has been confined to certain specific levels so as to determine what pitch within the equal-tempered scale an oscillator will have (no microtonal tuning adjustments are possible). In most digital and analog/digital hybrid instruments, all front panel-knobs and sliders are quantized.

quantizer: A module that accepts an incoming voltage and matches this as closely as possible at its output while confining the output to one of a series of equally spaced discrete steps. (Note: A quantizer is an analog module found on a few modular synthesizers, and is not to be confused with an analog-to-digital converter.)

R

RAM: Random access memory. All of today's digital-based keyboards contain RAM for storing sound data and other data. Typically, the user can write new data into RAM. See ROM.

ramp wave: See sawtooth wave.

rate scaling: See envelope tracking.

rate/level EG: A type of envelope generator in which the envelope shape is defined in terms of an ordered set of pairs of numbers, each pair consisting of a level (amount of envelope) parameter and a rate (speed or slope) parameter that determines how quickly the envelope will reach that level starting from the previous level. Synthesizers that use rate/level envelope generators include the Yamaha DX7 and the Casio CZ-101.

real-time mode: A situation in which events (such as keystrokes) are entered in computer memory at

a speed directly proportional to the speed at which they will be played back. The opposite of single-step mode.

regeneration: See resonance.

release: The final segment controlled by an envelope generator. The release portion of the envelope begins when the key is lifted. The release control determines how long the envelope takes to fall from the sustain level back to its initial level (usually zero). See sustain pedal.

release velocity: The speed with which a key is raised after being depressed. Release-velocity sensing is a feature on some velocity-sensitive keyboards, and is usually used to control the length of the release segment of the envelopes.

remote keyboard: A keyboard module that is not built into the same housing as the tone-generating circuitry it controls, but rather communicates with this circuitry via MIDI or some other data transmission system.

resolution: The fineness of the divisions into which an analog input is digitized (as in a sampling machine), or into which real-time input is quantized for memory storage (as in a sequencer or drum machine). The higher the resolution, the better the digital representation of the analog signal will be.

resonance: A mode of operation of a filter in which a narrow band of frequencies (the resonant peak) becomes relatively more prominent. If the resonant peak is high enough, the filter will begin to oscillate, producing an audio output signal even in the absence of an incoming audio signal. Filter resonance is also known as emphasis, regeneration, feedback, and Q.

resynthesis: The process of electronically approximating the sound of an acoustic instrument by analyzing its frequency and amplitude components and then using this information to control the operation of a synthesizer voice. Resynthesis differs from sampling in that the complete linear time-coherent digital representation of the acoustic waveform is no longer present in the synthesizer when the sound is being generated.

ribbon: A controller most often used for pitch-bending. The ribbon has no moving parts; instead, a finger pressed down on it and moved along it creates an electrical contact at some point along a pair of thin, flexible, longitudinal strips whose electrical potential varies from one end to the other.

ring modulator: A special type of mixer that accepts two signals as audio inputs and produces their sum and difference tones (but not, in a true ring modulator, the original signals themselves) at the output. The "ring mod" feature on some synthesizers does not produce true ring modulation but instead combines its two input sounds into some other musically useful set of overtones.

rolloff slope: The acuity of the cutoff frequency. When the rolloff slope is shallow (on the order of 6dB per octave) the frequency components beyond the cutoff frequency can still be heard, but at a volume reduced in proportion to how far past the cutoff frequency they are. When the rolloff slope is steep (24dB per octave or more) frequency components quite close to the cutoff frequency are so reduced in volume as to fall below the threshold of audibility. The terms two-pole (12dB per octave) and four-pole (24dB per octave) are sometimes applied to filters to describe their rolloff slope characteristic.

ROM: Read-Only Memory. A form of digital data storage whose contents cannot be altered by the user. An instrument's operating instructions and in some cases its factory presets are normally in ROM.

routing: Sending a signal from one place to another.

run: To execute a program.

S

sample: A digitally recorded and stored representation of a sound. Also, a single word of data that makes up a portion of such a recording.

sample-and-hold: A device that samples an incoming voltage to determine its level, and then puts out a signal at that level until the next time it is told to take a sample, regardless of what the incoming voltage has been doing in the meantime. Sample-and-hold units are often found in conjunction with an internal clock that tells them to take a sample at regular intervals of time, but on some synthesizers an external trigger can be used. The term "sample-and-hold" is used on some synthesizers to refer to a random step generator, *i.e.*, a sample-and-hold whose input is always a random noise source.

sampler: A keyboard or rack-mount module that records and plays back digital representations of acoustic sounds.

sampling: The process of encoding an analog signal by reading its level at precisely spaced intervals of time. Some form of sampling is used in an analog-to-digital converter to read the analog audio input and convert it to digital information. See sample, sampler, sampling rate.

sampling rate: The number of samples taken per second. When analog audio signals are converted to digital form, the sampling rate must be at least twice the frequency of the highest harmonic in the sound to be samples (the Nyquist limit) in order to prevent aliasing. Typical sampling rates range from 15kHz to 44.1kHz. See sampling.

save: To save a program or file from main memory to a peripheral device such as a disk drive.

sawtooth wave: A signal put out by an oscillator in which the voltage either rises smoothly from a lower value to a higher value and then falls suddenly back to where it started (positive-going ramp) or declines steadily from the higher value to the lower and then jumps back to the higher (negative-going ramp). An audio-rate sawtooth wave contains all the harmonics in the harmonic series, and has a bright, buzzy sound.

scale mode: A control mode that allows the user to alter the pitches of individual keys on the keyboard in relation to one another, resulting in non-equal temperaments.

scaling curve: A user-defined non-linear relationship between input and output.

Schmitt trigger: A device that puts out a pulse whenever the input voltage it is sensing rises above a certain (adjustable) threshold.

second touch: An additional control signal (found on some electronic organs) that is applied from the keyboard to a sound while a key is still being held down by exerting extra pressure. See aftertouch.

sequence: A set of voltages or keystroke commands and other data stored in a sequencer.

sequencer: A device that automatically puts out a user-determined set of commands, usually MIDI data or control voltages. Some sequencers exist in the form of software that runs on a general-purpose microcomputer, while others are built into dedicated hardware packages or into a keyboard instrument. A sequencer is usually found in conjunction with an internal clock, which determines its rate of playback. See digital sequencer, analog sequencer, polyphonic sequencer, sequence.

serial interface: A connection between two devices in which digital information is transferred one bit after another, rather than several bits at a time. MIDI is a serial interface. See parallel interface.

S/H: Sample-and-hold.

sidebands: Frequency components outside the natural harmonic series introduced to the tone by using an audio-range wave for modulation.

sine wave: A signal put out by an oscillator in which the voltage rises and falls smoothly and symmetrically, following the formula of the sine function in trigonometry. Sub-audio sine waves are used for vibrato and tremolo. Audio range sine waves sound very muted, since they contain only the fundamental, with no overtones.

single-step mode: A method of loading events (such as keystrokes) into memory one event at a time, which usually entails separately entering information about the timing (and perhaps other aspects, such as velocity) of the events. Also called step-time. See real-time mode.

single trigger: A type of keyboard logic sometimes found on monophonic synthesizers and on polyphonic synthesizers in unison mode, in which a new trigger signal is sent to the envelope generators only after an interval of time, however brief, in which no key was depressed. On a single-trigger keyboard, legato phrases can be played with several notes whose timbre and amplitude are governed by one continuing envelope. The opposite of multiple trigger.

sixteen-bit: Using sixteen-bit digital words to process and/or store audio data. See twelve-bit, resolution.

slave: Any device whose operation is linked to and governed by some other device called a master, such as a master keyboard or master oscillator. See master.

slope: The fourth segment of Korg's six-stage envelope generators. The slope control determines the speed at which the envelope will rise or fall from the break point to the sustain level.

SMPTE code: A standard protocol defined by the Society of Motion Picture & Television Engineers, used for synchronizing various devices such as tape recorders, motion picture projectors, and videotape players.

song: A list of sequencer or drum machine patterns that the machine will play back in the desired order. Some instruments also allow such information as tempo changes and patch-programming changes to be stored as steps in a song.

song position pointer (SPP): A type of MIDI data that tells a device how many sixteenth-notes into a song to begin its playback.

source: The oscillator, noise source, or external input that serves as the point of origin of the audio signal path.

split keyboard: A single keyboard divided electronically to act as though it were two separate manuals, with the output of each half being routed into a separate signal path.

split point: The point at which a split keyboard is split. On some instruments the split point is fixed, on others it can be moved from place to place but will be the same for all patches until manually changed by the user, while on still others its location can be stored in conjunction with other patch information, all of which can be called up simultaneously.

square wave: A pulse wave with a 50% duty cycle. An audio-rate square wave contains only odd-numbered harmonics, and has a hollow sound. A low-frequency square wave that modulates the frequency of an oscillator produces a trill.

state-variable filter: A filter whose response characteristics can be varied, for example from lowpass to bandpass to highpass, depending on the setting of a panel control or the fluctuations of a control voltage.

step input: See single-step mode.

sub-audio: Below about 16Hz (the lower thresh-

old of human hearing).

sub-octave generator: A circuit that puts out a signal whose frequency is equal to the frequency of the input signal divided by some integer, usually two.

subtractive synthesis: The technique of arriving at a desired tone color by filtering waveforms rich in harmonics, such as pulse and sawtooth waves. Subtractive synthesis is the type generally used on analog synthesizers. Compare with additive, FM synthesis.

sustain: The third of the four segments controlled by an ADSR envelope generator. The sustain portion of the envelope begins when the attack and decay portions have run their course and continues until the key is released. The sustain control is used to determine the level (between zero and the 100% peak reached at the end of the attack portion) at which the envelope will remain. While the attack, decay, and release controls are *rate* controls, the sustain control is a *level* control.

sustain pedal: The electronic equivalent of a piano's damper pedal. Some synthesizers respond to sustain pedal input by keeping the envelope in its sustain segment, as if the keys were still being held. On other instruments, the sustain pedal causes the envelope to switch to an alternate release time.

switch trigger: A type of trigger signal that consists of a sudden, brief drop in voltage. See trigger, voltage trigger.

sync: Synchronization. Two devices such as sequencers, drum machines, or arpeggiators are synced when the clock output of one is patched to the external clock input of the other, so that the timing of the notes they play will remain coordinated. Two oscillators are synced when the beginning of each new cycle on the master automatically triggers the beginning of a new cycle on the slave. When the slave oscillator is several octaves higher than the master, it will tend to lock onto one of the harmonics in the harmonic series for which the master is sounding the fundamental.

sync track: A timing reference signal recorded on tape, usually consisting either of a sync tone containing 24, 48, or 96 pulses per quarter-note or of SMPTE time code. A sync track is intended to be patched directly to devices such as drum machines and sequencers that will accept the appropriate clock input, as distinguished from a click track, which is mainly designed to be listened to by human musicians.

system-exclusive: A type of MIDI data whose format is specified by an individual manufacturer. System-exclusive data is used for transmitting sound parameter changes, patch memory contents, and sound samples from one digital device to another.

system real-time: A type of MIDI data, including clock data, active sensing, and start, stop, and continue messages.

T

tone mix: A term used by Casio to refer to internal two-voice layering.

touch pad: A controller that senses the presence of a finger, and on some models the position of the finger and the amount of downward pressure the finger is exerting, without any externally visible moving parts, and puts out corresponding control voltages. Also called a touch plate.

touch-sensitive: Equipped with a sensing mechanism that responds to variations in velocity or pressure with corresponding variations in a control signal output that is separate from the main output of the module. See velocity sensitivity, aftertouch.

track: (1) To be controlled by (as when a filter's

cutoff frequency tracks the keyboard, moving up or down depending on what note is played). (2) One of a number of independent memory banks in a multi-track sequencer.

transient: Any of the non-sustaining and non-periodic frequency components of a sound, usually of brief duration and occurring near the onset of the sound (attack transients).

transient generator: See envelope generator.

tremolo: A periodic change in amplitude. Compare with vibrato.

triangle wave: A signal put out by an oscillator that rises and then falls smoothly and linearly, with sharp corners between the positive-going and negative-going halves of the cycle. An audio-rate triangle wave has a muted sound similar to a sine wave but with a few weak overtones.

trigger: A signal sent out by a keyboard, sequencer, or clock that tells envelope generators to begin generating a new envelope. A trigger is typically of brief, fixed duration, as opposed to a gate, which usually remains in effect for as long as the key generating it is depressed.

twelve-bit: Using twelve-bit digital words to process and/or store audio data. See eight-bit, resolution.

two-pole: See pole, rolloff slope.

U

unison mode: A type of keyboard logic in which several or all of an instrument's voices are activated by a single key. On some synthesizers, all the voices sounding in unison mode may have the same pitch, while on others, a chord may be latched and then played in unison mode.

user: The person operating the computer, usually when a program is running.

V

VCA: Voltage-controlled amplifier. A device that responds to a change in voltage at its control input by altering the amount of gain of a signal being passed through it. VCAs are used for controlling the amount of both audio and control signals in some synthesizers.

VCF: Voltage-controlled filter. A filter whose cutoff frequency and (in a few cases) resonance amount can be changed by altering the amount of voltage being sent to a control input.

VCO: Voltage-controlled oscillator. An oscillator whose frequency and perhaps waveform can be changed by altering the amount of voltage being sent to a control input.

VDT: Video Display Terminal. See CRT

velocity data: A type of MIDI data, conventionally used to indicate how hard a key was struck.

velocity sensitivity: A type of touch sensitivity in which the keyboard measures how fast the key is descending while it is still in motion, or how hard it initially strikes the keybed. Velocity sensitivity emulates the touch response of the piano, though the velocity information can often be used to control other parameters of the sound than loudness. Compare with pressure sensitivity.

vernier: A pot used for fine-tuning.

vibrato: A periodic change in frequency. Compare with tremolo.

video monitor: See display.

vocoder: A device that continuously analyzes the frequency spectrum of one incoming signal (called the speech signal) and imparts analogous spectral characteristics to another (the carrier signal). The vocoder's output has the pitch of the carrier signal, with some or most of the timbral character and articulation of the speech signal.

voice: The output of a single audio signal path, or a

response from an instrument that acts as if it were coming from such an output. On a typical one-voice (monophonic) instrument, only one key at a time can be used to sound a note; on a multiple-voice (polyphonic) instrument, as many keys will sound simultaneously as the instrument has voices. The simplest standard voice is made up of a VCO, a VCF, and a VCA, together with the envelope generators that activate the latter two. *Note:* Some people use the term "voice" to refer to patch programs, creating some confusion about whether an instrument is capable of sounding (for example) 32 simultaneous notes, or whether it can sound fewer notes but hold 32 patch programs in memory at a time.

voice assignment: See assignment priority.

volatile memory: A type of memory whose contents vanish irretrievably if the instrument is shut off or unplugged. See memory, non-volatile memory.

voltage-controlled: Possessing the capability of being regulated or altered in some aspects of its operation by a specific type of analog electrical input (the control voltage).

voltage pedal: A foot-operated control voltage source.

voltage trigger: A type of trigger signal that consists of a sudden, brief increase in voltage. See trigger, switch trigger.

W

waveform: A periodic signal (such as a triangle, square, or sawtooth wave) put out by an oscillator. Different waveforms have different kinds of harmonic content, making each of them suitable for generating certain classes of sounds.

waveform modulation: A voltage-controlled change in the shape of the wave an oscillator is putting out, independent of any change in its frequency.

waveshape: See waveform.

wavetable: The set of numbers stored in a digital oscillator that govern what sort of waveshape it generates.

wavetable lookup: The process of accessing and putting out the numbers in a wavetable in some specified order.

wheel: A controller used for pitch-bending or modulation. The wheel is normally set vertically in a panel with somewhat less than half of its disc protruding in a position accessible to the left hand.

white noise: Random fluctuations in sound, weighted in such a way that there is equal energy per unit bandwidth throughout the frequency spectrum.

write: To transfer data from the computer to a peripheral, usually the disk drive.

write-protect: To protect the data on a disk from being over-written by covering the write-protect notch with a write-protect tab. Data may still be read from but not written to the disk.

write-protect notch: The small square cutout in one edge of the disk's jacket which is sensed by the DOS before it permits data to be written to the disk itself. If there is no notch, or if it is covered, data cannot be written to the disk.

write-protect tab: A small adhesive sticker used to cover the write-protect notch on a disk.

Z

zero crossing: A point at which a digitally encoded waveform or sample crosses the center value (conventionally zero) in the range of possible values. In some samplers, setting the start and end points of a loop at zero crossings is an important part of making smooth-sounding loops.

THE MIDI 1.0 SPECIFICATION

The MIDI specifications were made available to the general public early in 1983. At that point, however, there were still differences between the implementations of various manufacturers. Over a period of several months, the manufacturers ironed out these differences and came up with a standardized MIDI 1.0 specification, which is the standard in use today. The text here represents the full text of this basic specification as offered to the public by Sequential of San Jose, California. Since them, additions have been made to the specification, but the standards printed here still hold true. To obtain a copy of this and the more detailed specification, contact the International MIDI Association, 11857 Hartsook Street, North Hollywood California, 91607.

Document No. MIDI-1.0
Date: August 5, 1983

MIDI 1.0 SPECIFICATION

INTRODUCTION

MIDI is the acronym for Musical Instrument Digital Interface.

MIDI enables synthesizers, sequencers, home computers, rhythm machines, etc. to be interconnected through a standard interface.

Each MIDI-equipped instrument usually contains a receiver and a transmitter. Some instruments may contain only a receiver or transmitter. The receiver receives messages in MIDI format and executes MIDI commands. It consists of an optoisolator, Universal Asynchronous Receiver-Transmitter (UART), and other hardware needed to perform the intended functions. The transmitter originates messages in MIDI format, and transmits them by way of a UART and line driver.

The MIDI standard hardware and data format are defined in this specification.

CONVENTIONS

Status and Data bytes given in Tables I through VI are given in binary.

Numbers followed by an "H" are in hexadecimal.

All other numbers are in decimal.

HARDWARE

The interface operates at 31.25 (+/- 1%) Kbaud, asynchronous, with a start bit, 8 data bits (DO to D7), and stop bit. This makes a total of 10 bits for a period of 320 microseconds per serial byte.

Circuit: See Figure 1. 5 mA current loop type. Logical 0 is current ON. One output shall drive one and only one input. The receiver shall be opto-isolated and require less than 5 mA to turn on. Sharp PC-900 and HP 6N138 optoisolators have been found acceptable. Other high-speed optoisolators may be satisfactory. Rise and fall times should be less than 2 microseconds.

Connectors: DIN 5 pin (180 degree) female panel mount receptacle. An example is the SWITCHCRAFT 57GB5F. The connectors shall be labelled "MIDI IN" and "MIDI OUT". Note that pins 1 and 3 are not used, and should be left unconnected in the receiver and transmitter.

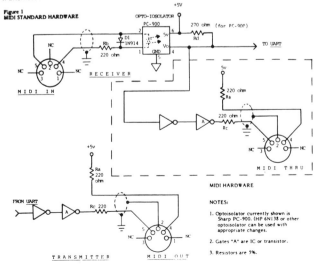

Figure 1
MIDI STANDARD HARDWARE

MIDI HARDWARE

NOTES:

1. Optoisolator currently shown is Sharp PC-900. (HP 6N138 or other optoisolator can be used with appropriate changes.

2. Gates "A" are IC or transistor.

3. Resistors are 5%.

Cables shall have a maximum length of fifty feet (15 meters), and shall be terminated on each end by a corresponding 5-pin DIN male plug, such as the SWITCHCRAFT 05GM5M. The cable shall be shielded twisted pair, with the shield connected to pin 2 at both ends.

A "MIDI THRU" output may be provided if needed, which provides a direct copy of data coming in MIDI IN. For very long chain lengths (more than three instruments), higher-speed optoisolators must be used to avoid additive rise/fall time errors which affect pulse width duty cycle.

DATA FORMAT

All MIDI communication is achieved through multi-byte "messages" consisting of one Status byte followed by one or two Data bytes, except Real-Time and Exclusive messages (see below).

MESSAGE TYPES

Messages are divided into two main categories: Channel and System.

Channel
Channel messages contain a four-bit number in the Status byte which address the message specifically to one of sixteen channels. These messages are thereby intended for any units in a system whose channel number matches the channel number encoded into the Status byte.

There are two types of Channel messages: Voice and Mode.

Voice
To control the instrument's voices, Voice messages are sent over the Voice Channels.

Mode
To define the instrument's response to Voice messages, Mode messages are sent over the instrument's Basic Channel.

System
System messages are not encoded with channel numbers.

There are three types of System messages: Common, Real-Time, and Exclusive.

Common
Common messages are intended for all units in a system.

Real-Time
Real-Time messages are intended for all units in a system. They contain Status bytes only--no Data bytes. Real-Time messages may be sent at any time--even between bytes of a message which has a different status. In such cases the Real-Time message is either ignored or acted upon, after which the receiving process resumes under the previous status.

Exclusive
Exclusive messages can contain any number of Data bytes, and are terminated by an End of Exclusive (EOX) or any other Status byte. These messages include a Manufacturer's Identification (ID) code. If the receiver does not recognize the ID code, it should ignore the ensuing data.

So that other users can fully access MIDI instruments, manufacturers should publish the format of data following their ID code. Only the manufacturer can update the format following their ID.

DATA TYPES

Status Bytes
Status bytes are eight-bit binary numbers in which the Most Significant Bit (MSB) is set (binary 1). Status bytes serve to identify the message type, that is, the purpose of the Data bytes which follow the Status byte.

Except for Real-Time messages, new Status bytes will always command the receiver to adopt their status, even if the new Status is received before the last message was completed.

Running Status
For Voice and Mode messages only, when a Status byte is received and processed, the receiver will remain in that status until a different Status byte is received. Therefore if the same Status byte would be repeated, it may (optionally) be omitted so that only the correct number of Data bytes need be sent. Under Running Status, then, a complete message need only consist of specified Data bytes sent in the specified order.

The Running Status feature is especially useful for communicating long strings of Note On/Off messages, where "Note On with Velocity of 0" is used for Note Off. (A separate Note Off Status byte is also available.)

Running Status will be stopped when any other Status byte intervenes, except that Real-Time messages will only interrupt the Running Status temporarily.

Unimplemented Status
Any Status bytes received for functions which the receiver has not implemented should be ignored, and subsequent data bytes ignored.

Undefined Status
Undefined Status bytes must not be used. Care should be taken to prevent illegal messages from being sent during power-up or power-down. If undefined Status bytes are received, they should be ignored, as should subsequent Data bytes.

Data Bytes
Following the Status byte, there are (except for Real-Time messages) one or two Data bytes which carry the content of the message. Data bytes are eight-bit binary numbers in which the MSB is reset (binary 0). The number and range of Data bytes which must follow each Status byte are specified in the tables which follow. For each Status byte the correct number of Data bytes must always be sent. Inside the receiver, action on the message should wait until all Data bytes required under the current status are received. Receivers should ignore Data bytes which have not been properly preceeded by a valid Status byte (with the exception of "Running Status," above).

CHANNEL MODES

Synthesizers contain sound generation elements called voices. Voice assignment is the algorithmic process of routing Note On/Off data from the keyboard to the voices so that the musical notes are correctly played with accurate timing.

When MIDI is implemented, the relationship between the sixteen available MIDI channels and the synthesizer's voice assignment must be defined. Several Mode messages are available for this purpose (see Table III). They are Omni (On/Off), Poly, and Mono. Poly and Mono are mutually exclusive. i. e., Poly Select disables Mono, and vice versa. Omni, when on, enables the receiver to receive Voice messages in all Voice Channels without discrimination. When Omni is off, the receiver will accept Voice messages from only the selected Voice Channel(s). Mono, when on, restricts the assignment of Voices to just one voice per Voice Channel (Monophonic.) When Mono is off (=Poly On), any number of voices may be allocated by the Receiver's normal voice assignment algorithm (Polyphonic.)

For a receiver assigned to Basic Channel "N," the four possible modes arising from the two Mode messages are:

Mode	Omni		
1	On	Poly	Voice messages are received from all Voice Channels and assigned to voices polyphonically.
2	On	Mono	Voice messages are received from all Voice Channels, and control only one voice, monophonically.
3	Off	Poly	Voice messages are received in Voice Channel N only, and are assigned to voices polyphonically.
4	Off	Mono	Voice messages are received in Voice Channels N thru N+M-1, and assigned monophonically to voices 1 thru M, respectively. The number of voices M is specified by the third byte of the Mono Mode Message.

Four modes are applied to transmitters (also assigned to Basic Channel N). Transmitters with no channel selection capability will normally transmit on Basic Channel 1 (N=0).

Mode	Omni		
1	On	Poly	All voice messages are transmitted in Channel N.
2	On	Mono	Voice messages for one voice are sent in Channel N.
3	Off	Poly	Voice messages for all voices are sent in Channel N.
4	Off	Mono	Voice messages for voices 1 thru M are transmitted in Voice Channels N thru N+M-1, respectively. (Single voice per channel).

A MIDI receiver or transmitter can operate under one and only one mode at a time. Usually the receiver and transmitter will be in the same mode. If a mode cannot be honored by the receiver, it may ignore the message (and any subsequent data bytes), or it may switch to an alternate mode (usually Mode 1, Omni On/Poly).

Mode messages will be recognized by a receiver only when sent in the Basic Channel to which the receiver has been assigned, regardless of the current mode. Voice messages may be received in the Basic Channel and in other channels (which are all called Voice Channels), which are related specifically to the Basic Channel by the rules above, depending on which mode has been selected.

A MIDI receiver may be assigned to one or more Basic Channels by default or by user control. For example, an eight-voice synthesizer might be assigned to Basic Channel 1 on power-up. The user could then switch the instrument to be configured as two four-voice synthesizers, each assigned to its own Basic Channel. Separate Mode messages would then be sent to each four-voice synthesizer, just as if they were physically separate instruments.

POWER-UP DEFAULT CONDITIONS

On power-up all instruments should default to Mode #1. Except for Note On/Off Status, all Voice messages should be disabled. Spurious or undefined transmissions must be suppressed.

TABLE I

SUMMARY OF STATUS BYTES

Status D7----D0	# of Data Bytes	Description
Channel Voice Messages		
1000nnnn	2	Note Off event
1001nnnn	2	Note On event (velocity=0: Note Off)
1010nnnn	2	Polyphonic key pressure/after touch
1011nnnn	2	Control change
1100nnnn	1	Program change
1101nnnn	1	Channel pressure/after touch
1110nnnn	2	Pitch wheel change
Channel Mode Messages		
1011nnnn	2	Selects Channel Mode
System Messages		
11110000	*****	System Exclusive

| 11110sss | 0 to 2 | System Common |
| 11111ttt | 0 | System Real Time |

NOTES:

nnnn:	N-1, where N = Channel #, i.e. 0000 is Channel 1. 0001 is Channel 2.
	.
	.
	1111 is Channel 16.
*****:	0iiiiiii, data, ..., EOX
iiiiiii:	Identification
sss:	1 to 7
ttt:	0 to 7

TABLE II

CHANNEL VOICE MESSAGES

STATUS	DATA BYTES	DESCRIPTION
1000nnnn	0kkkkkkk	Note Off (see notes 1-4)
	0vvvvvvv	vvvvvvv: note off velocity
1001nnnn	0kkkkkkk	Note On (see notes 1-4)
	0vvvvvvv	vvvvvvv ≠ 0: velocity
		vvvvvvv = 0: note off
1010nnnn	0kkkkkkk	Polyphonic Key Pressure (After-Touch)
	0vvvvvvv	vvvvvvv: pressure value.
1011nnnn	0ccccccc	Control Change
	0vvvvvvv	ccccccc: control # (0-121)(see notes 5-8)
		vvvvvvv: control value
		ccccccc = 122 thru 127: Reserved. See Table III.
1100nnnn	0ppppppp	Program Change
		ppppppp: program number (0-127)
1101nnnn	0vvvvvvv	Channel Pressure (After-Touch)
		vvvvvvv: pressure value
1110nnnn	0vvvvvvv	Pitch Wheel Change LSB (see note 10)
	0vvvvvvv	Pitch Wheel Change MSB

NOTES: 1. nnnn: Voice Channel# (1-16, coded as defined in Table I notes)

2. kkkkkkk: note# (0 - 127)
   kkkkkkk=60: Middle C of keyboard

0	12	24	36	48	60	72	84	96	108	120	127
		ac	c	c	c	c	c	c	c		
		+----------------piano range-----------------------+									

3. vvvvvvv: key velocity
   A logarithmic scale would be advisable.

0	1		64		127
off	ppp	pp p	mp	mf f	ff fff

vvvvvvv=64: in case of no velocity sensors
vvvvvvv= 0: Note Off, with velocity=64

4. Any Note On message sent should be balanced by sending a Note Off message for that note in that channel at some later time.

5. ccccccc: control number

ccccccc	Description
0	Continuous Controller 0 MSB
1	Continuous Controller 1 MSB (MODULATION WHEEL)
2	Continuous Controller 2 MSB
3	Continuous Controller 3 MSB
4-31	Continuous Controllers 4-31 MSB
32	Continuous Controller 0 LSB
33	Continuous Controller 1 LSB (MODULATION WHEEL)
34	Continuous Controller 2 LSB
35	Continuous Controller 3 LSB
36-63	Continuous Controllers 4-31 LSB
64-95	Switches (On/Off)
96-121	Undefined
122-127	Reserved for Channel Mode messages (see Table III).

6. The controllers are not specifically defined. A manufacturer can assign the logical controllers to physical ones as necessary. The controller allocation table must be provided in the user's operation manual.

7. Continuous controllers are divided into Most Significant and Least Significant Bytes. If only seven bits of resolution are needed for any particular controllers, only the MSB is sent. It is not necessary to send the LSB. If more resolution is needed, then both are sent, first the MSB, then the LSB. If only the LSB has changed in value, the LSB may be sent without re-sending the MSB.

8. vvvvvvv: control value (MSB)
(for controllers)

```
            0                                                 127
            +-------------------------------------------------+
           min                                               max
(for switches)
            0                                                 127
            +   -    -    -    -    -    -    -    -    -      +
           off                                                on
```

Numbers 1 through 126, inclusive, are ignored.

9. Any messages (e.g. Note On), which are sent successively under the same status, can be sent without a Status byte until a different Status byte is needed.

10. Sensitivity of the pitch bender is selected in the receiver. Ceneter position value (no pitch change) is 2000H, which would be transmitted EnH-00H-40H.

TABLE III

CHANNEL MODE MESSAGES

STATUS	DATA BYTES	DESCRIPTION
1011nnnn	0ccccccc 0vvvvvvv	Mode Messages ccccccc= 122: Local Control vvvvvvv= 0, Local Control Off vvvvvvv= 127, Local Control On ccccccc= 123: All Notes Off vvvvvvv= 0 ccccccc= 124: Omni Mode Off (All Notes Off) vvvvvvv= 0 ccccccc= 125: Omni Mode On (All Notes Off) vvvvvvv= 0 ccccccc= 126: Mono Mode On (Poly Mode Off) (All Notes Off) vvvvvvv= M, where M is the number of channels. vvvvvvv= 0, the number of channels equals the number of voices in the receiver. ccccccc= 127: Poly Mode On (Mono Mode Off) vvvvvvv= 0 (All Notes Off)

NOTES: 1. nnnn: Basic Channel # (1-16, coded as defined in Table I)

2. Messages 123 thru 127 function as All Notes Off messages. They will turn off all voices controlled by the assigned Basic Channel. Except for message 123, All Notes Off, they should not be sent periodically, but only for a specific purpose. In no case should they be used in lieu of Note Off commands to turn off notes which have been previously turned on. Therefore any All Notes Off command (123-127) may be ignored by receiver with no possibility of notes staying on, since any Note On command must have a correspording specific Note Off command.

3. Control Change #122, Local Control, is optionally used to interrupt the internal control path between the keyboard, for example, and the sound-generating circuitry. If 0 (Local Off message) is received, the path is disconnected: the keyboard data goes only to MIDI and the sound-generating circuitry is controlled only by incoming MIDI data. If a 7FH (Local On message) is received, normal operation is restored.

4. The third byte of 'Mono' specifies the number of channels in which Monophonic Voice messages are to be sent. This number, "M", is a number between 1 and 16. The channel(s) being used, then, will be the current Basic Channel (=N) thru N+M-1 up to a maximum of 16. If M=0, this is a special case directing the receiver to assign all its voices, one per channel, from the Basic Channel N through 16.

TABLE IV

SYSTEM COMMON MESSAGES

STATUS	DATA BYTES	DESCRIPTION
11110001		Undefined
11110010	0lllllll 0hhhhhhh	Song Position Pointer lllllll: (Least significant) hhhhhh: (Most significant)
11110011	0sssssss	Song Select sssssss: Song #
11110100		Undefined
11110101		Undefined
11110110	none	Tune Request
11110111	none	EOX: "End of System Exclusive" flag

1. Song Position Pointer: Is an internal register which holds the number of MIDI beats (1 beat = 6 MIDI clocks) since the start of the song. Normally it is set to 0 when the START switch is pressed, which starts sequence playback. It then increments with every sixth MIDI clock receipt, until STOP is pressed. If CONTINUE is pressed, it continues to increment. It can be arbitrarily preset (to a resolution of 1 beat) by the SONG POSITION POINTER message.

2. Song Select: Specifies which song or sequence is to be played upon receipt of a Start (Real-Time) message.

3. Tune Request: Used with analog synthesizers to request them to tune their oscillators.

4. EOX: Used as a flag to indicate the end of a System Exclusive transmission (see Table VI).

TABLE V

SYSTEM REAL TIME MESSAGES

STATUS	DATA BYTES	DESCRIPTION
11111000		Timing Clock
11111001		Undefined
11111010		Start
11111011		Continue
11111100	.	Stop
11111101		Undefined
11111110		Active Sensing
11111111		System Reset

NOTES:

1. The System Real Time messages are for synchronizing all of the system in real time.

2. The System Real Time messages can be sent at any time. Any messages which consist of two or more bytes may be split to insert Real Time messages.

3. Timing Clock (F8H)
The system is synchronized with this clock, which is sent at a rate of 24 clocks/quarter note.

4. Start (from beginning of song) (FAH)
This byte is immediately sent when the PLAY switch on the master (e.g. sequencer or rhythm unit) is pressed.

5. Continue (FBH)
This is sent when the CONTINUE switch is hit. A sequence will continue at the time of the next clock.

6. Stop (FCH)
This byte is immediately sent when the STOP switch is hit. It will stop the sequence.

7. Active Sensing (FEH)
Use of this message is optional, for either receivers or transmitters. This is a "dummy" Status byte that is sent every 300 ms (max), whenever there is no other activity on MIDI. The receiver will operate normally if it never receives FEH. Otherwise, if FEH is ever received, the receiver will expect to receive FEH or a transmission of any type every 300 ms (max). If a period of 300 ms passes with no activity, the receiver will turn off the voices and return to normal operation.

8. System Reset (FFH)
This message initializes all of the system to the condition of just having turned on power. The System Reset message should be used sparingly, preferably under manual command only. In particular, it should not be sent automatically on power up.

TABLE VI

SYSTEM EXCLUSIVE MESSAGES

STATUS	DATA BYTES	DESCRIPTION
11110000		Bulk dump etc.
	0iiiiiii	iiiiiii: identification
	. (0*******) . . (0*******) .	Any number of bytes may be sent here, for any purpose, as long as they all have a zero in the most significant bit.
	11110111	EOX: "End of System Exclusive"

NOTES:

1. iiiiiii: identification ID (0-127)

2. All bytes between the System Exclusive Status byte and EOX or the next Status byte must have zeroes in the MSB.

3. The ID number can be obtained from the MIDI committee. See Table VII.

4. In no case should other   or Data bytes (except Real-Time) be interleaved with System Exclusive, regardless of whether or not the ID code is recognized.

5. EOX or any other Status byte, except Real-Time, will terminate a System Exclusive message, and should be sent immediately at its conclusion.

RESOURCES

Hardware And Software Manufacturers

While this listing was up-to-date at the time of this book's publication, please note that manufacturers constantly bring out new products; from time to time they are also known to move, change names, and go out of business. Should you wish to contact one of these resources, and have no luck, try the National Association of Music Merchants (NAMM), at 5140 Avenida Encinas, Carlsbad, CA 92008 (telephone: 619-438-8001).

ADA Signal Processors, 7303D Edgewater Drive, Oakland, CA 94621. (415) 632-1323. MIDI accessories (signal processors, etc.).

Adams-Smith, 34 Tower St., Hudson, MA 01749. (617) 562-3801. MIDI accessories (SMPTE/MIDI translator); professional synchronization equipment.

Ad Lib, 220 Grand-Allee East, Suite 960, Ville du Québec, Québec, Canada G1R 2J1. (418) 529-1159. Or: 50 Stainford St., Boston, MA 02114. (800) 463-2686. Sequencing, educational, & entertainment software; interface card; musical instruments & accessories (keyboards, educational audio analysis equipment). IBM, Mac, IIe.

Advanced Digital Systems, 12440 Moorpark St., Suite 303, Studio City, CA 91604. (818) 766-1981. Portable IBM-compatible computers.

Aegix, P.O. Box 9488, Reno, NV 89507. (702) 329-1943. Editing & librarian software. ST.

Airdrum, see Palmtree Instruments.

Akai, Box 2344, Fort Worth, TX 76113. (817) 336-5114. MIDI instruments & accessories (samplers, synthesizers, wind & keyboard controllers, & automated mixers); professional audio.

AKG Acoustics, 77 Selleck St., Stamford, CT 06902. (203) 348-2121. MIDI accessories (signal processing); professional audio equipment.

Alesis, 7336 Hinds Ave., N. Hollywood, CA 91605. (213) 467-800   ᵔ¹ instruments & accessories (drum machine, s   ᵔ   ᵔer, signal processing devices).

Allen & Heath Brenell, 69 Ship St., Brighton, BN1 1AE United Kingdom. 44-(0273)-24928. Or: Five Connair Rd., Orange, CT 06477. (203) 795-3594. Professional MIDI-controlled mixing consoles.

Altech Systems, 831 Kings Hwy, Suite 200, Shreveport, LA 71104. (318) 226-1702. MIDI development software (Pascal, Basic, etc.); editing & compiling software. Mac.

Animated Music, 124 H Blossom Hill Rd., #494, San Jose, CA 95123. (408) 227-3959. Sequencing & notation software. ST.

Applied Research & Technology (ART), 215 Tremont St., Rochester, NY 14608. (716) 436-2720. MIDI accessories (signal processing, etc.).

Apple Computer, 20525 Mariani Ave., Cupertino, CA. (408) 996-1010. Computers.

Atari, 1196 Borregas Ave., Sunnyvale, CA 94086 (408) 745-2021. Computers.

Artisyn, P.O. Box 209, West Linn, OR 97068. (503) 295-1915. MIDI instruments (MIDI wind instrument controllers).

Audio Media Research (AMR), P.O. Box 1230, Meridian, MS 39301. (601) 483-5372. MIDI accessories (SMPTE/MIDI translator, etc.); professional audio equipment.

Austin Developments, 227 Marin St., San Rafael, CA 94901. (415) 454-9620. MIDI interface hardware. Mac.

Axxess Unlimited, P.O. Box 8435, Fort Collins, CO 80525 (303) 482-5656. MIDI accessories (MIDI destination mapping).

Bacchus Software Systems, 2210 Wilshire Blvd., #330, Santa Monica, CA 90403. (213) 820-4574. Editing & librarian software. IBM.

Bass Hit Productions, 203 E. 27th St., #47, New York, NY 10016. (201) 634-7381. Sequencing & librarian software. Tandy Color Computer.

Beam Team, 6100 Adeline St., Oakland, CA 94608. (415) 658-3208. Editing, notation, & sequencing software.

Beaverton Digital Systems, P.O. Box 1626, Beaverton, OR 97075. (503) 641-6260. Editor & librarian software. C64, ST, Mac.

Beetle, 120 N. Victory Blvd., Suite 101, Burbank,

CA 91502. (818) 841-9922. MIDI accessories (MIDI guitar controllers, switchers, etc.).

Blackhawk Data Corp., 307 N. Michigan Ave., Chicago, IL 60601 (312) 236-8473. Notation & sequencing software. IBM.

Blank Software, 1034 Natoma, San Francisco, CA 94103 (415) 863-9224. Editing, librarian, & processing software. Mac, C64.

L. Bosendorfer Klavierfabrik, c/o Kimball, 1600 Royal St., Jasper, IN 47546. (812) 482-1600. Computer-controlled & conventional pianos.

Brain Systems, 9526 Central Ave., Montclair, CA 91763. (714) 944-0913. High-speed portable IBM-compatible computers; sequencing & notation software; MIDI interface hardware. IBM.

Buchla & Associates, Box 5051, Berkeley, CA 94705. (415) 644-4444. Custom-built MIDI & non-MIDI computer-based instruments.

Caged Artist Productions, see Dr. T's.

Canadian MIDI Users Group, (CMUG), Box 1043, Belleville, Ontario, Canada K8N5B6.

Casio, 15 Gardner Rd., Fairfield, NJ 07006. (201) 575-7400. MIDI instruments & accessories (samplers, synthesizers, drum machines, sequencers, etc.).

C-Lab, Andrae & Co., Postfach 710446, 2000 Hamburg 71, West Germany. 49-(040)-6412255 or 49-(040)-486830. Sequencing & miscellaneous software. C64, ST.

Club MIDI Software, System Exclusive Products Div., Box 93895, Hollywood, CA 90093. (818) 788-3963. Librarian software. IBM.

Command Development, 11846 Balboa Blvd., Suite 135, Granada Hills, CA 91344. (818) 362-3550. Editing software. C64.

Commodore, Commodore/Amiga, 983 University, Los Gatos, CA 95035. (408) 395-6616. Commodore International, 1200 Wilson, West Chester, PA 19380. (215) 431-9100. Computers.

Compaq Computer, 20555 FM 149, Houston TX. (713) 370-0670. Computers (IBM-compatible).

Compu-Mates, 8621 Wilshire Blvd., Suite 177, Beverly Hills, CA 90211. (213) 271-7410. Sequencing, notation, scoring, editing, librarian software; MIDI accessories (patchers, switchers, etc.). ST, Mac, IBM.

CompuSonics, 2345 Yale, Palo Alto, CA 94306. (415) 494-1184. Magnetic disk audio recording & storage devices.

Computers & ME (Music Education), 10 Ashbrook Rd., Exeter, NH 03883-9733. (603) 772-4399. Educational (sight-reading) software. IIe, C64.

Computers & Music, 1989 Junipero Serra Blvd., Daly City, CA 94014. (415) 994-2909. Librarian, sampling, & development software.

Computer Music Systems (CMS), 382 N. Lemon Ave., Walnut, CA 91789. (714) 594-5051. Portable IBM-compatible computers & road kits.

J. L. Cooper Electronics, 1931 Pontius Ave., West Los Angeles, CA 90025. (213) 473-8771. MIDI accessories (memory, conversion, synchronization, switching, automation, lighting, & other devices).

Creager Peda-Band, c/o WEC, 2120 Arlington Ave., Atlanta, GA 30324. MIDI accessories (pedals, etc.).

Creative Solutions, 4701 Randolph Rd., Suite 12, Rockville MD 20852. (301) 984-2060. Music display & playing software. Mac.

CSL, 1616 Vista Del Mar, Los Angeles, CA 90028. Sampled sounds & effects on compact disc.

CTM Development, Case Postale 82, CH-1213 Petit-Lancy, 2 Switzerland. 41-(22)-33 22 43 Or 41-(22)-21 35 35 ext.3866. Computer-based musical instruments.

ddrum, P.O. Box 2668, Westport, CN 06880. Or: 1201 U.S. Highway One, North Palm Beach, FL 33408. (305) 622-0010. MIDI & non-MIDI instruments & accessories (drums, etc.).

Decillionix, Box 70985, Sunnyvale, CA 94086 (408) 732-7758. Sampling, sequencing, & waveform analysis software; MIDI accessories. IIe/+.

Delta Music Research, 1039 17th Ave #306, Calgary, Alberta, Canada. (403) 245-4919. Custom-built synthesizers & software.

Digidesign, 1360 Willow Rd., Ste. 101, Menlo Park, CA 94025. (415) 327-8811. Waveform analysis, additive synthesis, editing, & production/scoring software. Mac, ST.

Digital Music Corp., 21787 Ventura Blvd., Suite 124, Woodland Hills, CA 91364. (818) 704-7879. MIDI accessories (patching/processing devices, voice cartridges).

Digital Music Services, 23010 Lake Forest Drive, #334, Laguna Hills, CA 92653. (714) 951-1159. Editing & librarian software. Mac, IIe/+/GS. $179.95

Dr. T's Music Software, 220 Boylston St., Suite 306, Chestnut Hill, MA. (617) 244-6954. Editing, librarian, notation, sequencing, & miscellaneous software; MIDI interface hardware. Mac, IIe/+/GS, ST, C64, IBM.

Dominant Functions, P.O. Box 836155, Richardson, TX 75083-6155. (214) 783-9368 or (214) 696-4931. Sequencing & notation software. IBM.

Drumware, 12077 Wilshire Blvd., #515, Los Angeles, CA 90025. (213) 478-3956. Editing & librarian software. ST, IIe/+.

Dornes Research Group, 8 West 38th St., 9th Floor, New York City, NY 10018. (212) 966-5289. MIDI accessories (expression performance bar, mapper, etc.).

Dynacord, c/o Drum Workshop, 2697 Lavery Ct., #16, Newbury Park, CA 91320. (805) 499-6863. MIDI instruments (drums, controllers, etc.).

Electronic Arts, 1820 Gateway, San Mateo, CA 94404. (415) 571-7171. Sequencing, entertainment, & educational software. Mac, Amiga, IIGS.

Electronic Courseware Systems, 1210 Lancaster Drive, Champaign, IL 61821. (217) 359-7099. MIDI-based educational software. IIe/+/C/GS, C64, IBM, ST.

Elka, P.O. Box 1 - 60022 Castelfidardo, Italy. 39-(071)-970621. MIDI & non-MIDI instruments (synthesizers, etc.).

EMR (Electromusic Research Ltd.), 14 Mt. Close, Wickford, Essex, S11 8HG United Kingdom. 44-(70)-335747. Sequencing software; MIDI interface hardware. BBC B computer.

E-Mu Systems, 1600 Green Hills Rd., Scotts Valley, CA 95066. (408) 438-1921. MIDI instruments (samplers, drum machines, etc.).

Ensoniq, 155 Great Valley Pkwy., Malvern, PA, 19355. (215) 647-3930. MIDI instruments (samplers, synthesizers, etc.).

Fairlight Instruments, 15-19 Boundery St., Rushcutters Bay, Sydney, NSW 2011, Australia. 61-(02)-331-6333. Or: 2945 Westwood Blvd., Los Angeles, CA 90064. (213) 470-6280. MIDI instruments (CMI III) & accessories (pitch-to-voltage converter); sampling, sequencing, waveform analysis, & notation software.

Fast Forward Designs, Russ Jones Marketing Group, 13468 Beach Ave., Suite A, Marina Del Ray, CA 90291. (213) 822-7882. MIDI instruments (pedal controllers).

Forat Electronics, 11514 Ventura Blvd., Studio City, CA 91604. (818) 763-3007. MIDI instruments & repairs (Linn drum machines, sequencers, etc.).

Forte Music, Box 6322, San Jose, CA 95150. (415) 965-8880. MIDI retrofits of acoustic and electronic pianos; MIDI accessories (controllers, etc.).

Forté Sequencing, see LTA Productions.

Fostex Corp., 15431 Blackburn Ave., Norwalk, CA 90650. (213) 921-1112. MIDI accessories (SMPTE/MIDI translators, etc.); synchronizer/autolocator control & cueing software; professional audio equipment. IIC, IBM, Mac.

Freelance Music, see MusicWorks.

Garfield Electonics, P.O. Box 1941, Burbank, CA 91506. (818) 840-8939. MIDI accessories (SMPTE/MIDI translators, timing, synchronizing, & other devices).

Gentle Electric, P.O. Box 132, Delta, CO 81416. (303) 874-8054. MIDI accessories; editing & librarian software.

Giancarlo Giannangeli, Via Spartaco, 29-40100 Bologna, Italy. 39-(51)-531397. Software.

Great Wave Software, Box 5847, Stanford, CA 94305. (415) 325-2202 (also dist. by Passport). Sequencer & notation software. Mac.

Greengate Productions/Mainframe, 24 Missden Drive, Hemel Hempstead, Hertfordshire, HP3 8QR United Kingdom. Sequencing software; sampling & interface hardware. For DS3 keyboard instrument. IIe/+.

Grey Matter Response, 15916 S. Haven Ave., Tinley Park, IL 60477. (312) 349-1889. Instrument voicing & storage software updates (Yamaha DX7/DX7II).

Hinton Instruments, 168 Abingdon Rd., Oxford, OX1 4RA United Kingdom 44-(0865)-721731. MIDI interface hardware.

Hybrid Arts, 11920 W. Olympic Blvd., Los Angeles, CA 90064. (213) 826-3777. Sequencing, notation, librarian, editing software; MIDI interfacing hardware. ST, 130XE.

Hybrid Technology, Unit 3, Robert Davies Ct., Nuffield Rd., Cambridge, United Kingdom CB4 ITP. Music programming language.

Ibanez, c/o Hoshino USA, 1726 Winchester Rd., Bensalem, PA 19020. (215) 638-8670. MIDI accessories (signal processing, etc); instruments & musical accessories.

IBM, 900 King St., Rye Brook, NY 10573. (914) 934-4000. Computers; sound generating & interface hardware.

Intelligent Music Systems, P.O. Box 8748, Albany, NY 12208. (518) 434-4110. Editing, improvisational, drum machine, sequencing, & miscellaneous software. Mac.

International MIDI Association (IMA), 12439 Magnolia Blvd., Suite 104, North Hollywood, CA 91607. (818) 505-8964. Can provide lists of MIDI manufacturers, as well as MIDI specifications. Publishes newsletter.

Intercomp Sound, 129 Loyalist Ave., Rochester, NY 14624. (716) 247-8056. Sequencing & notation software. IBM, TRS-80.

Iota Systems, P.O. Box 8987, Incline Village, NV 89450. (702) 831-6302. MIDI-controlled mixer automation system.

IVL Technologies, 3318 Oak St., Victoria, British Columbia, Canada V8X 1R2. (604) 383-4320. MIDI accesories (pitch-to-MIDI converters, etc.).

Joreth Music, Box 20, Evesham, Worcestershire, WR11 5EG United Kingdom. 44-(0386)-831615. MIDI sequencing software. C64.

JMS (Jellinhaus Musik Systems), Martener Hellweg 40, 4600 Dortmund 70, West Germany. 49-(0231)-1719213. Sequencing & librarian software; MIDI interface & miscellaneous hardware. IIe/+, IBM, C64.

Juice Goose, 7320 Ashcroft, Suite 302, Houston, TX 77081. (713) 772-1404. AC mains power conditioners & voltage regulators.

Kahler, American Precision Metal Works, 2725 Gretta Lane, Anaheim, CA 92806. (714) 632-5280. MIDI accessories (timing devices).

Kaman Music, P.O. Box 507, Bloomfield, CT 06002. (203) 243-7106. MIDI accessories (pitch-to-MIDI converter).

Kawai, 2055 E. University Drive, Compton, CA 90224-9045. (213) 631-1771. MIDI instruments and accessories (synthesizers, drum machines, etc.); MIDI & non-MIDI acoustic keyboards.

Keyboard Technologies, 666 B West Union Ave., Montebello, CA 90640 Or: P.O. Box 1007 Burbank, CA 91507. (213) 725-6972. MIDI instruments (controllers, etc.).

Key Clique, 3960 Laurel Canyon Blvd., Ste. 374, Studio City, CA 91604. (818) 905-9136. Editing, librarian, & voicing software; modular equipment racks; educational videos; record production/distribution for MIDI artists.

Keytek, c/o Gibson, 641 Massman Drive, Nashville, TN 37210. (615) 366-2400. Also refer to Siel. MIDI instruments & accessories (synthesizers, sequencers, etc.); editing, librarian, & sequencing software; MIDI interface hardware. C64.

Korg, 89 Frost St., Westbury, NY 11590. (516) 333-9100. MIDI instruments & accessories (samplers, synthesizers, drum machines, signal processing, etc.); miscellaneous software; MIDI interface hardware.

Kurzweil Music Systems, 411 Waverly Oaks Rd., Waltham, MA 02154-8464. (617) 893-5900. MIDI instruments (samplers & synthesizers); sampling, sequencing, waveform analysis, & notation software. Mac.

LEMI/Felice Manzo, Corso Matteotti 37, 10121 Torino, Italy. 39-(100)-542654. Editing, librarian, & sequencing software.

Lexicon, 100 Beaver St., Waltham, MA 02154. (617) 891-6790. MIDI accessories (signal processing); professional a/v production equipment.

London Rock Shops, 26 Chalk Farm Rd., London NW1, England. 44-(01)-267-5381. Librarian & sequencer software.

LTA Productions, P.O. Box 6623, Hamden CT 06517. (203) 787-9857. Sequencing, editing, & librarian software. IBM.

Lyre, 1505 Chemin St.-Foy, Suite 101, Ville du Québec, Québec, Canada G1S 2P1. (418) 527-6901. MIDI instruments.

MacroMind, Inc., 1028 W. Wolfram, Chicago, IL 60657. (312) 327-5821. Miscellaneous software (a/v & music production).

Magic Music Machines, 1207 Howard St., San Francisco, CA 94103. (415) 864-3300. MIDI accessories & instrument repairs.

Magnetic Music/Texture, Rt. #1, North Smith Rd., Lagrangeville, NY 12540. (914) 677-8586. Sequencing & editing software. IBM.

MARC, 33 Cameron Circle, Atlantic Highlands, NJ 07716. (201) 872-1292. MIDI accessories (percussion triggers).

Mark of the Unicorn, 222 Third St., Cambridge, MA 02142. (617) 576-2760. Sequencing and notation software. Mac.

Meico Electronics, 35 S. Dishmill Rd., Higganum, CT 06441. (203) 345-3253. MIDI accessories (patch & controlling devices).

MicroMusic, Fruchtallee 19, D-2000, Hamburg 20, West Germany. 49-(040)-439-2919. Editing, librarian, educational, & sequencing software. C64.

Micro Performance, Oxford Synthesizer Company, 5 Gladstone Ct., Gladstone Rd., Headington, Oxford. MIDI accessories (sequencer).

Micro-W, 1342 B Route 23, Butler, NJ 07405. (201) 838-9027. Pre-recorded MIDI sequenced songs for sequencers & computers; MIDI interface hardware. IIe/+/C, ST, C64, various stand-alone sequencers.

MIDIcomp, The Teknecom Group, 13773 N. Central Exy, Suite 1444, Dallas, TX 75243. (214) 690-8480. Portable IBM-compatible computers; sequencing & notation software; MIDI interface hardware. IBM.

MID, Inc., 250 West 57th St., Suite 1527-40, New York City, NY 10107. (215) 262-4008 or (201) 560-8148. MIDI accessories (patcher, trigger devices, etc.).

Midimix, Box 161, Ashland, OR 97520. (503) 488-1023. MIDI accessories (splitter, merging, sequencing devices; cables).

Miditec, 453 Darwin Crescent, Thunder Bay, Ontario, Canada P7B 5W5. (807) 345-3077. MIDI retrofit hardware (for Korg pre-MIDI instruments).

MIDImouse Music, Box 272, Rhododendron, OR 97049. (503) 622-5451. Editing, librarian, sampling, & miscellaneous software. C64, IIe, various samplers.

Mimetics Corp., P.O. Box 60238, Station A, Palo Alto, CA 94306. (408) 741-0117. Sequencing, synthesis, editing, librarian, & miscellaneous software; MIDI interface hardware. Amiga.

Mongoose Cables, Box 13226, San Luis Obispo, CA 93406. (805) 549-9323. MIDI accessories (cables).

MusicData, Inc., 8444 Wilshire Blvd., Beverly Hills, CA 90211. (213) 655-3580. Sequencer, librarian, & miscellaneous software. C64, IIe/+.

Music Education Incentives, 328 E-1 1300 North, Box 599, Chesterton, IN 46304. (219) 926-6315. Computers; educational & entertainment software.

Musicworks, 18 Haviland, Boston, MA 02116. (617) 266-2886. Sequencing, librarian, notation, performance/mixing, & educational software; MIDI interface hardware. Mac.

Nady Systems, 1145 65th St., Oakland, CA 94608. (415) 652-2411. MIDI accessories (wireless MIDI transmitter); communications devices.

Neotek, 1154 West Belmont Ave., Chicago, IL 60657. (312) 929-6699. Professional mixing consoles (MIDI control optional).

New England Digital, Box 546 M, White River Junction, VT 05001. (802) 295-5800. MIDI instruments (Synclavier); professional audio/video production equipment; sequencing, waveform analysis, & notation software.

NoteWareCo, 4201 Via Marina, Suite 301, Marina Del Ray, CA 90292. (213) 822-1300. Chord notation/creation software. Mac.

Noteworthy Systems, see Gentle Electric.

Oberheim, 11650 West Olympic Blvd., Los Angeles, CA 90064. (213) 479-4948. Musical instruments & accessories (synthesizers, drum machines, sample player, EEPROM "burner," etc.).

Octave Plateau, see Voyetra Technologies.

Opcode Systems, 444 Ramona, Palo Alto, CA 94301. (415) 321-8977. Sequencing, editing, librarian, compositional/improvisational, notation, & film scoring software; MIDI interface hardware. Mac.

Optical Media, 485 Alberto Way, Los Gatos, CA 95030. (408) 395-4332. Optical CD-ROM mass storage devices.

PAIA Electronics, P.O. Box 14359, Oklahoma City, OK 73114. (405) 843-9626. MIDI accessories (merging, switching, patching, MIDI-to-CV, & time code devices); musical instrument & modification kits.

Palmtree Instruments, 5666 La Jolla Blvd., #81, La Jolla, CA 92037. (619) 546-8808. MIDI accessories (hand-driven MIDI controllers, etc.).

Paradigm, 1369 Concord Place, Suite 3-B, Kalamazoo, MI 49009. Librarian software. ST.

Passac, 64 Shepherd St., Chippendale, NSW 2008, Australia. 61-(02)-699-4416. Or: 759 Ames Ave., Milpitas, CA 95035. (408) 946-8989. MIDI & non-MIDI accessories (guitar controllers, preamps, pickups, etc.).

Passport Designs, 625 Miramontes St., Half Moon Bay, CA 94019. (415) 726-0280. Sequencing, notation, editing, librarian, entertainment, & educational software; MIDI interface hardware. Mac, IIe, IBM, ST, C64, C128.

Peavey Electronics, 711 A St., Meridian, MS 39301. (601) 483-5365. MIDI accessories (programmable effects & amplifiers, etc.); musical instruments & equipment.

Performance Computer Concepts, 2378 Sirius St., Thousand Oaks, CA 91360. (805) 493-1476. MIDI accessories (switchers, controllers, etc.); MIDI interface hardware. IBM.

Personal Composer (Jim Miller's Personal Composer), P.O. Box 648, Honaunau, HI 96726. (206) 328-9518. Sequencing & notation software. IBM.

PCS, Pfalzer-Waldstrasse 36, D8000 Munich 90, West Germany. Custom-built computer music systems.

Pianocorder, (formerly Marantz Pianocorder), c/o Yamaha Music Corp., USA, 600 Orangethorpe Ave., Buena Park, CA 90620.

PPG, Europa Technology, Inc., 1638 W. Washington Blvd., Venice, CA 90291. (213) 392-4985. MIDI instruments (PPG Wave); sampling, sequencing, & waveform analysis software.

Powertran Cybernetics Ltd., Portway Industrial Estate, Andover, Hants., SP10 3EM, United Kingdom. MIDI-controlled sampling & delay devices. BBC Computer.

Pro-Co Sound, 135 E. Kalamazoo Ave, Kalamazoo, MI 49007. (616) 342-0269. MIDI accessories (cables, etc.); cables, patch bays, & wiring harnesses (snakes); signal processing.

QRS, see Micro-W.

Quark Ltd., 16-24 Brewery Rd., London LN7 9NH, United Kingdom. MIDI accessories (switchers, etc.).

Quiet Lion, P.O. Box 219, Sun Valley, CA 91353. (818) 765-6224. Sequencing, notation, editing, & diatonic harmonizing (chords from one note) software.

RMD & Associates Inc., 5265 Grandview, Yorba Linda, CA 92686. (714) 777-3180. MIDI interface hardware & associated software. Universal RS-232-based (most computers).

RolandCorp, 7200 Dominion Circle, LA, CA 90040. (213) 685-5141. MIDI instruments & accessories (samplers, synthesizers, drum machines, signal processing, etc.); miscellaneous software; MIDI interface hardware; musical instruments & equipment. IBM, IIe/+.

RPMicro, 400 Main St., Hickory, PA 15340. (412) 356-4000. Portable IBM-compatible computers.

Sequential, 3051 North First St., San Jose, CA 95134-2093. (408) 433-5240. MIDI instruments (synthesizers, samplers, drum machines); production/sequencing equipment.

Serge Modular Music Systems, 572 Haight St., San Francisco, CA 94117. (415) 621-6898. Custom-built modular synthesizers; MIDI instrument modifications.

SIEL UK, Ahed Depot, Reigate Rd., Hookwood, Horley, Surrey, RH6 OAY United Kingdom. Or: **Siel USA,** c/o On Site Music, 2103 Sullivan St., Greensboro, NC 27405. (919) 272-5123. Also refer to Keytek. MIDI instruments & accessories (synthesizers, sequencers, etc.); editing, librarian, & sequencing software; MIDI interface hardware. C64.

Sight & Sound, 3200 S. 166th St. Box 27, New Berlin, WI 53151. (414) 784-5850. Miscellaneous entertainment & educational software.

Simmons Electronics, Unit 11, Alban Park, Hatfield Rd., St. Albans, Hertfordshire Al4 OJH, United Kingdom. 44-(727)-36191. Or: 23917 Craftsman Rd., Calabasas, CA 91302. (818) 884-2653. MIDI instruments (drums, mallet-percussion contollers, etc.); sequencing & sampling hardware; MIDI-controlled mixers.

Softwind Instruments, c/o Martin Hurni, Munstergasse 52, CH-3011 Bern, Switzerland. 41-(031)-22 28 20. MIDI retrofit for wind instruments.

Sonus, 21430 Strathern St., Suite H, Canoga Park, CA 91304. (818) 702-0992. Sequencing, editing, librarian, & waveform analysis software; MIDI interface hardware. IIe/+/GS, C64, C128, Mac, ST, IBM.

Sound Ideas, 86 McGill St., Toronto, Ontario, Canada M5B 1H2. (416) 977-0512. Sampler & sound effects libraries on Compact Disc.

Soundtracs, 91 Ewell Rd., Surbiton, Surrey KT6 68H United Kingdom. 44-(01)-339-3392. Or: AKG Acoustics, 77 Selleck St., Stamford, CT 06902. (203) 348-2121. MIDI-controlled professional mixing consoles.

Southworth Music Systems, 91 Ann Lee Rd., Harvard, MA 01451. (617) 772-9471. Sequencing & notation software; MIDI interface hardware. Mac, ST, IIGS.

SSSound, P.O. Box No.1, Kanie, Aichi, Japan 497. MIDI instruments (Sting electronic wind controller, etc.).

Standard Computer, P.O. Box 26, Plymouth, MI 48107. (313) 464-8562. Sequencing software, MIDI interface hardware. IBM.

Standard Productions, 1314 34th Ave., San Francisco, CA 94122. (415) 759-1756. MIDI accessories (power racks for modular synthesizers, etc.); notation software. Mac.

Steinberg Research, BND 228, 2000 Hamburg 28, West Germany. 49-(40)-789-8916. Or: c/o Russ Jones Marketing Group. 17700 Rayner, Northridge, CA 91325. (818) 993-4091. Sequencing & notation software; MIDI interface hardware. ST, C64, IIe.

Studiomaster, Chaul End Lane, Luton, Bedfordshire, LU4 8EZ, United Kingdom. 44-(582)-570370. Professional MIDI-controlled mixing consoles.

Sunn, c/o Fender Musical Instruments, 1120 Columbia St., Brea, CA 92621. (714) 990-0909. MIDI-controlled lighting mixer.

Suzuki, P.O. Box 261030, San Diego, CA 92126. (619) 566-9710. MIDI & non-MIDI instruments (synthesizers, etc.).

Synchronous Technologies, see PAIA.

SynthAxe, Four Seasons House, 102b Woodstock Rd., Witney, Oxford, OX8 6DY United Kingdom. 44-(0993)-76910. Or: c/o Russ

Jones Marketing Group, 17700 Raymer, Northridge, CA 91325. (818) 993-4091. MIDI guitar controller.

Systems Design (SD) Associates, 5068 Plano Parkway, Suite 1221, Plano, TX 75075. (817) 565-9210. Sequencing, notation, & librarian software; MIDI interface hardware. IBM.

TC Electronic, 120 County Rd., Tenafly, NJ 07670. (201) 384-4221. MIDI accessories (signal processing devices.)

Techniques Numeriques Avancées, BP14, F-30440, Sumene, France: 33-(67)-813711. Sequencing & miscellaneous software. UNIX (computer operating system).

TED, dist. by Capelle Music, 333 London Road, Hadleigh, Essex United Kingdom. 44-(0702)-559383. MIDI accessories (EPROM players, "burners," etc.).

Texture, see Magnetic Music.

360 Systems, 18730 Oxnard St., Tarzana, CA 91356. (818) 342-3127. MIDI instruments & accessories (merging & patching devices); digital playback systems.

TOA Electronics, 480 Carlton Court, S. San Francisco, CA 94080. (415) 588-2538. MIDI-augmented mixing consoles; professional audio equipment.

Valhalla, P.O. Box 20157, Ferndale, MI 48220. (313) 548-9360. Editing, librarian, & voicing software; related publications. C64.

Voyce Music, P.O. Box 27862, San Diego, CA 92128. (619) 549-0581. MIDI accessories (merger, switcher, splitter, programmer, etc.).

Voyetra Technologies, 426 Mt. Pleasant Ave., Mamaroneck, NY 10543. (914) 698-3377. Sequencing & librarian software; MIDI interface hardware. IBM.

Waveframe, 4725 Walnut St, Boulder, CO 80301. (303) 447-1572. Professional music/audio/video production equipment.

Wersi Electronics, 1720 Hempstead Rd., Lancaster, PA 17601. (717) 299-4327. MIDI & non-MIDI instruments & accessories (synthesizers, organs, drum machines, etc.).

Whirlwind, 100 Boxart St., Rochester, NY 14612. (716) 663-8820. MIDI accessories (cables).

XRI Systems-MICON, 10 Sunnybank Rd., Sutton Coldfield, West Midlands, United Kingdom. 44-(021)-382-6048. Sequencing & editing software. Sinclair ZX Spectrum.

Yamaha, Box 6600 Buena Park, CA 90622. (714) 522-9331. MIDI instruments & accessories (samplers, synthesizers, drum machines, signal processing, etc.); miscellaneous software; computers; MIDI interface hardware; musical instruments & equipment. CX5M, CX5MII-128.

Zeta Music Systems, 2823 9th St., Berkeley, CA 94710. (415) 849-9648. MIDI instruments & accessories (violin controllers, etc.).

INDEX

MMA. See MIDI Manufacturers
  Association
Mode select, MIDI and, 10-11
Modulation, MIDI and, 11
Monitoring, MIDI systems and, 93
Mono mode, 9-10, 18
Monophonic synthesizers,
  MIDI-equipped, 10
Moog, Bob, 1, 119
M-SMPTE, 4
Multi mode, 18-19
Multi-track sequencing, 74-75
Music notation, 82-85
Music transcription, 82-85
Musicworks, interface devices, 70
Mute, sequencer, 76

N

New England Digital Synclavier, 85
Note capacity, sequencer, 75
Note-off command, 26
Note-on command, 26

O

Oberheim, 1
Oberheim Matrix-12, 18, 81
Oberheim OB-8, 22
Oberheim Xk, 58
Oberheim Xpander, 18, 36, 51
Octave Plateau MIDI Guitar, 57
Octave Plateau OP-4001, 69
Omni mode, 9-10, 18
Omni-off mode, 41
Omni-on mode, 41
Opcode, interface devices, 70
Operating systems, personal
  computer, 61
Opto-isolator, 14, 48, 53
Overflow mode, 18-19

P

Pascal, 29
Passport, 66
  interface devices, 70
Passport MIDI Pro, 69
Patch data, editing, 81
Patch voicing, 80-81
Peek, 28-33
Performance controllers, MIDI
  systems and, 91
Perkins, Bill, 7
Personal Composer, 7, 83, 85
Personal computers, 60-65
  MIDI links, 4
  MIDI systems, 92
Pitch-bend, 42-43 MIDI, 11

Pitch-bend command, 28
Plauger, P.J., 29
Poly mode, 9-10, 18
Poly-off mode, 41
Poly-on mode, 41
Polyphonic key after-touch
  command, 26-27, 57
Powell, Roger, 56
PPG PRK-FD, 58
Preston, Billy, 56
Program change command, 27
Punching, sequencer, 76

Q

Quantization, sequencer, 76-78

R

Real-Time Clock, 33-34
Recording, sequencer, 75-76
RMD & Associates, interface
  devices, 69, 70
Roland, 1, 2, 7, 23, 80
  interface devices, 70
Roland 707, 50
Roland Axis, 57, 59
Roland Guitar Synth, 57
Roland Juno-10, 81
Roland Juno-106, 81
Roland JX-8P, 36
Roland MKB-300, 18, 19, 59
Roland MKB-1000, 18, 19, 51, 56,
  58-59
Roland MPU-401, 28-30, 47, 68
Roland MSQ-100, 19
Roland MSQ-700, 51
Roland RD-1000, 41
Roland SDE-2500, 22
Roland SPX-80, 33, 45
Roland Super Jupiter MKS-80, 36
Rossum, Dave, 5

S

Samplers, MIDI systems and, 91-92
Scholz, Carter, 33, 119
Scoring, 82-85
SEIL DK80, 81
Seiler Showmaster, 55
Sequencers
  MIDI systems and, 92
  timing of, 33-34
Sequencer software, 71-80
Sequencing, multi-track, 74-75
Sequential, 1, 2, 5, 47, 66
Sequential Multi-Trak, 18
Sequential Prophet, 81
Sequential Prophet 600, 1

ABOUT THE AUTHORS

Jim Cooper is the president of the MIDI Manufacturers Association and owner of JL Cooper Electronics. Through his company, Mr. Cooper has been the creator of many music technology devices. His column, "Mind Over MIDI", appears monthly in *Keyboard*.

Steve Cummings is a freelance writer specializing in computer technology. In addition to his music and computer interests, Mr. Cummings is currently pursuing further education in health sciences.

Steve De Furia writes two regular columns for *Keyboard*—"Software For Musicians", and "Systems And Applications"—and is the author of the *Synth Arts* instructional tapes. He has taught audio recording and electronic music at Berklee College of Music and worked as a studio musician and music software consultant. Mr. De Furia is also the co-author of several new instructional books and videos produced by Ferro Technologies.

David Frederick has been involved with electronic music since the age of seventeen, when he studied synthesizers and electronic music production with Allen Strange. While a product specialist at Passport Designs, he became an industry expert on MIDI and computer technologies. He was an assistant editor for *Keyboard* and co-authored *Beginning Synthesizer* and *Using MIDI*. Mr. Frederick is currently a product specialist and technical writer for WaveFrame Corporation.

Peter Gotcher is the president of Digidesign, a music software company, and writes the *Keyboard* column, "Computer For Keyboardists." Previously, Mr. Gotcher had been associated with Dolby Laboratories, and enjoyed a successful career as a San Francisco Bay Area drummer.

Ted Greenwald is one of *Keyboard's* assistant editors, and a Windham Hill recording artist. He has a degree in electronic music from Brown University and has done graduate work in film scoring at the University of Southern California.

Dominic Milano is the editor of *Keyboard*. He studied electronic music composition at the Chicago Musical College, and has written numerous articles on synthesis. He is active as a performer, programmer, and design consultant.

Bob Moog is an internationally celebrated designer of electronic musical instruments and the founder of Moog Music, Inc., which produced the first commercially-successful synthesizers. He has written and lectured widely on all phases of the electronic music medium. At present he is the vice-president of new product research for Kurzweil Music Systems.

Carter Scholz is a science fiction author, computer programmer, freelance writer, and performing musician. His short stories have been nominated for both the Hugo and Nebula Awards. Carter has been playing keyboards since he was four years old.

RECOMMENDED READING

ARP 2600 Owner's Manual, available from MDS, 4700 W. Fullerton, Chicago, Il 60639.

The Art of Electronic Music, compiled and with commentary by Tom Darter, edited by Greg Armbruster, A Morrow/Quill/ GPI Book, from GPI Publications, 20085 Stevens Creek, Cupertino, CA 95014.

Beginning Synthesizer, by Helen Casabona and David Frederick, a volume in the *Keyboard Magazine* library for electronic musicians. An Alfred Publishing/ GPI Book, from GPI Publications.

The Complete Guide To Synthesizers, by Devarahi, Prentice-Hall, Englewood Cliffs, NJ 07632.

The Complete Synthesizer, by Dave Crombie, Omnibus Press, London.

Computer Music Journal (quarterly), The MIT Press, Cambridge, MA 02142.

The Development And Practice Of Electronic Music, by Jon Appleton and Ronald Perera, Prentice-Hall.

Electronic Music, 2nd edition, by Allen Strange, Wm. C. Brown Company, 135 S. Locust St., Dubuque, IA 52001.

Electronic Music Circuit Guidebook, by Brice Ward, TAB Books, Blue Ridge Summit, PA 17214.

Electronic Music Production, by Alan Douglas, TAB Books.

Electronic Musical Instruments, by Norman Crowhust, TAB Books.

Electronic Musician (magazine), Mix Publications, 2608 Ninth St., Berkeley, CA 94710.

Electronmusic, by Robert De Voe, EML, Vernon, CT 06066.

Elementi di Informatica Musicale, by Goffredo Haus, Gruppo Editoriale Jackson, Milano, Italy.

The Evolution Of Electronic Music, by David Ernst, Schirmer Books, 866 Third Ave., New York, NY 10022.

Experimenting With Electronic Music, by Robert Brown and Mark Olsen, TAB Books.

Foundations Of Computer Music, edited by Curtis Roads and John Strawn, The MIT Press.

The IMA Bulletin (newsletter), International MIDI Association, 12439 Magnolia Blvd., Suite 104, North Hollywood, CA 91607.

Keyboard Magazine, GPI Publications.

MIDI For Musicians, by Craig Anderton, Music Sales Corp., Chester, N.Y. 10918.

Nueva Generacion De Instrumentos Musicales Electronicos, by Juan Bermudez Costa, 7, Spain.

Synthesis, by Herbert Deutsch, Alfred Publishing, 15335 Morrison St., Sherman Oaks, CA 91413.

The Synthesizer (four-volume set), published by Roland, Box 22289, Los Angeles, CA 90040.

Synthesizer Basics, compiled by the editors of *Keyboard Magazine*, a volume in the Keyboard Synthesizer Library, a Hal Leonard Publishing/GPI Book from GPI Publications.

Synthesizers And Computers, compiled from the pages of *Keyboard Magazine* and edited by Brent Hurtig, a volume in the Keyboard Synthesizer Library, a Hal Leonard Publishing/GPI Book from GPI Publications.

Synthesizer Technique, compiled by the editors of *Keyboard Magazine*, a volume in the Keyboard Synthesizer Library, a Hal Leonard Publishing/GPI Book from GPI Publications.

The Technique Of Electronic Music, by Thomas Wells and Eric Vogel, Sterling Swift Publishing, Box 188, Manchaca, TX 78652.

The Technology Of Computer Music, by Max Mathews, The MIT Press.

Using MIDI, by Helen Casabona and David Frederick, a volume in the *Keyboard Magazine* library for electronic musicians, an Alfred Publishing/GPI Book, from GPI Publications.

The Whole Synthesizer Catalogue, edited by Tom Darter from the pages of *Keyboard Magazine*, a Hal Leonard Publishing/GPI Book, from GPI Publications.

From *Keyboard Magazine* Books

▤ SYNTHESIZER AND COMPUTERS

A comprehensive overview, useful for beginners or seasoned pros, or anyone interested in the future of music. Includes discussions of digital audio, synthesis, sampling, MIDI, choosing software and interface hardware, and choosing the right computer. Also included is a section on Programming Your Own Software—which leads the reader step-by-step into the world of writing music software, and covers many insider's programming tips. From the pages of *Keyboard Magazine*, with articles by Steve De Furia, Dominic Milano, Jim Aikin, Ted Greenwald, Jim Cooper, Bob Moog, Craig Anderton, and other leading experts.
ISBN 0-88188-716-1 $12.95   From Hal Leonard Publishing.

▤ SYNTHESIZER BASICS

An introduction to understanding and playing today's electronic synthesizers, including What is Synthesis; What is a Synthesizer; Basic Concepts and Components; Synthesizer Sound Systems; Recording and Specsmanship. Written by leading experts, including Bob Moog, Jim Cooper, Dominic Milano, Roger Powell, and others; with helpful diagrams and illustrated examples throughout.
ISBN 0-88188-289-5 $9.95 ($12.95 after February 15, 1988).   From Hal Leonard Publishing.

▤ SYNTHESIZER PROGRAMMING

Don't be satisfied with factory presets! Get the most out of your instrument, whether it's a battered Minimoog or the latest digital dream machine. You can create your own unique sound with the concrete and understandable information in this practical introduction to programming and synthesis. With contributions by Wendy Carlos, Bo Tomlyn, and the editors and staff of *Keyboard Magazine*. Includes specific guidelines for the DX7, Oberheim Xpander, CZ-101, Roland JX8P, and JX10.
ISBN 0-88188-550-9 $12.95   From Hal Leonard Publishing.

▤ SYNTHESIZER TECHNIQUE

How to utilize all the technical and creative potential of today's synthesizers, with discussions of Recreating Timbres; Pitch-Bending, Modulation and Expression; Lead Synthesizer; Soloing and Orchestration. Hands-on practical advice and instruction by leading practitioners, including Bob Moog, Tom Coster, George Duke, Roger Powell, and others. Diagrams, illustrations, and musical examples throughout.
ISBN 0-88188-290-9 $9.95 ($12.95 after March 15, 1988).   From Hal Leonard Publishing.

▤ THE WHOLE SYNTHESIZER CATALOGUE

An extensive consumer guide to synthesizers, culled from the pages of *Keyboard Magazine*, the foremost publication of electronic keyboards in the field. Including evaluation and practical analysis of classic landmark instruments, current state-of-the-art hardware, and synthesizer/computer software.
ISBN 0-88188-396-4 $12.95   From Hal Leonard Publishing.

▤ THE ART OF ELECTRONIC MUSIC

The creative and technical development of an authentic musical revolution, from the Theremin Electrical Symphony to today's most advanced synthesizers. Scientific origins, the evolution of hardware, the greatest artists—including Tangerine Dream, Vangelis, Keith Emerson, Wendy Carlos, Jan Hammer, Kraftwerk, Brian Eno, Thomas Dolby, and others —in stories, interviews, illustrations, analysis, and practical musical technique. From the pages of *Keyboard Magazine*, and with a forward by Bob Moog.
ISBN 0-688-03106-4 $15.95   From Wm. Morrow & Co.

▤ BEGINNING SYNTHESIZER

A step-by-step guide to understanding and playing synthesizers with discussions of how to use and edit presets and performance controls. A comprehensive, easy-to understand, musical approach, with hands-on lessons in a variety of styles, including rock, pop, classical, jazz, techno-pop, blues, and more.
ISBN 0-88284-353-2 $12.95   From Alfred Publishing. (Item Number 2606.)

▤ USING MIDI

The first comprehensive, practical guide to the application of Musical Instrument Digital Interface in performance, composition, and recording, including: basic MIDI theory, using MIDI performance controls, channels and modes, sequencers, MIDI synchronization, using MIDI effects, MIDI and computers, alternate MIDI controllers, and more. A definitive and essential tutorial, from the editors of *Keyboard Magazine*.
ISBN 0-88282-354-0 $12.95   From Alfred Publishing. (Item Number 2607.)

▤ MULTI-TRACK RECORDING FOR MUSICIANS

How to make professional quality recordings at home or in the studio—comprehensive, creative, practical information including basic theory and up-to-date guidance on the latest equipment.
ISBN 0-88284-355-9 $12.95   From Alfred Publishing. (Available Summer 1988—Item Number 2608.)

To subscribe to *Keyboard Magazine*, write to *Keyboard Magazine*, Subscription Department, P.O. Box 2110, Cupertino, CA 95015

All prices subject to change without notice.